AN UNAUTHORIZED
BIOGRAPHY OF
THE WORLD

An
Unauthorized
Biography of the
World

ORAL HISTORY ON THE FRONT LINES

Michael
Riordon

BETWEEN THE LINES

An Unauthorized Biography of the World

© 2004 by Michael Riordon

First published in Canada in 2004 by
Between the Lines
720 Bathurst Street, Suite #404
Toronto, Ontario   M5S 2R4
1-800-718-7201
www.btlbooks.com

LIBRARY AND ARCHIVES CANADA CATALOGUING IN PUBLICATION

Riordon, Michael, 1944–
    An unauthorized biography of the world : oral history on the front lines / Michael Riordon

ISBN 1-896357-93-8

    1. Social problems–History.   2. Social justice–History.   3. Oral history.
I. Title.

HN17.5.R56 2004   361.1   C2004-904134-7

Front cover art: Margaret Adam, ArtWork
Cover and text design by David Vereschagin, Quadrat Communications
Printed in Canada

Between the Lines gratefully acknowledges assistance for its publishing activities from the Canada Council for the Arts, the Ontario Arts Council, the Government of Ontario through the Ontario Book Publishers Tax Credit program and through the Ontario Book Initiative, and the Government of Canada through the Book Publishing Industry Development Program.

CONTENTS

ACKNOWLEDGEMENTS

The author gratefully acknowledges
quotations from:

Mohawk Creation Story, told by Anataras (Alan Brant), Mohawks of the Bay
    of Quinte. http://www.tyendinaga.net/

I'll Sing 'til the Day I Die: Conversations with Tyendinaga Elders by Beth Brant.
    Toronto: McGilligan Books, 1995.

Night Spirits: The Story of the Relocation of the Sayisi Dene by Ila Bussidor and
    Üstün Bilgen-Reinart. Winnipeg: University of Manitoba Press, 1997.

*Strong as the Ocean: Women's Work in the Newfoundland and Labrador
    Fisheries,* edited by Frances Ennis and Helen Woodrow. St John's:
    Harrish Press, 1996.

Come and I Will Sing You: A Newfoundland Songbook, edited by Genevieve
    Lehr. Toronto: University of Toronto Press, 2003.

Power of the Unemployed, radio documentary produced by Kathryn Welbourn
    and Chris Brookes. St John's: Battery Radio Productions, 1996.

*Sea People: Changing Lives and Times in the Newfoundland and Labrador
    Fisheries,* edited by Helen Woodrow and Frances Ennis. St John's:
    Harrish Press, 1999.

Just Ask Rosie, play by Agnes Walsh. St John's, 2002.

A Man You Don't Meet Everyday, play by Agnes Walsh. St John's, 2001.

The Lifetime Struggle, radio documentary produced by Chris Brookes.
    St John's: Battery Radio Productions, 1995.

Testimonies of Pain and Courage, photo and testimony exhibit co-ordinated by
    Nelly Plaza. Project Counselling Service, Peru, and Inter Pares, Ottawa,
    Canada, 2003.

Comisión de la Verdad y Reconciliación/Truth and Reconciliation Commis-
    sion, Peru, 2003. http://www.cverdad.org.pe/ingles/ pagina01.php

*Patrick Lenihan: From Irish Rebel to Founder of Canadian Public Sector
    Unionism*, edited by Gil Levine. St John's: Canadian Committee on
    Labour History, 1998.

On All Fronts, video produced by Ottawa and District Labour Council –
Workers' Heritage Committee and Ground Zero Productions, 1997.

The Workers' City: A walking tour of Hamilton's East End. Booklet and
audiotape produced by the Workers' Arts and Heritage Centre, Hamilton, Canada.

The Crest of the Mountain: The Rise of CUPE *Local Five in Hamilton* by Ed
Thomas. Hamilton: Ed Thomas, 1995.

A Worker's Guide to Doing a Local Union's History by Ed Thomas. Ottawa:
Canadian Union of Public Employees; Hamilton: The Workers Arts and
Heritage Centre, 1999.

Dead but Not Forgotten: Monuments to Workers, by Ed Thomas. Hamilton:
Ed Thomas, 2001.

Tides of Men, website produced by Robert Rothon and Myron Plett,
Vancouver, 2003. http://www.tidesofmen.org

Women of Fire, video produced by IDL, Peru. Sponsored by the Project Coun-
selling Service, Peru, with the support of Inter Pares, Canada, and the
Peacebuilding Fund of the Canadian International Development
Agency (CIDA), 2003.

Robert Jackson radio interview with Dan Kerr, produced by Dan Kerr. Frost
Radio, WRUW, Case Western University, Cleveland, 2001.

"The Politics of Taste and Smell: Palestinian Rites of Return" by Efrat Ben-
Ze'ev. *Alpayyim* 25 (2003): 73–88. Also published in Arabic in *Al-Karmel*
76–7 (2003): 107–22.

"Packing Them In: A 20th-Century Working Class Environmental History,"
by Sylvia Hood Washington. Dissertation, Case Western University,
Cleveland.

The author also acknowledges with deep appreciation generous funding
from the Canada Council for the Arts and the Ontario Arts Council. It was a
pleasure to work with Maureen Garvie, who edited the manuscript with
finesse and a good ear for the human voice.

CHAPTER 1

Finding Voice, Making Sense

During a session of the 2001 Summer Institute on Oral History, at Columbia University in New York, a woman who teaches oral history in an academic setting said, "What Michael does is not oral history." Though I felt a little slapped, I didn't argue. In thirty years of doing this work, I've never called it that myself and had really only used the term to gain entrance to the institute.

In fact I had never *heard* of oral history until a few years ago when a friend who teaches history at Queen's University in Canada invited me to talk to a women's studies class – on oral history. "Why me?" I asked, "I don't know anything about it. I don't even know what it is."

"Michael," she said, in the measured tone of one who has shepherded many lost students, "it's what you do." Facing the task of talking to sixty-five or so young women, all budding deconstructionists, I put some time into figuring out what it is that I do, why, and how. That led to other talks, to the Columbia summer institute, and willy-nilly, to this book.

In New York I pursued my fellow institutee: How does she determine what qualifies as oral history, and what does not? (This is how I encounter people, and the world – I ask questions.) "Oh, I didn't really mean it," she said, embarrassed, then apologized. No need, I said. But I did wonder at the enormous human capacity for dogma. Even in this endeavour that all of us at the institute were celebrating as one of the most democratic vehicles possible for human expression, here was someone designating what does and what does not count.

Some of the people featured in this book call their work oral history, some do not. Some take issue with the term, but most don't care much what it's called. They just do it.

WHY ME?

I grew up twice colonized. Not knowing any better in the 1950s and '60s, I swallowed whole the official versions that I was fed: (1) Canadians are nice, and we defer to imperial authority – first the crown, then Washington; (2) homosexuals are sinful, criminal, and sick. I was nice enough, but as it turned out, a homosexual, and thus a bad guy in my own story. Offered salvation through electric shocks, I jumped at the chance. A few chaotic years later, nature triumphed over mad science and I came out, with a lingering suspicion of electrical devices and a powerful need to tell my own story, in my own voice.

In the larger picture, I've learned that tyrants hold power over us first of all by commanding our attention. Backed by convenient scriptures, they overwhelm us with their version of the world, which in time comes to seem more real than our own. In a media-soaked culture, they simply stupefy us.

As a writer, I think of my work – presumptuously, perhaps – as an antidote to stupefaction, both for myself in the doing of it, and for others in the reading/hearing/seeing of it. I work in a range of media: books and articles, film, video and radio documentaries, plays for stage, radio and, at one point, the street. Along the way I've recorded many hundreds of interviews with, among others, Mozambican farmers, inmates in federal prisons, traditional healers in Fiji, queer folk across Canada, Guatemalan peace-makers, Métis uranium miners.

Each of their stories adds an essential piece to the evolving human account, our shared work-in-progress. Together, they also help to counter, amend, and complicate the official version.

I absorbed my first official version from my imperial grandmother, who "raised" me on an ideology she called Noblesse Oblige: The world is made of two kinds of people – Us, walled up in castles, real or imagined, and Them, the rest of the humanity, out there, milling about on the vast, cold plains. The whole thing was elegantly simple. In here, Us. Out there, Them. Exactly as God intended. If we were not actually *in* the castle – we couldn't afford it, not on my widowed mother's salary – at least its great doors would swing open to me whenever I wished. It was only natural, by virtue of my provenance and breeding: white, Anglo, male, of noble lineage, and, of course, heterosexual. Each of these characteristics was held to be immutable, exactly as God intended.

Over Sunday lunch, we puzzled at French-Canadians clamouring to be *maîtres chez nous*, masters in their own house. The very idea! In the countryside where they belonged, my grandmother explained, they were such Good People, simple and innocent. But when they came to the city, they turned Bad. Nods around the table, as if we understood. I didn't understand, but should have by then. This is one of the great comforts of Noblesse Oblige, or any other ideology – Christianity, for example, or capitalism: once it's fully absorbed, you never have to think again.

Noblesse Oblige obliged me to be nice to the French-Canadian gardener while he waited in the porch, cap in hand, for his next instructions. Though being nice to *him* came easily to me, I did wonder: this beautiful, powerful man who could handle lilies without bruising them, yet could hoist me aloft with one hand – why did it feel as if I, at half his height, was talking *down* to him? But of course, he was one of Them.

Then the queer thing happened. I did my best – worst – to fight it. One afternoon in Athens, which my guidebook called the Birthplace of Western Democracy, I woke up. Wandering around the Mediterranean looking for myself, at this point I was only looking for the Acropolis. Atop a downtown building I saw young people holding up a banner, in Greek. On the streets below, swarms of buses gathered, their flanks and windows painted a dull grey. Men in uniform spilled out, clubs and guns on their belts. Streets emptied, shop doors closed. The young people disappeared from the rooftop. Soon they emerged on the street, choking and gagging – from tear gas, I assumed. Then they were forced through a gauntlet of clubs. I saw and heard the impact on heads and backs, young people hurled into buses like sacks of grain. A few broke free, ran to pound on shop doors. A door opened, hands pulled a refugee inside. Behind other doors, people shook their heads, Go away!

In one afternoon, at age twenty-eight, I woke up and saw the world from an entirely new angle. Shortly after, I returned to Canada and came out. Henceforth, I was one of Them.

In my safe deposit box at the local bank, I have four fading blue-bound volumes that document Us, my noble maternal line – the Gherardini of Tuscany, then the Geraldines of Ireland, from Florence in the tenth century to fade-out in the nineteenth. Here is the official version as it was fed to me: The people that matter leave records, they make history. By corollary, people who leave no records make nothing and have no value. This is why I do oral history.

My rough encounter with psychiatry taught me another sharp lesson, this one about memory and truth. In a cruel exercise called aversion therapy, based on Pavlov's work with dogs, three times a week Dr John Jameson administered electric shocks to my body while I stared at photos of naked men. With my foot on a pedal-switch, I could stop the shock only by moving to the next image. Enough of this, the theory went, and I would no longer find any pleasure in the bodies of men.

A few years later, I spotted the same John Jameson at a gay dance in a university gym. When I told others that he was there, they wanted to hitch him up to the nearest electric outlet. Instead I made an appointment to see him at his office; I would expose him in print, by then my chosen weapon. In that chilly interview, he told me, "Where I choose to put my cock has no bearing on how I function as a therapist." And this man was licensed to tinker with other people's minds!

Two decades on, a reporter with a mainstream Detroit newspaper wrote a story about my experience as a survivor of aversion therapy. Being a good reporter, he managed to track down Jameson, for his side of the story. The psychiatrist, who worked by then in kinder, gentler fields – smoking, fear of flying – told the reporter that he had never believed in aversion therapy and he had never done it, not to anyone, including me. It's not the Holocaust, but on an infinitely smaller scale the denial has a similar function, the wilful distortion of history. This is why I do oral history.

THE BOOK

If you're looking for a map, a line of argument to follow through the book, sorry, there isn't one. As always in oral history, the gold is in the stories. I invite you to encounter the chapters as you would a gathering of quite diverse and very stimulating people.

In the interests of full disclosure, I have to say, this book is not:

* an academic study. I wouldn't know where to begin, and in any case, it's been done, amply. On the other hand, I've encountered few books that make accessible to a wide range of readers the lived experience of doing oral history.
* neutral, objective, or balanced. I'm interested in telling the stories of passionate people engaged in challenging work, sometimes under dangerous conditions. In my book, passion is an asset, not a deficit.
* a how-to manual. I contend that oral history is far more an art than a science. No technique or approach shared in the book can be called definitive. They all illustrate how and why each person makes particular choices in particular contexts.

Having said what the book is not, I should say a little about what it is. Like most of my work it's a protest, in this case against:

- the killing strictures of the official version. Oral history celebrates diversity, of both the living and the dead.
- the privatization of life, the engineered disconnection of each of us from the others. Oral history demands, and celebrates, connection.
- wilful amnesia. As in the famous adage, "A country that forgets its history is condemned to repeat it." The same can be said of us all.
- the vast silence of mortality.

When New York oral historian Elisabeth Pozzi-Thanner accepted my request to interview me for the book (see chapter 12), one of the questions she asked was how had I chosen the people who are featured in it. I answered at almost Proustian length – edited in the final version – but I should have said, simply: "Given the nature and purpose of the book, I looked for people doing oral history with some of the most silenced communities and peoples in our world. I looked for people whose approach and questions I could respect, people who shape oral history to a variety of useful ends, and people who understand oral history – or whatever they may call it – as a tool for clarifying the past and reshaping the present."

That's a lot to ask. But then, these are remarkable people. When I sent one woman a draft of the chapter I'd written about her – I rarely do this, but in her case I wanted to be sure that nothing in the chapter would threaten her safety – she wrote back that it embarrassed her a little, because it made her out to be heroic. I replied that, since I had some idea of her capacity to be self-critical – we knew each other a little by then – I thought my assessment of her was probably as reliable as hers. I also said that I hadn't thought of her as heroic exactly, just thoughtful, compassionate, and brave.

In these desperate times, it is from people like her that I derive my hope for humanity, from "ordinary" people who refuse to give up their compassion or common sense, who stand against what I see as the rising tide of fascism. I'm writing *An Unauthorized Biography of the World* to honour such people, and their work.

I think of the book as an oral history of people who do a variety of things, all of which can be called oral history. The book is made of the techniques it explores. To gather material and impressions for it, I used the working method I've developed over the years – find people whose stories warrant telling, and ask a lot of questions: Who are you, why do you do this work, what drives you, what do you hope to accomplish? How do you build trust? What approaches and skills have you developed? What obstacles and dangers do you face? What ethical dilemmas? What do you give back? To what uses can this work be put? Where is its power?

FINDING VOICE, MAKING SENSE

During much of the research for the book, this was my working subtitle – *finding voice, making sense*. In the venal way of freelance writers who scramble for income, I dropped it because I feared it would drain impact from the provocative title, and thus might not sell. But I still like the idea. Both functions are essential to human life, but both are denied to most of humanity most of the time. The result: lives continuously marginalized, and a partial, impoverished historical record. This book looks at how engaged oral history, working from the margins, seeks to address these deficits.

Recently I led an oral history project with rural adults working towards their high-school diplomas. In our first encounters I was struck by their wary silence. None of them was accustomed to being heard, and few of them were used to asking questions of the world. Before they could gather other people's stories and voices, they would have to find their own.

We began by interviewing each other. We listened and recorded, listened again to what we heard, and asked more questions. People began to talk, began to listen with care, began to form their own questions and opinions. They found their voices.

Together, we concluded that people read the world in different ways, and that no reading can be taken without question as more authentic than any other. Even if only for a moment, we made some sense of a world that's usually opaque and out of reach.

Find voice, make sense. What else can we do?

CHAPTER 2

KANIEN'KÉHA/TS'EOULI

KANIEN'KÉHA

As far as our stories and legends
or myths, or whatever you want
to call them, as far as our information about our culture goes, I guess this is the oldest story that we have.
Some of the stories, they say, go right back to the time
of creation or the beginning of man. But this story goes
much farther into the past, beyond the beginning of
the earth or the world that we understand now. This
story begins way before any of that ever came into
existence. This story I call an Iroquoian creation story...

❁ Anataras (Alan Brant), Mohawks of
the Bay of Quinte

Later, much later, the Mohawk people lived in
what is now upper New York State. As the British
retreated in the American War of Independence, Mohawks who had
allied with them had to flee their ancestral homelands. In 1784, some
twenty families landed on the northern shores of the Bay of Quinte,
midway between Montreal and Toronto. As promised, the British lieu-
tenant-governor granted them a tract of land they called Tyendinaga,
93,000 acres of lakefront, wetland, meadow and forest. *Tyendinaga*

translates as "placing the wood together," strength in unity. Between then and now, through a series of manoeuvres bitterly familiar to indigenous people across North America, this land shrank to its current 18,000 acres. Of over 5,000 Tyendinaga Mohawks, about 2,000 live on the Territory.

After working as a hairdresser for twelve years, in 1990 Karen Lewis got the job of running the new Ka:nhiote Library. *Ka:nhiote* translates as "rainbow." The library overflows a tiny two-room bungalow on York Road in the Tyendinaga Mohawk Territory. With help from volunteers, Karen clears the snow, cleans the place, selects and catalogues the collection – books, magazines, videos, books on tape, and CDs. She stocks the usual Danielle Steeles and John Grishams that her readers demand, but one of her primary goals is to build a solid First Nations multimedia collection, so that people don't have to travel across the Quebec-U.S. border to Akwesasne, or up to Trent University in Peterborough, to hear their own stories.

I ask Karen how she selects materials. "I read the reviews," she replies. "I use Iroqrafts, a store at Six Nations, and also Goodminds.com – I trust their judgment to choose materials that do justice to First Nations people. When I started, it was hard to find good material. There was a lot of biased and stereotypical stuff out there – A is for Apple, I is for Indian, E is for Eskimo, that type of thing, books where we all live in tipis. But since the Oka crisis, a lot more decent information has come out."

In 1990, the municipality of Oka, west of Montreal, announced plans to extend a golf course already built on Mohawk land; the extension would destroy a cemetery and an ancient pine forest at Kahnawake. That March, Mohawk warriors set up camp on the contested land. For six months they were besieged by Quebec provincial police, then by 2,500 soldiers of the Canadian Armed Forces, with tanks, heavy artillery, and jets. By the time the siege ended, two Mohawks and one policeman had died. The siege sparked First Nations blockades on railways, highways, and bridges across Canada, including the bridge that links Prince Edward County, where I live, to

Tyendinaga Mohawk Territory. It also drew international attention to the long struggle by the first peoples of this continent to survive the European invasion.

> The continent remained, as it had been for uncounted centuries, empty. We think of prehistoric North America as inhabited by Indians, and have based on this a sort of recognition of ownership on their part. But this attitude is hardly warranted. The Indians were too few to count. Their use of the resources of the continent was scarcely more than that by crows and wolves, their development of it nothing.
>
> ❁ Stephen Leacock, *Canada: The Foundations of Its Future*,
> House of Seagrams, Montreal, 1941

"I've kept that book in the library just because it's so awful," says Karen Lewis. "But you know, it's not that unusual as an example of the way history was taught to many generations, including mine. No wonder there's so much prejudice and discrimination still around today."

As Karen builds the library, she's relearning her own story. "When I went to school here in the '50s, I didn't learn any history of Mohawk people at all. No, wait, that's not true. I remember there was one teacher who taught maybe two lessons about us – that's two days through the entire grade one to grade eight, and I'm pretty sure she wasn't supposed to do even that much. I remember she talked about the Peacemaker. But aside from that, all we got was the same empty-continent stuff as everyone else."

The Peacemaker, Tekanawite or Dekanawida, is believed to have been born near the Bay of Quinte. Historians estimate that in the mid-twelfth century – by the Christian calendar – he negotiated an enduring peace among five Iroquoian-speaking nations to form the Five Nations Confederacy; a sixth nation joined in 1713. Tekanawite also established the Great Binding Law of Peace, by which the Haudenosaunee, the People of the Longhouse, would be governed. It proved to be such an effective system of governance that it served as a template for the American Constitution and, much later, for the United Nations charter.

> My mother was a midwife and she made me go with her to birth the babies. And they said I was better than my mother. I says, how could that be? But I was good at that kind of work… We used to use Sweet Flag for the after pain. It healed the women right up. I always had quite a bit on hand, I used to go and get it in the spring when the water is up. We used to steep the root and drink it when we got a cold too. Mother used Bloodroot and I think she had seven different herbs she'd use for the women… The women would come to her for all kinda things, even how not to get babies. I learned a lot from her.
>
> ❊ Eva Maracle, in *I'll Sing 'til the Day I Die: Conversations with Tyendinaga Elders*, by Beth Brant

In the mid-1990s, Karen invited Beth Brant to do a reading at Tyendinaga. The Mohawk author is renowned as a poet, writer, editor, and speaker. Her books include *Mohawk Trail*, *A Gathering of Spirit: A Collection by North American Indian Women*, *Food and Spirits*, and *Writing as Witness: Essay and Talk*. Her poems, stories, and essays appear in a range of Native, feminist, and lesbian publications.

Inspired by her visit, the Ka:nhiote Library applied for a writer-in-residence grant from the Canada Council, and Beth Brant moved to Tyendinaga for six months. "She had never actually lived here, but she told us she always considered it home," says Karen. Beth's paternal grandparents had left Tyendinaga to find work in Detroit, Michigan. Beth was born there in 1941. Now a mother and grandmother, she still lives there with her partner, Denise Dorsz.

During her residency at Tyendinaga, Beth gave writing workshops and consulted with aspiring writers. Then Karen asked her what she would think about doing some interviews with local elders.

The idea was inspired by an oral history workshop that Karen had taken at a library conference. "I really liked the idea of the library being a keeper of history, holding our stories for generations to come," she says. "There's been tremendous change in Tyendinaga since I was a child, and I don't want that all to be lost. I want to keep some memories, other than just in my head. Everyone needs to know their roots, to know they're worthwhile."

When Karen was three, her father died from injuries he suffered fighting for Canada in World War II. Along with her mother and two sisters, she moved in with her grandparents: "I remember we would have meals together – sometimes my aunts would be there, and everyone would talk, so I'd hear all these stories from each of the generations. It seems to me that's not happening so much anymore. Children don't get to spend much time with their grandparents, maybe not even with their parents – the mother may be working a shift, everyone has to go to this meeting, that class, so people don't get to eat together like we did."

What does she think is lost by this? Karen replies, "I think I learned from my grandparents to have a certain – " (she hesitates) " – I don't want to say pride exactly, you know, because of the pride/sin thing. Let's say I learned a certain respect for my heritage."

To Karen, oral history is also a way to see more clearly. "We've been over-studied. When you look at where we live, we had contact very early with the Europeans, and we've been studied by them ever since – our way of life, our political system – there must be hundreds of anthropological studies on Iroquoian people. It's been useful in some respects, because without those studies, some things would probably have been lost. But you also have to realize that they didn't get the whole picture. For one thing, most of the studies were done by men, from a different society where men were the only important people. So they didn't even see the women – at least, they didn't see us as having any value, or making any significant contribution to the society we lived in. To get the whole picture, you have to look a lot closer than they did, and you have to understand what you're looking at."

Karen gave Beth a list of older people she thought might be amenable to sharing their stories. "Some of them were relatives, some not," says Karen. "Sadly, most of them are gone now. Eva Maracle was over a hundred, and just as sharp as a tack. She'd say things, you'd think, 'No, that can't be right,' but then you'd find it was, every time."

When Beth went to people's houses, before they'd tell her anything about themselves, first they wanted to know who she was. "When she told them about her grandparents, some people remembered them. That established her in a way, as someone who came from here, which gave her a certain acceptance. Then they would have tea, and they'd get down to their visiting and the interview."

Karen provided Beth with a list of about one hundred questions, which she had picked up at the oral history workshop. "It's pretty basic stuff, like who was your mother, your father, were there any momentous occasions at your birth, where did you live, what was school like, what did you do for work," she says. "Put them all together, and you've covered a person's whole life. Beth ended up using only about five of the questions, but they helped give the interviews a kind of coherent pattern."

I wonder what Karen means by "momentous occasions" at birth. "Well, for instance," she replies, "my aunt, who has now passed away, she used to say that when her mother was giving birth to her, the church was burning. Or the Titanic sank that morning, that kind of thing, it helps to set a date, which can be important, especially if you don't have access to other kinds of records."

By the time the interviews were done, it had become clear that the material was rich enough to warrant creating a book. Beth Brant hired a local woman to transcribe the tapes and her notes, then she edited the stories. "In editing," she writes in the introduction, "I wanted to convey the sense of orality and how Tyendinaga Mohawks have always recorded the way things used to be. Through elders' stories, we are given lessons on how to go about our lives in the best way we know how; values and traditions are imparted, warnings are given in the gentle and commanding presence of these voices."

My mother and dad spoke Mohawk. But I'll tell you something, in my generation we were not allowed to say one word of Mohawk language. If you did, you got the strap. So this is why we don't understand the Mohawk language, and that's a shame. And that was the government did that . . . The grownups always spoke the language to one another, and they did to us kids until we went to school, and then they were afraid to talk to the children in Mohawk, for fear of what might happen, if maybe the kids would be taken away, or punished. There was always a stool pigeon at school, "Oh, that so and so is talking Mohawk out there." Well, you got called in and the stool pigeon got the chocolate bar and you got the strap. You didn't dare say one word in Mohawk, not one word.

❄ Eva Maracle, in *I'll Sing 'til the Day I Die*

"I got no Mohawk language at all in school," says Karen. "I did get some from my grandfather, who spoke it more to me than to his own children. When he went to school he didn't speak anything but Mohawk, and like Eva said, he got punished for it. So when it came to his own children, he said, 'If they want you to speak English, then you'll need to speak good English, and it won't be as good if Mohawk is your first language.' Sadly for the language, there were more like him who said that. Occasionally a family would say, 'Okay, you have to speak English in school, but in this house you'll speak Mohawk.' That would have been better for the language. Anyway, my grandfather did speak some Mohawk to me, but he died when I was about eleven, and no one else spoke it around me, so it didn't stick."

In 2000, Karen joined with five other people to form the Tsi Kionhnheht ne Onkwawenna Language Circle. Their ultimate goal, they declared, was to make the Mohawk language, *kanien'kéha*, the living language of Tyendinaga. I ask Karen why it is so important to her that it be kept alive. "I think because it's so connected to our identity, and our beliefs," she replies. "There are lots of things we do, but often we don't recognize where they come from. Something as simple as corn soup, our people have made it for generations, you'll still find it served at a funeral, at a wedding, and on the big holidays we celebrate.

We just do it, but oftentimes we're not sure why. The reasons are buried in our past. I don't want that all to be lost. Maybe it's from growing up in that extended family, I knew from my grandfather that we came from New York State, I knew where our land was, I knew who we were. It wasn't that we talked about these things a lot, but somehow I did come to know them."

I mention having grown up immersed in anglophone contempt for the majority language of Quebec, and my subsequent understanding of the tumultuous nationalism that finally erupted there. Karen nods. "Of course. Language carries your culture, your identity, who you are. If you're supposed to blend into the mainstream, you have to forget about who you are and become someone else. But that doesn't work, because you're never allowed to be part of the mainstream, not fully. That's still the case for us, the racism is still there, it's just more subtle now, less in your face, more covered over. I kind of prefer it in your face, so it doesn't sneak up on you unexpectedly when you're not looking for it. I'm always surprised by it. You could see it when some of the young Mohawk men pushed the issue of their fishing rights, when they first went to fish in the Napanee River. Then you saw racism in your face all right – and not just to the people in the water fishing, but to the family members, the children. They were hollering at them, name-calling, swearing."

What does the language circle do to foster *kanien'kéha*? "Awareness of it was in such a bad state here that at first we tried to come up with ways to make people aware that it was even worth doing something about it," Karen says. "We started with the idea of language heroes – we would pick one person each year, and we'd celebrate their contribution to helping the language to live. Our first hero, Dorothy Lazore, is a Mohawk person from Akwesasne who's been teaching the language at the school here for about ten years. We had a big potluck dinner for her, it was a surprise, with family and friends of hers coming from Akwesasne and Kahnawake. Another language hero is Aida Doreen. She's always promoting the language – she'll use it if she knows you know some. We wanted to recognize that we value that kind of effort. We also did something for Aboriginal Day, we got the

Mohawk singers, and speakers from Kanatsiohareke and Kahnawake, they're good ambassadors for the language."

What about Karen – how's her own *kanien'kéha* coming along? She sighs. "I've gone to language classes for more than ten years. I've had four different teachers. But I'm not a very good student, I don't apply myself." She laughs. "The trouble is, I don't speak it every day, and I don't listen to it every day. I keep saying I'm going to, but somehow I don't get around to it." But with so few people around who can speak the language, how could she? "Well, that's the thing. You'd need to have people around you speaking it. My grandmother couldn't speak it when she married my grandfather, but she learned it from the people around here, because that's the only language they used when they got together. After one class I took with David Maracle, when he came back for the next session and started talking to us, I was surprised to find that I knew every word he said. But I couldn't have answered him. I guess you could say I'm a pretty fluent listener!"

A highlight of her language learning was a two-week intensive course at Kanatsiohareke in the Mohawk Valley. In 1993, led by Tom Porter, two dozen Mohawk families recovered three hundred acres of their ancestral lands in northern New York State. At Kanatsiohareke, the "place of the clean pot," they built a self-sufficient community, with a learning centre and library for the study of Mohawk language, culture, and spirituality. "We were about fourteen in a class," says Karen. "We lived where our people lived, communally as they did, and we used the language they used. It was quite emotional. It truly did cover all those mental, physical, emotional, and spiritual aspects. I think that was the best thing I ever did for myself."

The Tyendinaga language circle got funding to pay teachers to provide night classes, from beginners to intermediate. Students so far have ranged in age from twelve to sixty. "In the beginners course, the first thing you learn is the phonics of the language," says Karen. "It can be quite intimidating when you see it written down, because the words can be huge, they can contain whole ideas. So first off, you learn the sounds that those groupings of letters make."

Their next project is a full-time ten-month course, due to start in summer 2004. It will be led by David Maracle, a Mohawk from Tyendinaga, now a linguistics professor at the University of Western Ontario. "When David was a teenager, he spent a lot of time with the old folks," Karen recalls. "He always had a little book with him. He would ask them, how do you say this, or that, and he would write it down in his book."

> When we used to have Indian agents [federal government officials who directly controlled the reservations], they were the dictator. When I come back from overseas, we had a lot of veterans who had their money sent home, but we didn't know that the money was sent to the Indian agent who wasn't giving it to the families. So, we called a meeting and the agent came and said, "What's your business?" I says, "Yeah, I got some business and I say you've got too damn much say around here and you're stealing our money!" Oh, geez, he went up four feet in the air, grabbed his papers and ran down the road. But later, we got rid of him, and he cried like a baby when he had to go . . .
> ❖ Mel Hill, in *I'll Sing 'til the Day I Die*

I'll Sing 'til the Day I Die is a rich collection of unique voices and stories. I borrowed the slim volume from the Ka:nhiote Library; it's available at libraries and book stores across Canada. "Even though Beth Brant had to cut down the interviews quite a lot, she managed to keep people's voices," says Karen. "If you knew them, you'd say you could hear them speaking. It's quite lovely." The author donated her royalties to the library.

Now Karen is working on a second oral history project with the Tyendinaga research department, also funded by the Canada Council, to gather video interviews about how people lived on and with the land. This time she did some of the interviews herself. "We did work out some questions to ask, but I've found that it's not so important to be a good questioner as a good listener. You have your questions that you want answered, but sometimes people get talking, and you don't want to interrupt the flow just so you can go on to your next question. So you just watch, you see which questions they may have missed, you ask those, and that in turn sets off another whole flow of remembrance. If you pay attention, you can tell when they want to speak more. It's not just listening with your ears – you're paying attention on several different levels."

The first person Karen interviewed was one of her own aunts. I ask her if familiarity helped or hindered the process. "Neither of us was intimidated by it – basically it was a visit," Karen replies. "But even though I know her pretty well, she certainly said things that I didn't know. You don't often get the chance to talk in depth like that with people anymore. In days past, when people visited, they would stay a while. My aunt talked about when she was a child, and her grandfather would come to visit, he would stay for a week. You had to get there by horse and buggy – you didn't just drive over, stay ten minutes and then leave. So you got to talk more in depth than just about the weather and surface things like that."

As a keeper of history, does she have further projects in mind? "I wish we could do an oral history with everyone in the community," she says. "They don't even have to be that old, the life we lead changes so quickly. And the closer I get to being whatever old is [she's fifty-seven], the more I think that forty year olds have a story to tell. The fact that most of the people in the book have passed on – and now some of the people on our first list for the new project have too – that only reinforces my opinion that it's important to catch people's stories before it's too late. If you don't, think of all that knowledge and wisdom that you lose."

TS'EOULI

One spring day, when I was ten or twelve years old, I went to the town dump in Churchill with some neighbours and carried home food scraps in a little box tied on my back. There was nothing unusual about this. All of us went to the dump to look for food. But that day, when I came home and put the box on the table, my father stood near the window of our house. He was crying. As he stood there, he turned towards my mother and said, "I was once a leader for my people and my children. I stood tall and walked with pride and dignity. My people and my children never went hungry. When my family needed food, all I had to do was to go out on our land and hunt. I never came home empty-handed. The clothes I wore were the best – beaded caribou-hide jackets, beaded mukluks, and gloves. I would never wear anything that was torn or even a little ripped. That is how proud I was. I had the confidence of my people. Now, look at my baby daughter, bringing food thrown away by other people, so that I can eat." When he said this, I couldn't understand what he meant. I was too young. All I knew was that I loved my father and that it made me sad to see him cry.

❀ Ila Bussidor, in *Night Spirits: The Story of the Relocation of the Sayisi Dene*, by Ila Bussidor and Üstün Bilgen-Reinart

I made contact with Chief Ila Bussidor on a Sunday afternoon, in her three-bedroom, wood-heated house on the south shore of Tadoule Lake, in northern Manitoba. Tadoule (pronounced Ta-doo-lee) is derived from the Dene *ts'eouli*, which translates as "floating ashes." Chief Bussidor lives with her husband, Ernie, and their two younger kids, Roseann and Dennis; the two older ones, Jason and Holly, now live on their own.

I'd called to make an appointment to talk with Chief Bussidor by satellite phone the following week. "Oh no," she said, "I probably won't have any time during the week. The days go by so fast, there always seems to be a million things I have to do." My heart sank. It had taken a long time to find her. Then she added, "Why don't we talk right now?" I asked how should I address her, Chief Bussidor? She laughed. "Oh no, just Ila." She'd been vacuuming when I called, the machine run by the community generator.

Tadoule Lake is the most northerly community in Manitoba, not far from the 60th parallel, the border with Nunavut. When we spoke in early March, the winter road was still open. Cut through the bush by Ernie Bussidor and his friend Tom in the winter of 1998, it serves Tadoule Lake and two other northern communities. "That was quite a job," says Ila. "While they were cutting the road, they had to sleep outside at minus forty." In a month or so it will no longer be passable, and once again Tadoule Lake will be accessible only by air. The rush is on to get in as much fuel, building materials, and other heavy freight as possible.

I ask Ila about the million things she has to do: what does a normal work day look like for her? "Administration, paper work, that's a piece of cake," she replies. "It's dealing with people day to day that's the most difficult challenge. When you consider the history of what happened to our people in the last forty-eight years, it has left a tremendous scar on us. Being a leader in a community where people have a lot of problems that date back to that time, and most of the older people have died, now it's my generation that's responsible for taking care of the community. People are so wounded – let's say a family that lost a whole generation through all kinds of deaths in Churchill, freezing to death, house fires, getting beaten to death. If people haven't really recovered from all of that, it means a lot of problems. And our children, who are in their twenties now, they're also affected by what happened to us. I think we still haven't addressed healing in a proper way. I don't know if there is a proper way of doing it – it's a huge job, maybe going to take another lifetime to do it. Maybe those little wee children growing up now, five years old, twelve years old, maybe they'll have a better life than I had when I was a child."

For more than a thousand years, the Sayisi Dene lived in the forests and on the open tundra of what is now northern Manitoba and Nunavut, moving with the seasons and the caribou.

I remember a time when there were no white men around us, and the people had to survive on the land. This was a very long time ago. The people were instinctive and strong like the caribou and the wolves in this harsh territory. Their sense of direction when they travelled was unfailing, as if the directions were imprinted on their minds. They didn't need a map. They just knew where to go.

Survival was hard work. To eat, we had to hunt or fish. To stay warm, we had to make caribou-hide clothes. For shelter, we had to make our own teepees. There were no shortcuts. We did every-thing by hand. We went everywhere on foot. Never once did any-one complain about the hard work. No one ever got angry because there was so much work to do. We had to co-operate, there was no time to argue. It was just the way our life was.

    ✾ Betsy Anderson, one hundred years old, interviewed in her
one-room cabin at Tadoule Lake for *Night Spirits*. She
spoke in Dene, translated by Ila, her granddaughter.

In August 1956, the year after Ila was born, the government of Canada forcibly removed the Sayisi Dene from their traditional lands and livelihoods and dumped them on the outskirts of Churchill, a military and trading town on Hudson Bay in northern Manitoba.

The plane came with three white people plus the pilot. They said they came to move the people. The people never replied. We took whatever we could with us, we left behind our traps, our tobog-gans, our cabins, and we got into the plane. When we got out in Churchill, there were no trees. The wind was blowing sand on everything. We didn't know what to do next. We couldn't do anything there. We couldn't go trapping. We couldn't set a net. There was nothing to hunt. We were in a desperate state. We had nothing to live on.

    ✾ John Solomon, Sayisi Dene elder, in *Night Spirits*.
He was thirty in 1956.

Over the next two decades the Sayisi Dene disintegrated. The book documents 117 deaths between 1960 and 1977, almost half of them by house fires, freezing, drowning, car accidents, or murder. Thirty-two children died from malnutrition or preventable illness. "The rest of us, the survivors," says Ila, "we carry the scars, and the memories."

In 1985, Ila met Üstün Bilgen-Reinart (see chapter 4), a current-affairs reporter with CBC-TV in Winnipeg. Ila was taking a Native communications course in Thompson, Manitoba, and Üstün wanted to talk with her for a documentary she was making on the community at Tadoule Lake. "She interviewed me as one of the young people who had to leave the community to get skills I needed, which was not going to happen in Tadoule Lake."

Three years later, Ila became chief of the Sayisi Dene. She asked Üstün to help her tell the story of her people – by then they had picked up their friendship again. "She said, 'Why not do it yourself?' but I didn't have the confidence for that. I needed somebody to help me, and I chose her. We did an outline of what needed to be done to put this story together, and we applied for funding. She and I went to Churchill together, and she came up to Tadoule Lake, I don't know how many times, so we could do the interviews."

I ask Ila why she felt so powerfully compelled to document the Sayisi Dene story. "I wanted to be a voice for my father and my mom," she says, "and a lot of those other people whose lives were cut off, so they never had the chance to tell their own stories. Because of my own pain after I lost my parents in 1972, I remember when I left Churchill – I was living with a family and going to school in Guelph at the time, but I had come back home for Christmas. As the plane left Churchill, I could see the streetlights of Dene Village down there, and I said to myself, 'If I ever come back here again, I will make something out of my life, I'll honour my mum and dad, so they will never be forgotten.' I was seventeen years old. It was like a little seed, something I planted within myself."

Perhaps the seed had been planted earlier. "I always wrote poems when I was a child, and I read a lot," says Ila. "Then as an adult I started reading articles written by professors getting their Ph.D., studies on my people, and I could see that a lot of this information was inaccurate. When I was about sixteen, I saw a thesis done by somebody called Skip Coolidge, who lived for maybe two summers with us in Dene Village. We were just little kids then, we were his buddies, and then he wrote that it was a big drunken mess and nothing more. When I read that, I was really shocked and saddened. A lot of it was true, but the way he wrote it, it was like it was done through a second set of eyes, from somebody who wasn't really there. I read a lot of stuff like that, and I thought this is bullshit, I lived this story, I could tell it better."

She writes in the book, "It is sad we did not have the skills, knowledge, and resources to speak for ourselves during those terrible years. When I was a young girl, I often wished I could help my parents, although I did not fully understand something that I could feel was so wrong. I wondered, How can I make something right out of a terrible situation? Telling my story now might correct some of the outsiders' misconceptions about my people. Our story may show the government what a terrible mistake they made when they uprooted my people."

According to the historical account, "mistake" is a generous word to describe yet another crime against the Sayisi Dene. As happened to many others, in brief negotiations with inadequate translation, the Sayisi were persuaded to sign on to Treaty Five in 1910. In return for "surrendering" thousands of square miles of their traditional territory in northern Manitoba, the Dominion of Canada promised $5 per adult per year, an annual visit by a doctor, and a reservation, 160 acres per registered family. Families registered. The promised land never materialized.

> When the treaty registration was over, the white man said to the Dene: "From this day on, you will never be in need of food supplies. This will always be provided for you. Have a feast and then you will celebrate this day. It's an event which is celebrated all over this country."
>
> . . . Today, eighty-five years later, I live in a little matchbox house with no running water or proper heat. Of my eleven

children, nine have died alcohol-related deaths during our days
of poverty in Churchill. I often wish I had a picture of my children
who died, so I could look back and remember what they looked
like. But I don't.

The white men haven't kept their promises. They have all the
power now because they have our land. But as the only person
alive who remembers that historic day in 1910, I have something
that the white men don't have: my memory, which is as clear as it
was when I was a child. I am richer than they are in that sense. I
am a wealthy woman.

❁ Betsy Anderson, in *Night Spirits*

To gather the stories, Ila interviewed twelve survivors of the Churchill
years, some of them close relatives. Some interviews she did jointly
with Üstün, some on her own. With the older people, who spoke little
or no English, she did the interviews in Dene, then translated them
into English.

I ask her about her mother tongue. "Until I was about two and a
half my language was Dene," she says. "My parents were still living in
North River then, about thirty miles inland from Hudson's Bay – a few
families tried to make a go of it there. But then I was taken to the hospital in Churchill with some kind of sickness. An army doctor kept me
at the hospital for about six months, even after I got well. He didn't
want to give me back to my parents, he begged them to give me over to
his care – can you imagine that? But there was no way my mother
would let me go. Anyway, when I went back to my parents, I was speaking a mixture of English and Dene."

In the intervening years, her Dene language skills faded. "To translate from Dene into English was really hard. You have to be fluent in the
language to get the real meaning. Sometimes I would have to check a
word that I didn't understand, somebody would have to translate that
word for me. I think Dene has more depth and meaning to it than English. Say you want to use the word 'sun' – in Dene the word for that can
mean two or three different things. Depending on how you phrase it,

it can also mean time, clock, or watch. There are no swear-words in Dene, no really harsh words like F-you in English. I think it's a really beautiful language. When you say a word, it's not just a word, it's part of your spirit."

I ask her about *Sayisi Dene*: Could these words be translated? "*Dene* means person, people, any human being," she says. "I guess more recently, after the Europeans came over, we had to start to name different people – white man, Inuit, Cree. But still, if you mean people in general, you say *Dene*, people. If you see somebody walking toward you, let's say on the ice of a lake, and you can't see who it is yet, you say *Dene*, which means it could be anybody. *Sayisi* means 'of the east.' So we are the eastern Dene, the eastern people."

Ila's own story runs like a dark river through *Night Spirits*. Üstün recorded it in a series of long, wrenching interviews. For Ila, the hardest part was going back to Dene Village, a deeply haunted place for her, particularly since Christmas Eve, 1972.

> After the show ended [*she had gone with friends to a movie at the army base*], we got on the bus to go back to Dene Village. Another girl, named Alice, got on the bus after us and she came beside us. "The bus driver said there was a house on fire in Dene Village," she said. We all thought it must be one of the empty houses at the end of the road.
>
> Usually when the bus goes to Dene Village, it just turned around and let people out, but this time it drove all the way through the village. As it was turning the corner, I saw the house that was burning. I thought it was Alexander's house. As we got closer, everyone stood up in the bus to see. I was sitting next to the window and I heard one of the girls say, "That's your mom and dad's house!"
>
> By the time I stood outside in the crowd, the roof had caved in. The whole house was on fire. The cops were there. There was no way anybody could get out.
>
> ✣ Ila Bussidor, in *Night Spirits*

Ila's dark river winds from the ashes of the fire through alcohol, drugs, rapes, and attempted suicides, until it reaches a clear northern lake, about four hundred kilometres west of Churchill. In 1973 a group of Sayisi Dene survivors left Dene Village and went back to the land. They set up camp on the shore of Tadoule Lake, a traditional fishing spot. From here the wild Seal River tumbles through spruce forest, eskers (post-glacial sand and gravel ridges), tundra, and rapids to Hudson Bay. People voted unanimously to ban alcohol in their new community.

Ila flew in for the first time the next summer and returned to stay the following winter. "It was most beautiful place I had ever seen, even though people were living in tents and hand-made cabins. The Department of Indian Affairs didn't put in a bunch of money to help people rebuild their lives. They had to do it on their own."

I wonder about the skills needed to survive in the northern wilderness: did people still remember them? "It was very hard with so many of the older people either dead or so wounded that they couldn't help much," says Ila. "I learned everything I could from my older sisters, my aunties, and other older women. Though I knew we couldn't live like that any more, I wanted to learn just so I could do these things: how to tan caribou hides, how to make mukluks and mitts, how to put a net in the lake the proper way so you catch fish, how to get wood – everybody has to burn wood here for heat, but you don't just go into the bush and chop any old tree. I learned how to tell which was tamarack and which was green wood, just by looking at them. Now, thirty years later, of course those ways are gone. My kids listen to current music, they have access to the Internet, to satellite TV, they dress just like what you see in Toronto. We know what's happening all over the world, according to CNN and the CBC." Suddenly she laughs. "I forget what your question was, I got carried away there!" So did I.

The Sayisi Dene had to relearn other skills basic to life. Ila and her husband, Ernie, have been together since 1976. In *Night Spirits* they talk about the demons they carried with them from Dene Village. Ernie says, "I would drink and then I would hit her and then I would sober up and I would be remorseful. It was a cycle. She would forgive me, we would go through a honeymoon phase. But our honeymoon phases became shorter and shorter. The terrible thing was that I knew something was very wrong – but I had no idea what it was, or why." The cycle continued after their first child was born, and the other three.

Says Ila: "We go for a while without violence, and then it erupts. I have too much hurt and bitterness in me. I throw all that at him and he can't take it. I say things to really hurt him because I can't hurt him physically – he is stronger than me. That's when I bring it out in him. He has to hurt me back so he starts hitting me." She describes lying to a doctor to cover up for Ernie after he had broken her eardrums.

In one of her last interviews with Üstün Bilgen-Reinart, Ila says, "I made a decision not to abuse alcohol the way I had seen it abused at Camp-10 and Dene Village. It has made a big difference. But I still struggle with it. If I had kept drinking the way people at Dene Village had, maybe I wouldn't be alive today. Maybe Ernie would be in jail. As a sober person, I have the strength to recognize a lot of things and to try to make some corrections. Slowly, our relationship is getting healthier."

Ernie adds, "I would say Ila and I get along better now. When we age together, I hope we will settle down and be close to each other. If you're willing to stick it out that long, you can work things out in the end."

Night Spirits was published in 1995 to immediate critical acclaim. "A must-read book," said the *Winnipeg Free Press*. "A historical masterpiece," said *Indian Life*. The *Winnipeg Sun* called it the "Manitoba book of the year, a Canadian holocaust memoir." "A creative and courageous act of individual and collective grieving," said Jean-Guy Goulet of Saint Paul University in Ottawa.

In Tadoule Lake, reactions to the book were mixed. Ila was no longer chief at the time. "When the book came out, a lot of fighting happened within the community, and the leadership basically laughed at me," she says. "I think it was partly jealousy, but more because people still don't know how to acknowledge some of these terrible things that happened to us. At the beginning I was really hurt, but then I thought, it's too late, I can't take it back, I did what I could, and what's stopping you people from doing something instead of attacking what I did? About a year later, I was sitting in the band hall with a bunch of people, there was a card game going on. Someone came up behind me and put their arms around me. I could feel her face against my cheek. I looked up and saw a young girl, her name is Brenda. She said, 'I read the book. Now I know why my parents are the way they are.' She said 'Mahsi' – thank you. That made it okay."

How does Ila assess the book herself? "When I talk about a voice for the many who lost their lives in Churchill, I see this book as being their voice. Along with Üstün, we made sure those voices are going to be here for a long time." There she stops. It's enough.

In the opening chapter, "My Story," Ila says, "By telling the true story of my people and my family, I am beginning a journey that's very important for my life and for my children. This is a good day to begin to travel the road towards healing. "

I ask Ila how her journey is going. She hesitates, a long silence. Then she says, "I think as long as I live, there will always be pain in my heart for what I lost. But no matter what happened to you, you can't get stuck there. Some of my generation, and the generation before me, they were so messed up by what happened in Churchill. So many bad things that maybe they haven't acknowledged, and they can't move forward. I see people that have educated themselves, they even have a degree, they could work anywhere, but I see them on the streets of Thompson, drunk, not able to hold a job. The way I see it, to move on, you have to go back and acknowledge what happened, no matter how bad it was, or how painful it is to relive. Only then can you let it go, or maybe you have to live with it. Each time you talk about it, you get stronger and stronger. For myself, I can't say I'm completely healed. Probably I will never be. But if I didn't go back to Dene Village and start doing the story, I don't think I could have done the things I'm doing today. I haven't done a whole lot but, like you, I contribute a small piece to this mission – I call it a mission, to get justice for the people. I don't know – " She trails off, perhaps embarrassed. But she knows.

> This relocation destroyed our independence and ruined our way of life. More than 100 of my people, one-third of our population, died in the Churchill Camps because of this unplanned, misdirected government action. This didn't happen a thousand miles from here, or a hundred years ago . . . It happened to my people, my family, thirty to thirty-five years ago. It seems like only yesterday, and it affects us still today.
>
> ❂ Ila Bussidor, testimony to the Royal Commission on Aboriginal Peoples, Thompson, Manitoba, June 1993

Once again chief of the Sayisi Dene, Ila has become known as a passionate, articulate advocate for her people. "I will take it as far as I can," she says, "so some day my children and grandchildren will benefit from whatever can be done to resolve this issue." It's part of the journey. I think it's the primary reason Ila agreed to talk to a stranger from the south, a white man writing a book on oral history.

The *Winnipeg Free Press* reported that three European human rights observers, consultants to UNESCO, would visit Tadoule Lake to document the impact of the forced relocation, and stalled negotiations with the federal government over compensation. The article quotes Arne Peltz, a Winnipeg lawyer representing the Sayisi Dene First Nation: "We were told this was an expedited file, but there has been no indication of a decision or a time frame . . . I think the presence of the observers will require the government of Canada to account for its handling of the situation." That was in September 2001.

Two weeks before our conversation in late winter 2004, Ila flew to Ottawa to meet – again – with officials at the Department of Indian Affairs. "We've been after them forever about compensation," she says, "but they tell us they don't have a mandate to deal with this matter. Without that, all this meeting and talk, it's meaningless. It's frustrating. But at least we have our foot in the door. I think maybe what we need to do is make a lot of noise, make a public statement. This has been outstanding for too long. We've been through how many different prime ministers since then. Maybe it's time we have to say, 'If you don't do this for us, we'll go ahead and sue the Canadian government for all the damages you've done to us.' Who knows, maybe that will speed it up."

Ila is about to turn forty-nine, "maybe halfway through my life." At 103, her grandmother, Betsy Anderson, is still on this earth, still living at Tadoule Lake, though blind and frail. Ila and Ernie fish in the summer; in the fall he hunts caribou, and she dries the meat. Ernie was chief of the Sayisi Dene in the mid-'90s. "When you look at him," says Ila, "you wouldn't know he's Indian. He looks like a white man, you know, with the blue eyes? He was a product of the Churchill days, when the army was there. But he was brought up by his grandparents, so he knows the language really well. He's also a drum singer, and he has helped to revive our traditional hand games." Ernie leads the youth drum group, a project to help pass on Sayisi Dene traditions and values.

Now Ila is a grandmother herself. "Cody is Holly's first child," she tells me. "He's going on seven months, and he's the most beautiful, beautiful thing in my life right now. Everything is about him. I think he's being over-loved – I don't know, can you be over-loved? After the pain I went through, now I'm getting something in return. Over half of my life I cried for the loss of my parents, but now it's like they have been given back to me. I think they live through me, and they will live through my children, and my grandchild."

 LAND AND LIFE

At the deep heart of many First Nations grievances is land. While European and then Canadian
invaders have seen it as a commodity, theirs to take, for First Nations
people it has always been the basis of life. So it is for the Sayisi Dene.

After years of negotiation, finally in 1996 the Sayisi Dene reached
a tentative agreement by which the federal government would grant
them 23,000 acres of land – land that had been taken from them – and
$580,000 for economic development.

In the meantime the government had reached a settlement with
the Inuit to create Nunavut, the first self-governing First Nations territory in Canada, two million square kilometres north and west of
Hudson Bay, above the tree line to the North Pole. The Inuktitut word
Nunavut translates as "our land." "But all the time they were negotiat-
ing, they knew there was a third party involved," says Chief Ila Bussidor: " – us – because our traditional territory overlaps with the land
the Inuit were claiming as theirs. But they excluded us, they didn't
even invite us to table. And we were in no position to fight, because of
the ordeal we'd been through."

Still, fight they did. In 1993 the Sayisi and the neighbouring
Dene nation went to court to assert their treaty rights. The Inuit
agreed to freeze 106,000 contested acres within the proposed boundaries of Nunavut until the case was settled. But in 1997 the Inuit cut

off negotiations and sought dismissal of the Dene court challenge. The case resumed; now the Dene had the full support of the Assembly of First Nations.

Nunavut was born April 1, 1999. "At the eleventh hour," says Ila, "when the prime minister and all the officials were about to go up to Iqaluit [the capital of the new territory] for the celebrations, we took people from here and from the next Dene community, the Oteinadi Dene of Lac Brochet, to protest in Ottawa. Somebody in Winnipeg donated $50,000 to the cause, so we could pay for the travel – it's very expensive from here. So we had our seventeen drummers, the elders, and the young people standing out there on Parliament Hill."

Jane Stewart, minister of Indian Affairs at the time, had agreed to meet with the two Dene chiefs. "The lawyers and the grand chiefs came in with us," says Ila. "She said she had fifteen minutes for us, twenty minutes at the most. We talked for a while, but it wasn't getting anywhere, so I said to this other Dene chief in our language, 'Tell everybody else to leave, and we'll see what we can do by ourselves.' Some of the grand chiefs didn't like that, but they left anyway. Then this other chief from Lac Brochet – he had just come on, he was a couple of years older than me – he had a stab at it, he said we'll go to court. I said to him in Dene, 'The reason we're here is we were in court already. If we go back there, it's a step backward, we can't allow that.' He said, 'Well then, you try.'"

Ila spoke to the minister as she did to me, person to person. "It didn't need lawyers or long speeches. I just re-echoed how important our traditional territory was to us and how unjust it was for them to exclude us from that traditional land. I said, 'You go out there, you tell the young people, the old people, that as minister of this country you have nothing for them, they came here for nothing. You go tell them because I'm not going to do it for you.' I guess I cornered her. She said, 'Okay, we'll start a process.' She came out there with us, the chiefs were there, and the media, there was no way she could back out of it. That's how the negotiation started."

Five years later, negotiations continue. "It's so slow," says Ila. "I wish they'd speed it up a bit. But there's been progress, which is good.

We stand to regain about 4.5 million acres of our traditional territory. With that comes harvesting rights, rights to minerals, all that. This could make a big difference for us."

DELGAMUUKW

The oral histories were used in an attempt to establish occupation and use of the disputed territory which is an essential requirement for aboriginal title. The trial judge refused to admit or gave no independent weight to these oral histories and then concluded that the appellants had not demonstrated the requisite degree of occupation for "ownership." Had the oral histories been correctly assessed, the conclusions on these issues of fact might have been very different.

❁ *Delgamuukw v British Columbia,*
Supreme Court of Canada, 1997

Towards the end of the nineteenth century, settlers of European origin began to occupy the wooded valleys of central British Columbia. Over the next hundred years, the people who had lived there for centuries tried to win recognition for their traditional rights to the land. All their efforts were ignored or rebuffed by a succession of governments, provincial and federal.

In 1984, Gitxsan and Wet'suwet'en hereditary chiefs launched an action in the British Columbia Supreme Court, claiming title to 58,000 square kilometres of ancestral territory. In the longest First Nations land claim trial in Canadian history to that point, the chiefs broke new ground for oral history as evidence. In previous trials, anthropologists and other non-Native "experts" had provided evidence, but in this case key testimony was given by Gitxsan and Wet'suwet'en elders, who spoke about their people's centuries-old relationship to the land.

In 1991 the judge, Allan McEachern, released his ruling. He dismissed most of the chiefs' claims, along with their oral evidence of historical attachment to the land. He described the pre-colonization life of their people as "nasty, brutish, and short," with "no written language, no horses or wheeled vehicles. . . . " He concluded that the Gitxsan and Wet'suwet'en had no interest in nor any rights to the lands in question. Not surprisingly, the decision generated a storm of outrage, including a UN report that condemned McEachern's ruling.

After the B.C. Court of Appeal upheld the decision, the Gitxsan and Wet'suwet'en took their case to the Supreme Court of Canada. Its historic ruling in 1997 overturned those of the two lower courts. It confirmed that aboriginal title does exist in British Columbia, that it includes a right to the land itself – not just the right to hunt, fish or gather – and that when dealing with crown land, the government must consult with and may have to compensate First Nations whose rights are affected.

The Supreme Court also ruled that from now on, due respect and weight must be accorded to First Nations values and history as conveyed through their oral traditions.

The decision was widely considered a milestone in treaty negotiations, reverberating as far away as Australia, where aboriginal peoples have been struggling as long and hard to reclaim stolen lands as their counterparts in North America. The Supreme Court ruling is also regarded as a milestone in validating oral history as evidence.

Joan Holmes and Christine Dernoi do historical research for First Nations land claims. Each has her own firm in Ottawa, the locus of federal power. "When I started in 1983," says Joan, "oral history wasn't considered to have any value at all. The government position was that the documents were all you needed to look at, they told the whole story. But First Nations people kept saying, again and again, 'That is *not* the whole story, far from it.' Either that story was completely contrary to what they believed and how they understood history, or it was grossly incomplete, the whole perspective was wrong."

Both women came to land claims work in the early 1980s with degrees in anthropology. I asked why this training was useful. "Because at least you would have heard the word 'Indian' in some way that wasn't an insult!" says Christine, "You'd be surprised how rare that was in the early '80s. Also, anthropology is about valuing other cultures on their own terms."

How does oral history actually figure in their work? Christine replies, "When you're looking for specific kinds of information relevant to a case, I or someone else would set up the questions, possibly with a lawyer, in consultation with the First Nation. In one case, a First Nation kept being relocated for over a century – they kept losing the ground under their feet, either it was expropriated or sold. We wanted to hear from each generation, why did they think they had to move, what happened in each move, where did they go, what did they lose – or gain, as the case may be. We already knew what had happened according to the documents, the paper trail, but we also wanted to hear people's own perceptions."

Joan Holmes worked with a First Nation whose reserve had been split by a hydro line shortly after World War II. "Based on what we knew from the paper trail," she says, "we drew up a slate of questions to clarify what people remembered from when the lines were put through: how it happened, what kind of arrangements were made with the chief and council, what they remembered about the construction – some of them had worked on it, or their fathers had – and what land was taken from them. We also asked about life on the reserve before the development: where people lived, how they used the land, what had changed after the development, and how people felt about the whole thing. The questions were quite structured, to get some consistency in the material. People in the band did the interviews. Then we did transcripts from the tapes and sent them back for people to look at. We added all this information into the report, interspersing the document history with what people from the community had to say."

Though the researchers pursue specific topics, oral history often reveals a rich portrait of real lives behind the technicalities of the legal case. Joan worked recently on a project in northeastern Ontario, documenting land occupation and use. "Mostly we talked to people in their sixties and older who had grown up in the bush. They could tell you in minute detail what kind of plants were used for what, how they left signs in the bush to communicate with each other on the trap-lines – if they needed help, or were moving from one spot to another – and what kind of wood they used in smoking meat to give it a particular taste. One woman told me her grandmother taught her never to mix two kinds of wood in a meat-smoking fire. Everyone talked about how much it disrupted their way of life when the registered trap-line system came in after World War II in Ontario. For generations, they had decided as a community how to use the land, and how to pass it on – for example, when someone was getting old, they would need a trap-line that was more accessible. Now all of that was replaced by government regulations. Some of them lost their family trap-lines. If they didn't use it for a year or two – if they were letting it rest, or if a family death or sickness meant they couldn't use it for a while – the ministry would give it to a white trapper."

During interviews for this project, Joan was jolted repeatedly by accounts of how the government had seized children to place them in church-run schools. "One woman talked about how an RCMP officer would come with the Indian agent – this was someone who knew where people would be, how many children they had and of what ages, because they had to register in order to get treaty payments – and as soon as the children reached school age the Mounties would come and take them away. It was heartbreaking to hear people talk about losing their children like that." Joan is a mother, with two sons.

"I've been told that some people actually hid their children," Christine adds. "They never registered them, choosing to forego the treaty annuity – a significant sacrifice for people with hardly any income – rather than have their children taken away. One woman told me they hid the children so they'd keep their language – the ones who went to school lost it. If they knew the language, they could be told the stories, then they'd be the carriers of the culture. For people that rely on oral tradition to pass down their history and their way of life, if you don't have your children, that's the end of the line."

Joan interviewed a woman whose grandmother had hidden her and two cousins in the bush when the Mounties were coming. "So this

woman grew up without ever going to school," she says. "The government argued that it seized children for their own good, so they could
learn to read and write. This woman didn't have any of that, and she's
the most marvellous person, articulate, intelligent, sophisticated. You
can feel her groundedness, her confidence – I just loved her. She also
told me how lonely she'd sometimes been as a child, just her and a few
cousins with all the adults. Sometimes she used to wish that she'd gone
with the other children."

I ask Christine and Joan what practical impact they see the *Delgamuukw* decision having had on oral history – was it as significant in
practice as it was on paper? Joan replies, "I'd have to say that people
have been paying a bit of lip service to it – 'Okay, you can have an oral
history component in your study, we'll agree to fund that.' But on the
government side, people still don't really believe in oral history unless
it's substantiated by the written record. You hear it all the time, 'I can
hardly remember what's happened in my own life. How can people
claim their oral history is accurate?' It's pretty well recognized that oral
history isn't that good on specific times – typically it collapses time
frames – and everybody remembers the same thing in different ways.
But those aren't adequate reasons for dismissing it as a valid source of
information. It certainly helps if the oral history is at least consistent or
understandable within the context of the written record. Where there
are differences between the two, it's worth asking why – why did people
who wrote the record have one view, and First Nations people another?"

Since this seems rather abstract to me, I ask for an example. "The
Howard case," says Christine. "The Williams Treaty was signed in 1923
with Chippewas north and west of Peterborough. It turned out they
didn't get any hunting rights in that treaty, so they went to court to
see what happened. In the trial the crown produced a First Nations
witness who said, 'We surrendered all our hunting rights.' Unfortunately the First Nation didn't have a witness to counter that. Which
leaves the document, the treaty, and it says nothing about preserving
any hunting rights. But where did the crown find this person, and how
did the First Nations lawyers miss him?"

Joan adds, "With oral history, often you have to check, where did this person get their information? If someone says, 'This is what happened,' and you press them a little – 'Why do you think this, how did you learn this?' – sometimes you discover that they read it in a book. Though people may treat that as oral history, because it came out of somebody's mouth, it may only be their opinion, and a second-hand opinion at that. So when someone says, 'Yeah, we gave away all our hunting rights,' you have to ask, 'On what basis does he say that?'"

"The first question that comes to mind is why would people who have survived for millennia on hunting and gathering suddenly give up their right to hunt, knowingly, of their own free will," says Christine. "It doesn't make any sense."

Joan nods in agreement. "If you take what this person said in court – 'We surrendered our rights' – and then you go back and look at the whole massive pile of transcripts from 1923, all 800 pages of them, when the government commissioners had an inquiry before they wrote the treaty, you find many elders saying, 'When we make our treaty, you must ask the government about our hunting and fishing rights, because the other day when I was out hunting, I got stopped by a farmer, so I want to make sure I can still hunt there.'"

Christine explains, "What we're talking about here aren't hunting rights on the reserve but on traditional hunting grounds. These rights are guaranteed in some treaties – which is why people don't need licences to hunt or fish. But for some strange reason, in the Williams Treaty hunting rights were left out."

Joan continues, "Again and again through the transcripts, you find this concern to ensure that hunting and fishing rights are maintained, and you find the commissioners saying, 'We'll take that under advisement.' So when you look at that kind of written history, the commission transcripts, and then someone says, 'Oh yeah, we gave up our rights,' they just don't match."

"Who knows, this person may have assumed that they gave up their hunting rights *because* it wasn't written there in the treaty," says Christine.

Only quite recently has the written record been subjected to the same critical scrutiny as oral sources. Says Joan, "Sometimes by following the paper trail, you'll find that the same people have been coming to the Indian Department [as it used to be called] generation after generation with the same grievance, but the department keeps saying, 'You have no grounds.' Then you look at department correspondence, and you find that the letter of response in 1950 is exactly based on the wording in the letter of 1930, which is exactly based on the wording of the letter written in 1890. Each of these went into the file, and each time a response was needed, they just looked up the last letter and repeated it! Eventually, by sheer repetition, this becomes 'the truth.' That's how the written tradition entrenches itself, but yet the written is believed and the oral isn't!"

"Especially if it's coming from Indians," Christine adds.

In the Williams Treaty case, the researchers discovered that the written record provided more support for the First Nations interpretation than did the oral testimony. More often, the opposite is true. But in either case, First Nations contend – backed now by the Supreme Court – that the spirit and intent in which a treaty was made are at least as important as its contents. "What we're dealing with is a long, long history of discommunication between governments and First Nations," says Christine. "So we need to investigate the different understandings, the different intentions that the two cultures had when they signed the treaty. What were they thinking? What did they want?"

To gather oral histories across cultures demands a particular quality of attention, says Joan. "Sometimes when I ask a question, and the answer doesn't seem to relate at all to my question, at first I used to get frustrated. But eventually I started to realize that they *were* answering my question, only it was in terms they considered to be important. What it requires of you is a different kind of listening."

"If you pay attention," says Christine, "you'll learn more about the people you're interviewing, and then you can ask better questions."

Joan agrees. "When I read over transcripts of interviews I've done, I notice that when you start with something big and general, it's like peeling away the layers of an onion, people go into more and more detail – like those people in the bush who talked about which kind of wood to use for smoking meat."

For several years Christine has been gathering oral and written research on Treaty 9, which covers a huge swath of northern Ontario and affects the survival of forty-nine First Nations, now allied as the Nishnawbe Aski Nation. Governments argue that the Native chiefs agreed to *surrender* their land. The First Nations counter that they agreed only to *share* it. The difference in one word reveals not only inadequate translation but fundamentally opposed understandings of the human connection to land.

> Our Father, we beg you to tell those who possess lands above Long Sault *[on the Ottawa River, northwest of Montréal]* to live in peace with us as we will tell our young people not to trouble them. Capt Fortune mistreats us often, he forbids us to fish, forbids us hunting partridge and prevents us from taking wood to warm ourselves, when we are chastized by the wind and the rain; we have decided in Council that we will ask you to observe to Lord Dorchester *[governor-general at the time]* our Father, that we have not sold our lands above Long Sault . . . Although we can prove no title that those lands belong to us, would one have the cruelty to grab them from us? Have we not always been the peaceful possessors of these lands? Would one want to use force to take lands from us that our fathers handed down to us and that we had hoped to pass on as our children's heritage?
>
> ❁ Petition 84, by Chiefs of the Algonquin
> and Nipissing Tribes, 1791

One form of written record that has proved useful in land claims research is the Indian Petition, a written record from an oral source. "I've worked with a lot with petitions from the Algonquins, in the Ottawa Valley up to Lake Nipissing," says Joan. "From the time of the British conquest, they wrote – or rather they spoke, then the missionaries, usually, would write down – these petitions to the government in defence of their hunting grounds. They say 'We are these people, our forefathers have occupied this land since time out of mind,' then they describe the territory by its geographical features. There are whole strings of these petitions, each one written down, but what they recorded was oral history. For us, they're important sources to identify traditional territories."

Christine is working on land claims that hinge on such petitions. "But you know, some people just won't believe what they read. I've come across land claims where the Indians have clearly identified their territory in these petitions – in oral testimony which someone else recorded – but then the government officials won't even believe *that*, or they won't take into account, which amounts to the same thing."

"Really it's not so much the particular record that's distrusted, whether oral or otherwise," says Joan. "It's the source – the First Nations. A lot of the reason we're doing the work we do today is because in the past what different First Nations people said wasn't believed."

Christine laughs, then says, "I shouldn't laugh about this, but it is *so* absurd. For years one First Nation had been telling civil servants that they don't have a reserve, and for years Canada kept telling them, 'Yes you do, it's right here on the map,' and they'd say, 'No, that belongs to someone else.' This went on for eighty years – imagine, eighty years! – until finally someone took the trouble to research it. And eventually the government had to admit, 'They're right, they were never given a reserve.' But how much time and money and effort did it take to prove their point?"

Joan adds, "Partly it stems from racism, but also from the assumption that since the Indians have an interest in this land, surely they'll stretch the truth. They'll say whatever they have to, therefore everything they say is suspect. Whereas the crown is some-how above manipulating information, the records are true, untainted, and objective, because that side – *our* side – has no self-interest. That's the blindness of our society. We really want to believe we're the good guys."

Christine: "I think the prejudice against oral history comes partly from the fact that it's easier and more comfortable for many academics to sit in the archives than to go out and talk to actual people."

Joan: "I also think this whole reverence for written documents, and contempt for oral sources, has its origins in the scientific, empirical way of thinking that's so characteristic of European culture, as opposed to the more spiritual approach that you find in oral traditions."

From where they stand, what needs to change for land claims to work better? More funding? Of course that would help, says Christine. "But there's something else which is at least as important: more face-to-face contact. In my experience, though obviously they need resources, First Nations aren't interested in being dealt with as if they were making some kind of insurance claim – 'Here's the list of damages, here's your cheque, that's it, goodbye.' This would never satisfy a First Nation, never. It's not what they're after. Sitting down face to face and talking about things, that's very important in First Nations tradition. They want to see who's there. But government people are very slow to understand this. In one case I've been working on, this First Nation filed a caution in the 1970s and eventually went to court in 1985. But between 1972 and 1985, while they had a whole series of negotiations going on with Canada and Ontario, not once did they get to meet face to face with the government side, not until 1983. Can you believe that?"

"As soon as people meet face to face, somehow they get tied into the story of what's happening," says Joan, "It becomes more personal, they're implicated. It's so much easier to dismiss people if they're just something abstract on paper, rather than individuals you've met and talked to. In any meetings I've been in about land claims, if the purpose of the meeting is exploratory – 'This is who we are, this is what we think this is about – '"

Christine cuts in, "Some people call those bum-sniffing exercises."

They both laugh, then Joan continues: "Always the First Nations people insist on telling their version of the story. They'll say this claim is about this, but then they'll talk about it personally, 'My grandfather lived on this land, then there was this surrender and this is what happened to him.' A lot of oral history comes out. Whether it's on the agenda or not, people on the First Nations side will probably get up and talk about their own experience. You can see people on the government side rolling their eyes, looking at their watches, wishing they could get out of there. But if you keep going to meetings like that, if you stay with it and you listen, slowly you start to understand what it's really about."

ILA AND PAUL

When Paul Martin became Prime Minister of Canada, hopes were raised for a less combative relationship between the federal government and First Nations. Martin pledged a new, more co-operative approach. By way of signalling the shift, in December 2003 the new prime minister asked a First Nations elder to perform a smudging ritual at his swearing-in ceremony in Ottawa. The ancient rite of blessing with smoke from burning sage was a first for any incoming prime minister.

More concretely, in January 2004, Paul Martin announced that the proposed First Nations Governance Act would be scrapped. Introduced during the tenure of the former prime minister, Jean Chrétien, it had sparked angry protests across Canada. While its proponents claimed the new bill would make the country's 633 Native reserves more fiscally accountable, critics argued that it would only reinforce the colonial status of First Nations.

Chief Ila Bussidor and other First Nations leaders have seen many prime ministers, and promises, come and go. They continue to face a heavily overburdened land claims system in which a specific claim can take twenty years and enormous cost to reach resolution. The current Indian Affairs settlement budget has been capped for several years at a maximum of $75–100 million annually, hardly enough to settle fourteen cases a year, which is far fewer than the number of *new* cases being filed each year.

Still . . . .

The weekend before we talked, Ila Bussidor was one of six chiefs invited to meet Prime Minister Martin at a First Nations hockey tournament in Thompson, Manitoba. "The red carpet was rolled out for him at the arena," she says. "He dropped the puck, and pictures were taken. We sat up there with him, pretending the game was really interesting." She chuckles. "Then we went into a closed area and had a meeting with him. I spoke with him about the relocation, and the land claims negotiation we're under right now. I handed him a copy of *Night Spirits*. I said, 'I want you to have this, it's the story I'm talking about.' They wanted a picture of him holding it, so Paul Martin and I had our picture taken with the book. I said to him, 'I know you're very busy, you meet hundreds of people all over the place, but maybe this story will make you remember this person you talked to in northern Manitoba.' Probably he'll forget my name and what I look like, but maybe he'll remember what I said. That human connection, it's so important. Anyway, we'll see what happens."

CHAPTER 4

Umut/Hope

How I used to work! I would get up before sunrise
to knead bread – fifteen, sixteen loaves. Then to the
fields. We were growing wheat, broad beans, chick-
peas, rye. The rye was so high that you'd get lost in
those fields. We had three cows that I milked. That's
how I spent my life. Everything we ate, we produced
ourselves. At night, when I finally went to bed, I used
to be so tired that I'd lie down as if I were dead . . .

Our work was hard all the time but until these
foreigners came here, we had peace. This mine has
destroyed that peace. How would we have known
that in our old age we would become activists
and protesters?

⚙ Süyet Ünek, seventy-five, interviewed by Üstün
Bilgen-Reinart in the village of Ovacik, Turkey

When Üstün Bilgen-Reinart returned to Turkey in
1998 with her husband, Jean, they thought they
would stay only a year. She had been a long time away and wanted to
spend time with her elderly parents. But very soon she rediscovered
her love for Anatolia, one of the oldest continually inhabited regions
on earth, between the Aegean and the Black Sea. "I had forgotten the

richness of this place," she says, "the abundance of fruits, vegetables and flowers, the riotous vitality of nature in the spring, the softness of the climate, and also the layers and layers of human heritage on this land. For me all of these are treasures."

Born in the Turkish capital Ankara in 1949, Üstün started seeing a young man in her mid-teens. "In Turkish society, that meant we walked to the school bus together," she says. When she finished high school at seventeen, they married. He won a scholarship to McGill University, so they moved to Montreal. A year later Üstün left him, fell in love, remarried, and moved to Winnipeg, where she enrolled at university and gave birth to two children.

When her husband committed suicide in 1977, she decided to stay in Canada. I ask her why. "I knew that for a young woman with two children there would be a lot of social pressures in Turkey," she replies. "I would be expected to move back with my parents, or if I did not, there would be a lot of eyes on me – if I went out with a man, the neighbours would talk, and I certainly couldn't entertain a man in my own home. I wanted to be free to do any of these things."

From 1974 on, Üstün worked in radio, first programming international music on a private station, then doing a variety of scripting, hosting, and making short documentaries for the Canadian Broadcasting Corporation in Winnipeg. "But what I really wanted to do was news and public affairs," she says. "So one day I went up to the TV newsroom and said I'd like to work here. They said I probably wouldn't be qualified, but they'd try me out." Within a year she was a full-time reporter with the daily TV current affairs show *Twenty-Four Hours*. A few years later she was invited to work for *The National*, the apex of the CBC-TV news pyramid.

"At first it was the honeymoon," she says. "They loved me, I was a fresh face, a fresh voice. Also they liked the ethnic presence – they're fond of that at *The National*, as long as the content remains absolutely mainstream. But I was never at ease in that environment, and I began to feel increasingly isolated. They kept telling me I didn't fit in with *The National*'s style, I was too passionate, too biased."

This was not the first time Üstün came up against the demon Bias. "Throughout my years at the CBC, I had the reputation – well, at best I was seen as the conscience of the program or something like that, and at worst, biased. I was always questioning the dominant line taken on anything, the so-called mainstream point of view, which I thought was a bias in itself. I tried to argue that what they called objectivity was simply a matter of parroting the dominant viewpoint, and as soon as you questioned that you were accused of bias!"

In my own experience, the CBC came noticeably under attack from right-wing and corporate forces in the late 1970s, when they were moving aggressively to reclaim ground they had partially lost through the previous decade. By the late '80s, under the Tory fiscal axe, the public broadcaster had been fairly well tamed. In 1986, a satirical radio play of mine about a Washington plot to seize Canadian water was aired once on the AM network, then pulled by the head of programming before its usual second broadcast on the FM network. Whether he got an official complaint or was simply doing his job as internal censor remains unclear. In Winnipeg, Üstün had a parallel experience, which sharpened during the volatile national debates in the months leading up to the "free trade" election of 1988.

"At the time there was a growing movement against the North American Free Trade Agreement that Mulroney was pushing. I was strongly opposed to it, and I wanted to do stories that would reflect its real meaning and potential costs. But I remember being told very clearly by someone higher up in the editorial line that we would not be spending much time on stories critical of free trade. I got the clear impression that if I wanted to continue at the CBC, I should not push on issues about which I had a passionate feeling, and the higher I climbed in the hierarchy, the more careful I would have to be."

In the late 1980s Üstün covered a variety of aboriginal issues, often working with high-profile leaders like Ovide Mercredi and Philip Fontaine of the Assembly of Manitoba Chiefs. "I loved my work," she says, "but I remember wishing I could be free of the CBC so that I could openly take sides. To me, in so many of these issues there was clearly a right and a wrong. But at the CBC you could never say this is wrong, you always had to include the opposing voice, which almost always was the dominant official voice. You were supposed to sit on the fence as if you had no view, no judgment of your own, which of course is impossible."

At *The National* the constraints were more sophisticated. "I was always told, 'Üstün, you're free to do what you want, tell any story you want, this is a democratic institution.' Of course there's some truth in that. I had then and still do have a lot of affection for the CBC, and when I look at the global media now, it's not hard to see how much further the sham of objectivity has gone. Also I don't take a simplistic view on this, I know that when you're passionately committed to something, you can easily get carried away and lose fairness. At the same time, it was very clear to me that there was this huge, dominant – let's say, hegemonic – culture, and as soon as you began to dig and question critically that dominant point of view, you were automatically seen as sliding into bias."

After the honeymoon cooled and comments about her "passion" and "bias" started to escalate, Üstün was bumped from *The National* reporter job by the return of the previous incumbent. But she refused to settle back into local news; instead she went to Europe for a holiday. On her return, a CBC Winnipeg executive created a new job for her as social affairs reporter, free to choose her own stories "except during emergencies." Then a journalist friend, Susan Riley, became executive producer of *Country Canada*, a network farm show that aired Sunday afternoons out of Winnipeg. She persuaded Üstün to co-host the program. "It was amazing," says Üstün. "This program existed only because the CBC mandate required it. It was never meant to be anything, and hardly anyone watched it, so we were able to do some wonderful things – environmental stories, what was going on in the food industry. That was a period of real excitement for me."

In the early '90s their bold new *County Canada* began to draw viewers, and, inevitably, corporate attention. "Very suddenly there was a coup d'état," says Üstün. "Susan was dumped, and I was told that from now on, I would be just a reporter." Susan went to law school, and now works on aboriginal land claims for the federal government. Üstün continued to work for a while at *County Canada*. During a shoot in Quebec she met Jean Burelle, and a long-distance relationship developed. "By then I was becoming very disillusioned with the CBC, and I began to think, do I really want to spend the rest of my life in Winnipeg? What do I really want to do?"

TADOULE LAKE

In 1985 Üstün made a documentary on Tadoule Lake, a small Sayisi Dene community in northern Manitoba (see chapter 2). Along the way she became friends with Ila Bussidor, a young woman who was chief of the Sayisi Dene at the time. A few years later Ila told Üstün she wanted to tell the story of her people but didn't know where to start. Would Üstün help? "The issue of appropriating voice was very prominent then," says Üstün, "and in any case I feel strongly that being able to tell your own story is a way of gaining power. I know that to be true for women, and I believe it's true for any people who've been denied access to the means of building their own history. So I urged Ila to write the book herself, and I would help as needed. If she couldn't write it down, I suggested she use a tape recorder and talk it out. At least that would loosen things up."

Finally, at Ila's insistence, Üstün agreed to collaborate on a book. Sharing a Canada Council grant with Ila, she returned to Tadoule Lake to record interviews with survivors of one of the cruelest crimes in Canadian history. For more than a thousand years, the Sayisi Dene lived in the forests and on the open tundra of what is now northern Manitoba and the Northwest Territories. In 1956 the government of Canada forcibly removed them from their traditional lands and livelihoods, and dumped them on the outskirts of Churchill, a military and trading town on Hudson Bay.

Night Spirits documents the disaster that followed, and, more than two decades later, the long, painful journey of the Sayisi Dene towards healing. The book weaves a detailed, wrenching historical account, researched and written by Üstün, with extensive segments from interviews she and Ila recorded with Sayisi Dene who endured the Churchill years. For Üstün, working on the book was another step in her own journey of discovery.

Of the first interview they recorded, she writes: "Ila and I headed to the one-room cabin of Ila's almost 100-year-old granny, Betsy Anderson. The sky was steely grey, with crimson streaks to the west. The air smelt of wood smoke as it always does in fall and winter at Tadoule Lake. The wind carried a powdery snow.

"Inside, a kettle was boiling on the woodstove, the steam rising from its spout fogging the windows. We put our tape recorder on the little table beside the bed, and Ila began the interview. They spoke in Dene. Granny Betsy's low, raspy voice rose slowly, deliberately, between coughing spells. She smoked. And she laughed every once in a while, a gleeful cackle. Hours passed; the room became dark and filled with smoke."

I ask Üstün how she experienced the shift from reporter to oral historian. "When I started doing the interviews, I remember feeling two things," she replies. "First, I no longer had to maintain even the appearance of so-called objectivity. I finally had the freedom that I'd been craving. The other thing I had was time. As a journalist you know what you want, and when you get it, you cut. Hardly ever do you have time to hear more, to go deeper. But Native people, especially in this community, aren't used to speaking in such a linear way. They have a beautiful way of expressing themselves, in a circular manner – they start with the most urgent things, then they tell you the background, then eventually they come back full circle to where they began. This made for very long interviews. Then I would go back to Quebec [where she worked on the book] and listen, listen, listen to the tapes. With the older people who spoke only Dene, Ila and I ran the tapes in a hotel room in Winnipeg, she translated orally, and I typed. Her translation of the answers was never as detailed as the original responses, so always I had more questions. Back we would go to fill in the gaps – this was not very economical, I'm afraid! Eventually I collected almost forty tapes."

One of the people that Üstün interviewed was Ila Bussidor herself, past and future chief of the Sayisi Dene. At the beginning of the book Ila pays tribute to her co-author "whose encouragement, amazing perseverance, and hard work carried me through the pain of remembering many dark moments in my past, and who always managed to make me laugh and see the good side of life."

The raw candour of Ila's account reveals not only her determination to be heard but also the degree of rapport that had developed between her and the woman to whom she would entrust the story of her life. A fragment:

> The first summer at Dene Village, I was just twelve years old. One beautiful warm day in July of 1967, around mid-afternoon, my parents were already drinking with some people. I did my chores as quickly as I could so that I could go and play with my friends outside. I finally got out of the house and walked down the street looking for other kids to play with. The only person on the street was a Dene man walking towards me. He was about twenty-five years old, or older. He stopped me and when I tried to walk around him he started blocking my way. I stopped. I could tell right away he had been drinking, but he wasn't drunk. He knew what he was doing. I don't know what he said to me or what I answered, but I was lured behind a house. The next thing he slugged me in the face. He kept slugging me till I blacked out.
>
> When I came to, my head was spinning and I couldn't see. The man was gone. When I tried to stand up I kept falling, and then I noticed he had ripped off my clothes. They were scattered on the ground . . .
>
> ✿ Ila Bussidor, *Night Spirits: The Story of the Relocation of the Sayisi Dene*, University of Manitoba Press, Winnipeg, 1997

ANATOLIA

The year after *Night Spirits* came out, Üstün
returned to her beloved Anatolia. Jean took a leave
of absence from his job in Quebec, and Üstün got work teaching English at the Middle Eastern University in Ankara. The first summer they explored the region on a motorcycle. Üstün was particularly drawn to the lush, green plateau around Bergama, a town of about fifty thousand not far from the Aegean, renowned as Pergamum in Hellenic and Roman times for its great library and medical centre.

In Canada she had heard that villagers in the area were trying to block the development of a gold mine which, they said, posed a mortal threat to their farms. "I was immediately interested," she says. "Villagers in Turkey had never done anything like this before. They've never had any power, never any say in what happens to them. In a way, in the Turkish context villagers are the aboriginal people. They work very hard, toiling on the land, and for centuries they've been buffeted by economic forces, political whims, and now globalization. I knew that for villagers to engage in civil disobedience against a foreign mining corporation was extremely unusual." She decided to investigate.

Not surprisingly, at first the villagers were reluctant to answer any questions. Though Üstün spoke Turkish, she looked urban and had arrived with a foreigner – all of which meant she could be a spy for the mine. When a few people did consent to talk with her, cautiously, she was struck by the clarity and depth of what they said: The mine would poison their land and give nothing back. They didn't want anything to do with it, they would defend their lands, to the death if necessary, but would use no violence, nor would they break the law.

"Clearly this was not some marginal group trying to attract attention. These were people who knew what was happening, and they knew that the power they faced was the greatest in the world, a transnational corporation [Normandy Mining, based in Australia]. In Turkey, foreign investment is almost sacred. They had researched all this, they had discussions with university professors, engineers who knew what damage gold mines have done all over the world. They were so focused, so courageous, so restrained in their resistance, I fell in love with them and decided to support them. After all, I was fifty years old, I was free of the CBC, I had a right to take a stand!"

She had also done some research of her own. On every continent where gold has been mined, indigenous people have been killed and displaced, farmland, forests, and natural habitat destroyed, rivers, lakes, seacoasts, and fish poisoned with arsenic, mercury, cyanide, and sulfuric acid. "I knew that these horrible things happened in other places," she says, "but now I was actually witnessing it in the country of my birth, and just when I was rediscovering the glorious nature of the place. This is the most fertile, most densely populated region in Turkey. Seventy million people live in this country, compared to Canada's thirty million, who live on thirteen times the surface of Turkey! To bring this devastating industry to this place seems to me a terrible kind of violence."

We were looking for a leader. We tried all the party leaders, no one took us on. In the end, we went to Oktay [Konyar, aged fifty-nine]. "This is what we're up against," we said. We knew him well. I know him from his childhood. He is married to a woman from the village of Saganci. "We need someone to lead us," we said. "What do you say?"

"I'll come to the villages and see how solid you are," he said. He came around and visited all seventeen villages. "Do you give me the authority to lead you?" he asked. "Will you stand by me?" We all said yes. We'll be behind you.

After he became our leader, the struggle took on a new shape. It became action oriented. We all have land here so we swore to perform civil disobedience until the mine would leave our lands. Everyone swore to stick together.

After that, we set up committees in each village. Ten-people committees. Here, I was the head of the committee. Oktay was coming to us and telling us "tomorrow, at such and such a place . . . You let your villagers know . . . We'll march . . . or we'll

perform disobedience in a particular place . . . Everyone should be
ready at such and such a time."

❀ Munir Aldaş, 64, interviewed by Üstün in the
village of Ovacık, fifty metres from the mine

Üstün began to support the villagers' demonstrations. "They
didn't allow outsiders into their demonstrations," she says. "They were
very careful in how they defined what kind of support they did and did
not want. But they accepted that a few supporters at the university
would pay for their buses when they were going to Istanbul for a
demonstration. We have also provided food and a place to stay when
they come to Ankara – they're extremely poor people, they don't have
the money to go to even the cheap restaurants."

When forty-five villagers came to Ankara for a demonstration,
Üstün invited them to her home, on the first floor of an eight-storey
apartment block. She cooked soup, chicken, and rice, which the villagers ate sitting on the floor. "When they arrived, the whole neighbourhood filled up with police cars, but all that was happening is these
people were coming for supper!"

Supporters arranged to sell some of the villagers' olive oil in
Ankara, directly rather than through a merchant. "Their olive oil is
wonderful, but very soon no one will buy it because of the cyanide
used in gold mining. Already some merchants won't buy their products, which is a terrifying thing for people who depend so much on
selling what they grow."

I ask Üstün to describe the "restrained resistance" that moved her
to support the villagers. "It was always very dignified," she says. "Men
would strip from the waist up – this is unheard of among villagers,
who are normally very prudish – they would walk in large numbers
under the rain, sit and block a road. Or they would circle around the
mine in a kind of vigil, the women in *shalvar* [traditional ballooning
pants] and the men carrying torches. They were walking on their own
land, not the land of the mine, but even this terrified the mine owners,
so they brought in the army."

When the gendarmes arrived, I said to them, "Son, when this thing operates and poisons us, do you think you'll be safe from it? Don't you think you too depend on the land?" The police said to us, "C'mon, go home and milk your cows. Your grandchildren are waiting for you. Go home."

No, we didn't leave. We were fighting for our lands. "Aren't you the people of the same country?" we asked them. And then they felt all over us as if we were terrorists, and they were looking for guns. "Why are you doing this?" We asked them. They said "Go home, we don't want you to be hurt."

"Why should you hurt us anyway?" we answered them.

❀ Nazgül Yoldaş, aged sixty-two, interviewed
by Üstün in Pınarköy village

The villagers' protests included a march to Gallipoli, the site of a notorious attack on Turkey during World War I by troops from Britain, France, New Zealand, and Australia. After nine months, with 100,000 soldiers killed and another 250,000 injured on both sides, European commanders withdrew their surviving troops. The villagers wanted to draw attention to this new assault on their land by the Australians.

In 1997 the villagers sued Normandy Mining for contravening the Turkish constitution, which states that "everyone has a right to live in a healthy environment." The Turkish State Council, the country's highest court, ruled that the mine was indeed violating the constitution and should close. The government commissioned a report which concluded that the mine had improved its safety standards. In April 2001 the minister of Health issued Normandy a one-year trial permit. The villagers continued to resist. In February 2002 a regional court ruled that the trial permit violated the public good and issued an injunction against the mine. It was to close by April. Defying its own laws, the government passed legislation permitting the mine to continue production. The villagers continued to resist.

By now they were up against an even larger force: Colorado-based Newmont Mining had acquired Normandy to become the largest gold-mining corporation in the world. In addition to scandals over massive discharges of lead, arsenic, and mercury from its operations in the United States and Indonesia, Newmont faced charges of bribing Vladimiro Montesinos, Peru's former spy chief, now in prison, to ensure that Peruvian judges approved Newmont's bid to control the Yanacocha gold mine, the largest in Latin America.

To protest the illegal action of the Turkish government, villagers came to Ankara by overnight bus and gathered at the Ministry of Health before it opened for the day. With copies of the court ruling hanging from their necks, they sat quietly on the curb. Squads of heavily armed riot police and gendarmes surrounded them. When the gendarmes tried to move the villagers, their leader gave a signal, and they all lay down on the pavement.

"This made it very difficult for the gendarmes," says Üstün. "The villagers were very kind to them, they would offer them olives, cheese, and loaves of bread that they had brought with them. The gendarmes, many of them villagers themselves, didn't know what to do. If these were students or civil servants demonstrating, they would simply beat them, but how could they beat these middle-aged and elderly people offering them food? This was what the villagers did. The women would march barefoot without ever shouting insults at anyone or engaging in any kind of behaviour that could be seen as provocation. They had slogans, but they were never shrill. Everything they did was nonviolent, and very unexpected."

Since her return to Anatolia, Üstün had been working on a book about the region, a kind of love story. *Mountain Mother, Earth Mother: Notes from Anatolia* will be published in Canada. But then her encounters with the villagers gave birth to a new project. Much had been written on the Bergama resistance, but all of it by engineers or professors of metallurgy. No one had told the stories of the villagers, from their own perspective, on the ground. "Since the government betrayed its own people, there is an embargo on the story in Turkey," says Üstün. "The large media outlets have almost entirely stopped talking about Bergama. I feared that unless people told their stories now, they would be lost. One woman said to me recently, 'Right now as we talk to you we are disappearing, they are killing us, we are facing our end.' It became a central purpose for me to be instrumental in their ability to leave a document for future generations."

This passion to provide outlets for silenced voices – where does it come from? "Could it be that having grown up in a society where young girls were severely controlled, I developed a deep distrust for authority very early on?" she replies. "My father was an intelligent, decent, but extremely controlling person. I had to rebel against him, and against the society that had formed me, especially because I questioned and challenged and rejected all the roles that were considered appropriate for women. Yet, I remember that becoming a mother also politicized me, by making the world a more important place than it had been until then. Now I had a child that I loved so ferociously that the world mattered to me. I identified with my vulnerable baby, and all vulnerable people. Does this make sense? And once you begin to hear the silenced voices, the process takes you along."

After Üstün won the trust of Oktay Konyar, their chosen leader, other villagers agreed to share their stories with her. "However, in some villages where people had been bought by the mine, the dynamics were a lot more tricky. I would go there unannounced, sit at the village coffee shop, and wait for people to talk to me. The women in villages don't go to the coffee shops, it's only men there, so basically I acted as if I were a man. Eventually someone would offer me tea, they would pull their chairs around, and we would talk. When I turned on the tape recorder, some would resist, some opened up – you know, that's how it is with people."

> At the beginning, women didn't go to meetings. We used to ask "What's a meeting?" The mayor, Sefa Taşkin used to come with some men from the cities and we used to just look at them from behind our curtains.
>
>   The first time I went to a meeting was when they said "Women should come" to a meeting at the wedding hall in our

village. We went there shyly, quietly. The men sat in the front, the women at the back. None of the women spoke. We didn't know Oktay Konyar yet. He has become our leader, but what kind of a man is this?

Soon after that first meeting, women began to go to all meetings. And after that, women became the ones in the front lines . . .

❀ Müberra Özyaylalı aged fifty-three, interviewed by Üstün in the village of Çamköy

I asked Üstün how she approached the women for interviews. "I just talked to them," she says, with a warm laugh. "It was easy, I'm a woman, we had lots to talk about!" Before the resistance developed, village women played no role in public life. "It was an amazing change. In a village where a man would not have allowed his wife to go even to her mother's place without another woman going along, now he wouldn't blink when someone knocks twice on the window – one knock, the man has to go, two knocks, the woman – so the woman grabs her basket of olives and cheese and bread, she runs to the minibus waiting outside in the dark to take her to Ankara or Istanbul. While she's gone, the men look after the children, they make breakfast, they send the children to school. The men had even got used to seeing the women on television, so my coming on the scene asking questions to the women was not threatening at all."

In the interviews, Üstün undertook to explore not only stories of resistance but also what was at stake for the villagers: the texture of their daily lives, working on the land. "They work with the rhythms of the seasons, the light, the sun, and the rain. This is what they know. They told me that olive trees never die – if you prune them in the right way, they're immortal. I didn't know this. So I wanted to make a record of how hard they work, how gruelling their lives are, and yet how they love this life, because they work with the soil, and it gives back."

She also wanted to fathom how isolated villagers with little formal education had built such a complex, sophisticated movement. "I remember that in Canada, NGOs would hold workshops on civil disobedience – it's not something you can just do. How could large numbers of people, including women, leave their families, get on a bus, go to a big city and do these courageous, creative acts of disobedience? That was stunning to me."

I ask her what obstacles she encountered in doing the interviews. "Villagers did not have a tradition of working with words – with the land, yes, but not with words," she says. "In the beginning they would say, 'Oh yes, it was very hard, we went everywhere, we did lots of things.' Then, silence. I kept asking questions in different ways: 'When you were little, what kinds of stories would your parents tell you? What songs were sung in the region? In the bus going to the demonstration, did you sleep, did you talk, were you worried?' The villagers had learned to be very careful in what they said, because if they were going to do an action, and out of affection they told someone, of course word would travel, and they'd be arrested on the way, so they had to change the way they related even to each other. Not knowing these things beforehand, I had to find ways of asking questions that would elicit such details. But then eventually a kind of invisible tap would be turned on, and they would talk to me."

After more than a decade of resistance, hundreds of meetings and actions, how well are people able to reconstruct their memories? "Of course there were gaps, it's inevitable," says Üstün. "I would ask, 'Do you remember you tied tins to your ankles, you carried your animals with you and went in a procession on the highway, the tins banging as you walked?' He looks at me. He can't remember the details. But then I would ask someone else, 'When there was that cyanide spill in Romania, you protested, didn't you?' She says, 'Oh yes, we tied those tins around our ankles, we carried the animals on our shoulders, and we did this. . . .' So it comes out like that."

Since one of her goals is to document the villagers' resistance for future generations, how concerned is she with the accuracy of their memories? "I find that from a distance, people do remember things differently," she replies. "For example, a woman told me that in one demonstration she offered a bowl of olives to the gendarme, she said to him, 'This is what we are defending.' But then purely by chance I found a video of this action – the gendarmes always tape demonstrations, and by Turkish law they are required to make it available, on request, to the people who were taped – and in the video I see that this actually happened, but the woman who offered the olives was not the same person who told me the story, it was someone else!" She laughs. "But really, in the bigger picture it's not so important, is it? When people embellish things or misremember details, I don't interfere."

Why not? As a journalist, she does have to be concerned with accuracy, doesn't she? "Yes, of course," she says. "But there is a kind of truth even in the embellishments. I want their truth to remain as they see and define it. At the same time, I also do an enormous amount of work with archives, court and government records, police videos, newspapers, any documents I can find. The Bergama book is structured similarly to *Night Spirits*, where the oral histories are framed by my narrative voice. That frame, as in traditional journalism, has to be tightly constructed so that times, dates, events are as accurate as possible – the documents have to confirm objectively what events took place when and where. After I've taken care of that, always there is this human process, the interaction between my consciousness and theirs, but in the end, it's their voices telling their stories."

WE KNOW THE LAND!

The book was released in October 2003. The title *Biz Topragi Bilirik!* translates into English as *We Know the Land!* For the official launch at a major book fair in Istanbul, a group of villagers joined Üstün and a panel of scientists and geological engineers at the podium. "It was breathtaking," says Üstün. "'This is our book,' they said, 'we are the ones who own it.' That night they went in a huge group to Istiklal Caddesi, a street in the downtown area, and they entered several large bookstores – an elderly woman told me this – they said, 'Do you have our book?' 'Yes,' the booksellers said, 'here is your book.' People recognized them. They have become well known in this country."

I wonder about the shifts that Üstün has made from radio to television and now to print, which tends to have a more limited reach than the electronic outlets. She wants people to know what happened at Bergama. Does she regret losing access to the larger public? "I'd love to have made a documentary on the Bergama resistance," she says. "But that takes a lot of financial resources, a lot of time, and a team of professionals, while you can write a book by yourself. When I did have access to the great media, when I was working at *The National*, I have never felt as stifled in my life, before or since. In broadcast journalism I was painfully aware of how much you end up reporting out of context – one day it's breaking news, maybe it's still in the lineup the next day, but the third day you may never hear of it again. The whole thing becomes a strange kind of soup, which I think has two effects. It depoliticizes people. When you can't make connections between cause and effect, between the roots and consequences of events, how can you interpret things in a rational way?"

And the second effect? "That constantly changing soup wipes out memory. Events and people don't just disappear. They are still there and they still have consequences. But as far as the news is concerned they simply drop into thin air. A year later we may wonder what happened to that person, that story, but it's gone, vanished from memory. I value memory. In Anatolia I find myself cherishing this sense of a very long history. I consider that history to be memory too, memory of the whole human adventure. So I want to resist, even in a small way, this wiping out of memory. I want to salvage it in any way I can."

I comment that in the human journey, land and memory seem vitally connected. The disconnection from both in the general population renders most of us dangerously indifferent to the elimination of the peoples most deeply rooted in the earth, and in the kind of long memory that's needed to survive on it – how to read the seasons, how to prune olive trees so they become immortal. "Absolutely," says Üstün. "I find a very similar relationship to land and memory in both aboriginal people and the villagers of Bergama. Both have this fundamental connection to the land – it is your mother, and if you injure it, you can't be whole yourself. Once you've lost that connection, once you forget, you can destroy anything. I get very worried that the very sources of human life are in the process of being destroyed. We seem to have lost the wisdom that should tell us we're destroying our own means of survival."

The Newmont gold mine has been operating in Bergama since spring 2001. By August 2003, when Üstün visited with a chemistry professor from the university, the villagers said that many people were sick and there were a lot of cancers, of the intestines, prostate, and breast. "We wondered if this wasn't too soon for such diseases to occur," says Üstün. "Could this be an expression of people's overwhelming anxiety? But then in the first week of September, a young mineworker stepped on a sharp object in the mine, and although the wound was treated, it grew cancerous, and he died. Another mineworker was fired in September because he had advanced cancer and could no longer do heavy work. Several others are very ill. In early November the medical doctor at the mine resigned, saying she was not being allowed to do her job. She said there were accidents at the mine every day, and mine officials were hiding accidents and illnesses. At the book launch, a village woman said many young women had lost their breasts to cancer. The geological engineer on the panel explained that quartz dust raised by dynamite explosions might be the culprit. A professor of metallurgy said that chemicals used in the extraction of gold are also carcinogenic. We are calling for a thorough, systematic health check in the villages surrounding the mine, but so far, the Ministry of Health has not responded."

Are people leaving the land? "Oh yes," says Üstün. "The villagers who can afford to are going away. One example: Çamköy, a village fifty metres away from the mine, had 120 houses. Now, only about forty are occupied. Vandalism of empty houses has become a problem. Those who remain don't have the money to go anywhere else. No one wants to buy their land except the mine, which wants to expand. In fact the remaining villagers are despairing because some of the people who were in the resistance for many years are now considering selling their lands to the mine so they can go away."

For Üstün the book has a second purpose: a warning. The last time I spoke with her, the Turkish parliament was considering new legislation that would open up to unrestricted mining "all formerly protected areas such as olive groves, coasts, forests, agricultural lands, national parks and cultural/historic sites, without requiring any Environmental Impact Study." "If this book can make some politicians think twice and slow down that process," she says, "it will have been useful."

In July 2003 she spoke against the legislation at a Turkish parliamentary hearing. She continues to expose its dangers and inherent hypocrisies wherever she can. I found one of her articles on the website of JATAM, an Indonesia-based network of NGOs "working on behalf of human rights, gender, the environment, and indigenous people's rights impacted by mining policy and activities."

Opposing transnational corporations can be a dangerous occupation. The villagers have been subject to continuous harassment and arbitrary arrest. When the book came out, village leader Oktay Konyar called to congratulate Üstün on finally having made it onto the list. Which list, she asked. The MIT list, he replied. It stands for Milli İstihbarah Teşkilatı, the national intelligence agency.

Within one harrowing week in November 2003, bombings in central Istanbul targeted two synagogues, the London-based HSBC bank, and the British consulate, killing fifty-one people. One of the suicide car bombs exploded in the same neighbourhood where, two weeks earlier, the villagers had eaten supper with Üstün before their book launch. How does she deal with the potential of risk to herself?

"I'm aware that Turkey is a dangerous place," she says. "But it's not only Turkey, it's the whole world. In Canada I often encountered this notion that people should avoid exposing themselves to danger, the assumption that it was possible to be safe from harm. Here, I don't have such a notion. I don't do foolish things to expose myself to danger,

I hope, but I do feel compelled to write and speak about things that matter to me. If I become so anxious to protect myself that I can't speak up, then it limits my life. I don't want to be grandiose about it, but I do feel that if I can say what I know to be true, whether that's dangerous or not, then I'm a more joyful human being."

Given the apparent defeat of the villagers' resistance, and the escalation of violence in the world, I asked if she still has hope for non-violent resistance. "A lot of hope," she replies. "I think resistance, even under hopeless circumstances, is a hopeful act. Non-violent resistance can be very powerful. In Bergama, it delayed the operation of the mine by one whole decade. That's an amazing accomplishment. If I lost hope in non-violent resistance, in art, in music, and in kindness, I would drown in despair."

> The resistance developed in secret. The villagers were going to protests and actions of disobedience in the night. They were organizing themselves. I, as a civil servant, did not enter the events.
>
> One night I was sitting at the coffee house; someone came into the coffee house and told us the villagers had occupied the site. There were some incidents of fires and vandalism of cars, but everyone knew that the miners had done those things as provocation. The villagers had touched nothing.
>
> It's important to note one thing: in all these actions, they never harmed anyone, they never resorted to violence. They did everything they could to draw attention to their plight. I see the resistance at Bergama as a popular resistance that sets an admirable model that should be studied at schools.
>
> ❁ Yusuf Kaya, retired teacher in the village of Çamköy

"Hope" seems to me a fitting title for this chapter. When I asked Üstün for the Turkish equivalent, she replied, "'Hope' is an ironic title, I'm afraid. The struggle in Bergama is now over, defeated – and other gold miners have begun preliminary drilling at various sites in Anatolia.

As Arundhati Roy said in Mumbai [the site in India of an International Monetary Fund meeting], 'If you have natural resources, you're done for. Gold is a curse.' However, your use of the word gives me hope. In Turkish, it is *umut*. A good word."

To be real, to be more than vain, hope needs grounds. What are hers? "I derive hope from the fact that people can walk five hundred kilometres with their olives, cheese, and bread, to speak up," Üstün replies. "I derive hope from the warm friendship that has sprung up between me and Greek anti-gold-mine activists during this struggle. [Greece and Turkey have been in conflict for centuries.] I derive hope from human creativity, from Dostoyevsky, from Nazim Hikmet, a Turkish communist poet who died in the '60s, from Yunus Emre, a fourteenth century Turkish mystic poet, from Camus, Mozart, Verdi, Schubert, Bach, from Goya, Picasso, Abidine Dino [a Turkish painter who died in 1993]. I derive hope from very simple pleasures such as swimming in the Aegean sea, and sipping the glass of wine that my husband, Jean, has just brought me. In short, I love life. I need to generate hope in myself so I can continue to love life."

CHAPTER 5

THE MESSENGER

MARTIN KAUFMAN: Hello. My name is Martin. I am
going to be interviewing Mr Ronald Nitengale.
How are you doing, Mr Nitengale?

RONALD NITENGALE: Pretty good.

MARTIN: The first question I would like to ask is how
long have you been living in Chicago?

RONALD: I was born in Chicago. I have been here fifty-
nine years.

MARTIN: Fifty-nine years.

RONALD: The community I'm in, I wasn't aware of all
of this until, I am saying maybe the last six, seven
years. And that's when they, the community, they
had community protests about the dump in Hillside,
which is the next suburb over. And I really never
gave the dump any other thought other than you
could always smell the smell. And to me that was
just ... part of, you know, its being a dump. You live
near it, you're going to smell the dump. And as the
community was protesting about the dump and
everything, then I became aware of all of the side
effects and what actually was happening. Fumes
coming in to the air, noxious fumes, poisonous

fumes. Then I became aware of what we were not
only smelling but breathing and taking in. And also I
became aware of the side effects from all this. And
then looking around and from conversations with
people I learned about the other environmental haz-
ards that we were affected by. . . .

MARTIN: Have you ever lived near heavy industries?

RONALD: It seems like I have always lived near a heavy
industry. When I was in the city there was always –
well, as a kid I used to live down the street from the
coal dump. Not a coal dump, where the coal came
from. You know the coal yard. There was always
some type of industry. Paint factories, recycling, not
dumps but I guess you would say it would be a
junkyard. There was always a junkyard. Cars . . .
motors, things like that. . . .

Martin Kaufman is sixteen, African-American, and
Catholic. One of seven teens in a day-long work-
shop at the Chicago Historical Society, he interviewed two older
African-Americans about the changes in environment they had experienced over the years in their Chicago neighbourhoods. The interviews
are a key component in a major oral history project, Environmental
Justice and Memory, organized by historian Sylvia Hood Washington.

"History is nearly always written by the conquerors," she says,
"which means no voice for the common person. Right now, in my opinion, most environmental history is written from the perspective of
corporate growth, while the voices of people impacted by that growth
are silent. I feel driven to hear those voices."

That drive is rooted in the lost paradise where Sylvia Hood Washington grew up.

In the 1940s her parents joined the Great Migration from rural
south to industrial north. Through the first half of the century, close to
a million African-Americans fled the south to escape sharecropping – a

system of agricultural exploitation little better than slavery – the collapse of the cotton industry, and the lynch mob, still a grim possibility in mid-century Alabama, where her parents had lived. The migrants sought jobs and safety in northern cities ringed by industry: New York, Pittsburgh, Detroit, Chicago, Cleveland.

Sylvia's father found work at the Ford motor plant in Cleveland, Ohio, as a skilled labourer welding engine blocks. In her Ph.D. dissertation she writes, "I have only one childhood memory of his worksite: belching smoke from gargantuan buildings that grew upward like Jack's beanstalk with an almost suffocating odor. I was constantly reminded that this place and the industrial conditions in this working space were unnatural and deadly. It was why both of my parents pushed all of their children to go to college; they did not want us to be subjected to the debilitating spaces of the industrial workplace."

Her parents set up house at a safe remove, in the Lee-Saville area between Cleveland's outer ring and the suburban communities on its southeast side. "In this place of my childhood and young adult life, were looming trees, arching lazily over small frame houses . . . . They filled this space with the sweet fragrances of green apples, peaches, and pear trees. Among the trees and small neatly kept homes were daffodil, rose and tulip gardens. You could even find vineyards on white trellised tunnels, which greeted you as you walked into the front yards. It seemed like everyone had their own vegetable gardens, filled with corn, turnips and mustard greens, green peas and green tomatoes, squash and sometimes okra." Sylvia recalls childhood rambles through the woods, along creeks where people would fish for their supper.

By the mid-1970s, people noticed that outsiders had started to dump garbage in their woods. A few years later Sylvia's father, Lorenzo Hood, told her they were now also dumping PCBs and other chemicals. After the 1976 ban on PCBs in the United States, the cancer-causing chemicals were often dumped illegally in the nearest convenient spot, where they would poison the environment and food sources for decades. "By the late '60s and early '70s, some of the clear brooks had turned a reddish brown and the tadpoles started dying. My father and many of the adults in my neighborhood made it a point to tell their children that this turn of events was environmentally 'unnatural' and had occurred because the people dumping knew they could get away with it in neighborhoods like ours." This would be her first lesson in environmental justice.

In the early 1980s, the state government of North Carolina announced that a new landfill for toxic waste would be built in Warren County, as a repository for PCB-contaminated soil from other parts of the state. Consistent with practice throughout the south, the site chosen for the dump was in a low-income, mostly African-American community. Civil rights and environmental activists forged an alliance to protest the landfill, accusing the authorities of environmental racism. More than five hundred people were arrested, including clergy, community leaders, and a member of Congress. In 1982 the movement for environmental justice was born.

At the same time, with a science degree and a major in human communications, Sylvia landed a job as the first female environmental chemist at the Lakeshore Power plant in Cleveland. Her job was to interpret regulations embedded in two new federal laws, the Resource Conservation and Recovery Act and the Toxic Substances Control Act, and to convey the relevant contents to plant technicians. "For example," she says, "if they dumped lime into the lake, the pH would be so high it would kill all kinds of stuff out there. I had to make sure people didn't do that." She would also package data for the company's legal and public relations departments. The company had already been the target of protests from community groups when its faulty electrical equipment leaked dangerous chemicals in their neighbourhoods.

One day Sylvia saw her cousin fishing on the outtake channel from the plant. She knew that the water discharged from boilers and turbines is so hot and under such pressure that inevitably it pollutes the water with dissolved metals. There was also the matter of chemicals used to clean the metal parts. She asked her father to tell the cousin he should fish somewhere else.

In her next job, as an environmental engineer with the National Aviation and Aeronautics Administration, she dealt with the political and environmental impacts of nuclear systems. Listening to her fellow engineers, she became increasingly uncomfortable with their disdain for ordinary citizens, especially those who presumed to question nuclear safety. She explains: "Corporate engineers know that people in these little community groups don't have the kind of access to technical knowledge that they have, and they don't have money to do the research they need in order to articulate their side of the argument, so basically they're no competition in public hearings."

By then a mother with two young children, Sylvia deepened her commitment to the Catholic church. As a catechist (religious teacher) she focused on biological and environmental ethics. Finally the tension between her beliefs and her professional role became untenable.

Since I don't think of conventional religion as being committed to environmental issues, I ask her to explain the dissonance. "It's simple," she replies. "I think everyone has a right to life. The Catholic church believes in the right to life, which means we believe every human being has a right to be born without being corrupted by industrial pollution. Research from the National Institutes of Health and the National Institute of Environmental Health Sciences shows that when women are exposed to lead, mercury, and other industrial chemicals while they're pregnant, it can do severe and lasting genetic damage to their children. That is immoral to me. Even if I wasn't Catholic, it would still be immoral to me."

When her husband, a banker, was relocated to Chicago, Sylvia resumed work on her Ph.D. on the history of science, technology, and the environment. "As I got into my research, I became more and more interested in the way that environmental history is being written. The conventional approach looks at how technology transforms nature, but hardly at all at how it transforms people's lives. Acid rain doesn't just kill lakes and trees – it changes people's lives! Those who can't escape an area that's being devastated – which generally means the poor, regardless of colour – they can see that their environment is being transformed, and they can see that it's doing them harm. I began to realize that these are the kinds of stories I wanted to tell, on a very deep level."

She began with the story of her own awakening. In her dissertation, subtitled "A 20th Century Working Class Environmental History," she writes, "As I grew older I started remembering trips, around 1967, to visit our relatives who had chosen to stay in the city. As soon as we left our neighborhood the outside environs took on gradations of muted greens and shades of gray. Sometimes the neighborhoods we would pass through began to look like the black and white pictures on television. Driving deeper into the city, the air lost its sweet smell of fruit trees and took on the pungent odor of rotten eggs . . . . We were driving through Cleveland's flats; and on a bad day the clouds of dark gray smoke would engulf the cars passing through with the choking smells of industrial pollution. I eventually learned that the place with the clouds and pungent smells of industry was also a place where people not only worked but also lived with their families."

Sylvia was surprised to find that not everyone welcomed her thesis. It was blocked from publication, twice, she says. "There's an elitist mentality at work here. There are some historians – not all of them, but some – who don't want this kind of history to be out there. When environmental historians work for major institutions that get their funding from industrial corporations, they are not going to speak out. In fact their task is to speak *against* this kind of work. I've actually heard historians say, 'Oh, those poor blacks, those poor working class whites, they don't really care about themselves or their children, they'll gladly trade away the environment for a job.' When I hear that I'm in shock, I say, 'Of course they care, what is wrong with you?' Given an informed choice, no human being will trade their lives or their children's future for a job."

At the first oral history workshop in the Environment and Memory Project, in August 2003, an elderly Chicago resident vividly confirmed Sylvia's argument. "We knew we were being poisoned," he said, "but we didn't think anybody cared. They've been doing these things to us all along. People tried to do something about it, but city hall wouldn't listen to us. Then we were afraid if we pushed too hard, we'd lose our jobs. But we knew we were being poisoned, and we were very upset about it."

For Sylvia, the project offers an ideal vehicle to draw out voices like this man's that have been bullied into silence. "It's almost a cathartic process," she says. "People who didn't have a voice before, now their voices matter, at least to someone. I think that's very important, it begins to address the despair that sometimes happens in communities that have been silenced."

Her partner in the project is the Knights of Peter Claver, a black Catholic lay organization formed in 1909 by Josephite priests in Alabama, as an alternative to the Knights of Columbus, from which blacks were barred. Unlike its counterpart, says Sylvia, the Knights of Peter Claver welcomes women and children. St Peter Claver was a Spanish Jesuit assigned to convert and care for African slaves in South America. Canonized in 1888, he was named the "patron saint of the Negroes in America."

When they sought funding for the Chicago project from the U.S. Conference of Catholic Bishops, they learned that in its ten-year environmental justice program, this would be the first time the USCCB had ever funded an African-American organization. The Conference did penance with its largest single grant ever, and its first for a public environmental history.

Chicago is an appropriate setting. Built in the 1940s by the municipal housing authority, Altgeld Gardens rises from a landfill site, now cut off from the city by railroad tracks and two interstate highways and virtually engulfed by hazardous waste sites, incinerators, sewage treatment facilities, paint and chemical factories, and steel mills. Sylvia's forthcoming book, *Packing Them In*, recounts this dismal chapter in Chicago's history. "Even if housing projects like this were okay in the beginning," she says, "these neighbourhoods never got the same kind of protection by zoning laws that white neighbourhoods did."

Studies at Altgeld Gardens have found high concentrations of poly-aromatic-hydrocarbons, PCBs, lead, asbestos, and pesticides, along with a variety of airborne pathogens from mountains of sludge at the sewage treatment plants. Not surprisingly, many residents suffer from birth defects, learning disabilities, near-epidemic asthma, emphysema, diabetes (which has been linked to PCB exposure), and the highest incidence of lung cancer in the greater Chicago area. For years, neighbourhood activists have been fighting for basic remedial action from the city, with little success.

In Bellwood, one of the pilot parishes for the oral history project, residents have been waging a long battle against a municipal incinerator in their neighbourhood. Solid waste incinerators are notorious for emitting acid gases, heavy metals, and chlorinated organics, all of which cause serious respiratory illnesses. Incineration also produces an ash residue with high concentrations of toxic metals. Routinely dumped in landfills not equipped to handle hazardous materials, this bottom ash threatens water supplies.

Another urgent environmental justice issue in Chicago is asthma, a chronic respiratory disease and the most common chronic illness in American children. Airborne pollutants are widely understood to trigger asthma. Attacks vary from mild to life threatening. Between 1996 and 2001, reported cases in the United States shot up by more than 45 per cent. Asthma mortality is also rising sharply; non-Hispanic blacks are 200 per cent more likely to die than non-Hispanic whites, 160 per cent more likely than Hispanics. In Chicago, over 10 per cent of inner-city kindergarten children suffer from the disease, almost double the national rate.

"If you look at where African-Americans live in Chicago," says Sylvia, "some of the neighbourhoods are practically surrounded by highways. Historians talk about the big urban renewal projects here in the '50s, when they purposely located new highways to separate black neighbourhoods from white. The incomplete combustion products from all those cars causes a huge amount of air pollution, of the type that triggers asthma."

Many low-income and minority children are forced to live in older housing, much of it in decay, providing comfortable habitat for roaches and rats. Both can also trigger asthma.

Older housing also features poor ventilation and lead paints. "Chicago is like ground zero for lead poisoning," says Sylvia. "O study found over 40 per cent of African-American children had ra lead in the blood way in excess of government allowable limits established that lead causes lowered IQ, violence, and elevat ity." A recent study from the University of Illinois also lin' sure to hypertension.

The Environmental Justice and Memory project has tives: to document the experience of African-American Catholics in areas of known environmental inequity in Chicago, from their own perspective and memories, and then to connect their stories back to local environmental history. The end goal is to promote environmental literacy, and thus greater public participation in the forming, and re-forming, of environmental policies that affect these communities.

It begins with the interviews, of which Sylvia plans to gather more than two hundred. The majority will be conducted by African-American youth, selected by Knights of Peter Claver chapters in the three pilot parishes. After training sessions at the Chicago Historical Society, the fledgling oral historians seek out elders to interview in their home parishes. For their first workshop, Sylvia prepared the questions and coached the seven participants through their interviews. "Mostly I walked around and listened. I encouraged them to talk, not to just run through the questions one to ten, because that does not get what you want, but to try and elicit a dialogue with the person, like the one we're having now. I asked one student to stop, and I started asking the questions, to get the conversation flowing. I wanted them to see how that works."

How does it work? I ask. How do you get the conversation to flow? "It's my culture," she says. "I talk to older blacks the way I'd talk to family members. When I grew up, we had cousins, aunts, and great aunts all coming through the house. We're finding that our kids are removed from that, because of changes in American culture across the board. A lot of them don't have any opportunity to talk to older people. So basically I had to show the kids how to break the ice. You don't just approach this person as an object to be analyzed, but – 'let's have a dialogue here.' It's sort of like sitting at my mother's kitchen table."

Sylvia also had to confront the fear of being awkward, a powerful inhibiting force in adolescents. One young man told her that if he didn't say anything, he wouldn't end up sounding stupid. "Don't look at it that way," she replied, "think of it as a discovery – this person knows something that might be fascinating for you, they are a resource." Once he got into it, she says, "this kid who said 'I can't do this,' he just took over the interview! The woman he was interviewing happened to be the first resident of the public housing unit he lived in, so she was really telling him about his own environment. His eyes got big as saucers, it was so funny! If he had seen this woman on the street, I don't think he would ever have talked to her. He was so enthralled the conversation continued on after the interview stopped. *That* is what we want."

At the same workshop, Martin Kaufman interviewed Bob Miller, a Chicago resident since 1954:

> MARTIN: Could you describe the difference in environments of the neighborhoods? Different neighborhoods you stayed in?
>
> BOB MILLER: Well, down on 35th Street when I was coming up and I would come over to visit, one of the big things you had was the stench that you would get from the stockyards, the Chicago stockyards to the west of that area. Plus the fact that growing up in Gary and in Chicago . . . right after the Depression when we threw our garbage out it would come to the point many times of overflowing, because they didn't have the adequate garbage pickup. And so it was a breeding place for – I can remember the maggots and the flies and so forth and so on. Chasing the rats, trying to catch them, trying to kill them . . . Oh man, let me tell you about the roaches. You see, that's an environmental hazard too. We used to play games. Open the door and come in, walk into the kitchen and then turn the light on real quick. And when you turn the light on you look and roaches

were everywhere. And it looked like they paused, waiting for you to move. And when you moved they went every which way. We used to play games to see who could kill the most roaches. That was an environmental health hazard. We didn't know it then.

I ask Sylvia to explain the goal of the project, "to promote environmental literacy." What does that mean? "When you live in a neighbourhood and you say, 'This is how it is, this is how it's always been,' that may not be true," she replies. "So one aspect is for people to understand there were trees in their neighbourhood once, there was grass, there was clean water and air, there was an environment that wasn't degraded. The question is, how did it become degraded? What policies, what decisions led to this situation? Also, for example, in Bellwood, there are kids there who don't know what's going on, but when they interview adults involved in the fight to stop this incinerator, then they gain knowledge about their community. That's what I mean by environmental literacy. Why does asthma happen? When we kicked off this grant, I had a session with about 350 black Catholics in Newark, New Jersey. I talked about environmental issues, then there was this *outpouring* of stories, it was incredible. People said, 'We didn't have asthma when we left Mississippi, Arkansas, Alabama. We didn't have these issues with Attention Deficit Disorder.' Then kids would say, 'Well, what happened?' What happened was a significant change in their environment, going into an urban setting with lots of pollution, into older housing with no windows and lead paint on the walls. These kids want to know, 'Where do I live when I grow up? How do I get the lead paint off the walls? If we're forced to stay here, what can we do to make the place less damaging?' That," says Sylvia, "is what I mean by environmental literacy."

Given the current regime in Washington – climate change denied, Kyoto shut out, the Clean Air Act gutted, the SuperFund (for cleaning up toxic sites) gutted, the Environmental Protection Agency's budget slashed, and a growing list of other crimes against both the environment and humanity – I comment that this seems a particularly difficult time to be promoting environmental literacy.

"You know what's amazing to me?" says Sylvia. "We had Rachel Carson 1962, Earth Day 1970, Warren County 1982, and da-da-da, but when I did a presentation recently with twenty- and twenty-one-year-old science students at Northwestern University, hardly any of them had ever heard of environmental justice or environmental racism! Northwestern doesn't have even an environmental studies course. Neither does the University of Chicago. What you do have since the 1970s are environmental *science* programs that do not deal with issues of ethics or justice but only prepare people to work in corporate America, to run the industrial processes and to interpret the environmental regulations that are being dismantled before our eyes."

Since she seems determined to find a place for herself in an academic world that hasn't made her particularly welcome to date, I ask Sylvia about the advantages and constraints of working in that milieu. "I do have to give credit to DePaul University," she says. "They actually want me to teach courses on environmental justice and ethics. That's because it's a Catholic university, with a specific mission for peace and social justice. It would be quite a different story at a secular university that gets its money primarily from industry."

Founded in 1898 as a school for the children of immigrants, DePaul is the largest Catholic university in the United States, with 23,000 students and seven campuses throughout metropolitan Chicago. "I'm going to create an environmental justice externship there," says Sylvia. "Students will have to work a minimum of thirty hours with an environmental justice group in the community. It will be a great learning experience for them, and it gives me an advantage as an academic that most environmental activists don't have – usually they're overwhelmed with how much work has to be done and how little resources are available to them."

And the constraints? "Well, I don't believe I'm ever going to get a traditional history teaching job. I'm writing history of the people, a kind of bottom-up history, and most historians aren't comfortable with that, especially if their own work is tied into corporate funding. I'm not naïve, I knew that when I made this decision there'd be a political penalty involved. I think I'm a threat to more traditional environmental historians. Their biggest complaint is that they're at the mercy of the corporate scientists and engineers. Because most of them never trained in the sciences or did poorly in them, they can't effectively counter the arguments posed by these people. Now here comes me, a scientist and engineer with a doctorate in natural health, and even more dangerous than someone else with similar credentials because I have fifteen years' first-hand knowledge of how corporate America operates. Plus I'm not writing from some abstract point of view, I write as someone who has actually experienced environmental inequality, as an African-American. Put all of that together, and it gives me a certain kind of weight. How can they ever be comfortable with that?"

Given her own assessment of academe, I wonder, would she really want a traditional history teaching job? She hesitates, then replies, "In an ideal world where all is fair – which we know does not exist – I would love to be a tenure track professor and to have graduate students working on these topics. But being a realist, I also know that it would take a very brave soul in a history department to hire someone like myself to do this kind of research." She leaves it at that.

At the November 8 oral history workshop, thirteen-year-old Sarah Washington interviewed ninety-three-year-old Mary Walker:

SARAH WASHINGTON: When were you born?

MRS WALKER: I was born March the 25th, 1910.

SARAH: You said you lived in Ida B. Wells?

MRS WALKER: Yes.

SARAH: Describe it. It was nice back then?

MRS WALKER: Oh, it was beautiful when I first moved into Ida B. Wells in 1941. . . . Everything was just beautiful. Flowers, green grass. We even had the kids who were supposed to keep the kids off the grass. If one of these little parole officers saw you on the grass then he took you to your parents. And your parents could give you a good jacking up about walking on the grass. And we had flowers and everything. The kids in the afternoon would go to Madden Park. They had a swimming pool there. And they had a field house. And they had activities for the kids there. The neighbors were very good neighbors who were so proud of living in such a beautiful place. Visitors came from all over the world to see this new project. It was something that hadn't been tried before. And so everybody kept their houses clean, windows shining, curtains all clean. And in the evening the parents would get the kids all cleaned up, we would go down to the park, and different churches would come with their choirs and sing and entertain us. It was just a beautiful place to live. . . . Well, of course everything is changed now. It's just a disaster. I can't believe that such a beautiful place could be so destroyed. When you think about all the flowers and the green grass and kids playing in nice clean clothes and everything else, and now it's just so different.

The four buildings in the Ida B. Wells project are gradually being demolished by the Chicago Housing Authority to make way for a new mixed-income development. The CHA's ambitious ten-year plan to transform the city's public housing calls for a net loss of 14,000 units for low-income families. According to the Urban Institute, more than half of the households still living in Ida B. Wells report annual incomes of less than $5,000.

As the walls come tumbling down, I ask Sylvia what obstacles she sees standing in the way of positive change. She pauses a moment, then says, "I believe that people – regardless of colour and especially if they're caught up in class – want to believe that other people suffer because they don't work hard enough. If you argue that it's not about working hard enough, but us allowing policies to be put in place that hurt other people, generations of them, I don't think people want to hear that. We don't want to feel responsible for doing bad things to other people. We don't want to hear that we benefit from the suffering of others. And when we talk about environmental justice, we are not talking about slavery, we are talking about current practices. It's not about, 'Well, don't blame me for what my grandpapa did,' it's about things we are doing right now, decisions we make every day. But looking at it that way would call people to action, and I don't think most of us want to be called to action. We want to be left alone, we don't want to be bothered. We want environmental histories written that say these people don't care about themselves, so we're not responsible. We didn't do anything, and therefore we don't have to do anything."

Still, and always, people continue to organize and resist however they can, in Ida B. Wells, in Bellwood, in Altgeld Gardens. With a historian's long view, Sylvia connects their struggles directly back to memories of her own childhood. "I grew up with parents who I realize now were community activists in their own way, especially my mother. In fact they were part of a national movement of African-Americans that started in the '20s and '30s, people who said we have to clean up our own neighbourhoods, we have to protect ourselves from harm until the government acts on our behalf. They knew better than to wait for the government to take action. You cannot wait for a knight in shining armour to come along on a horse, you have to do it for yourself, you have to inform yourself and your children about environmental issues, because that shining knight may never come."

In the apparent absence of any shining knights on the horizon, how does she define her own role? Sylvia thinks, then says, "I consider myself to be a messenger. My job is to give people voice, and to help them make informed choices. I don't want to get them stirred up or start a riot or anything. If I'm an activist, it's only for people to have as much control of their lives as possible, regardless of what's happening around them. Regardless of who's in office, a Clinton, a Bush, whoever, people still have to make choices. In order to make reasonable choices, you have to understand the situation you're in, how it came to be the way it is, and what kind of options you've got. Different people see different parts of the picture. I think I've been fortunate enough to see the whole picture, and I have an obligation to communicate that to people, so they can understand what they're dealing with.

"Like my cousin out there, fishing on the outtake channel, and then there's me, sitting in my office, knowing what's in that water. Am I going to keep my mouth shut, for a pay cheque? Do you see what I'm saying?"

CHAPTER 6

THE GALE BEGAN TO RISE

On the twenty-fifth of August the gale began to rise,
Which left so many orphans and took so many lives;
Left there to stay for their last day, their friends to see
    no more,
For the ocean wave it rolled that day like it never
    rolled before.

       ✤ Ray Hepditch and others, Southeast Bight,
       1976, from *Come and I Will Sing You:*
       A Newfoundland Songbook, edited
       by Genevieve Lear

"These songs reflect the social history of the people," says Anita Best, who collected the songs with Genevieve Lear. We're talking over strong tea in Anita's kitchen, warmly sheltered from a blizzard that blew into St John's off the Atlantic last night.

"Some songs are factual accounts of events that never got recorded in any other way – there were no newspapers, nobody to write about a little schooner going down in Placentia Bay, so we can regard the songs the same as we do newspaper accounts. In studying folksongs, you realize that sometimes the dates change – because, you know, twenty-five doesn't rhyme with heaven! – but the names and places are usually correct, and the story is always authentic. I've never been convinced of the historians' argument that documents are more reliable. I'd say you have just as much reason to believe what someone remembers as what someone has written down."

> I was 25 when I got married, and I had three children when I was working on the beach. I could work with anyone, but in the morning sometimes I sat on the bed and me legs be that stiff and tired I could hardly get me stockings on. 'Twas hard managing it. I used to have short nights. I had to be up every night to do for me children and the house 'cause when it was daylight I was not in the house. Then every night, stars in the sky, you'd take your two buckets and bring in a barrel of water for the next day. I used to set me gardens too in among that.
>
> ❈ Louise Belbin, in *Strong as the Ocean: Women's Work in the Newfoundland and Labrador Fisheries,* edited by Frances Ennis and Helen Woodrow

"With the closure of the fisheries here, which came upon us in the early '90s," says Helen Woodrow, "I found myself wondering why this large group of hard workers – capable individuals, articulate men and women – why had they remained so invisible? Why were they now being made to do these 'civilizing' education programs, computers and the so-called life skills type of thing? We got the idea to try and give voice to some of their experience, to tell the story from another point of view. For the women, we were moved by the notion that their work had never really been valued, never truly understood, these women who had made so many sacrifices to try to earn a dollar, and the way things go, they were lucky to get that much."

The "way things go" features strongly in Newfoundland songs and stories. When I flew to St John's via Halifax in early December, I could see why. At the gate in Toronto, the pilot told us cheerfully, "The weather in Halifax is getting a little more dynamic, so we're taking on some extra fuel. Heavy snow is expected this afternoon in St John's. We'll assess the situation once we get to Halifax." After we lurched into Halifax and the plane had been de-iced, the pilot said, "The weather in St John's is somewhat dynamic and evolving. Rest assured we'll use a conservative approach, and if it doesn't look like a good operation there, we'll come back to Halifax."

After sailing smoothly for a while over dusk-tinged clouds, the plane descended, shuddering. Through a maelstrom of snow and gathering darkness, I caught glimpses of rough land below – or was it ocean? As soon as I could breathe again – on the ground, with the terminal in sight – I thought, though the weather must be the fiercest, least explicable force that Newfoundlanders have had to endure over the centuries, surely it's only one of many.

ANITA BEST

In 1948, the year before Newfoundland joined the Canadian confederation, Anita was born on the south shore of Merasheen Island in Placentia Bay. When she was twelve, her father moved the family to St John's. "He was of the opinion that Joey Smallwood – a demon in our life history – would soon be telling people where they had to live." A few years later the Newfoundland government did force people to leave the outports for resettlement in more populous areas.

"My father's life was a misery after that," says Anita. "At home he was an elder in the community. He was known as really smart. Though he never got past grade six himself, he would help people with their high school exams, geometry, algebra. He found all of that quite easy. But in St John's he never could find work that would use his intelligence, so he became a janitor, a night watchman. The Merasheen community was scattered by then, so there was no one for him to be a leader of. He became very embittered. It destroyed him."

A whole generation of outport Newfoundlanders shared the same sense of dislocation. "If you talk to anybody who underwent resettlement, you'll find that for a lot of them it shaped their lives in many ways – emotionally, artistically, politically," Anita says. "You're uprooted, your life is gone, your community is gone, you've lost that familiar circle that sustained you, and you have no real home to go back to. It no longer exists. Merasheen Island is summer cabins now. People go there for holidays. Many people around the world must experience that kind of forced migration and exile, the dispersing of whole communities. I grew up in that tradition too – I didn't decide to go away, for example to better myself, but *boom*, it was gone. There was no natural closure."

Anita says her mother experienced the move to St John's quite differently. "She came into her own. She became the leader of family, the main breadwinner. She rose to the occasion because she had to, which she would never have done if we'd stayed on the island. My mother would never go back to the Bay, she couldn't possibly. Out there she would simply have had to carry on in her traditional role."

In 1973 Anita began to record Newfoundland songs and the people who sang them. "My father was a singer and a storyteller. When he died, it suddenly occurred to me that I would never have any record of that. I started to collect other people's songs so they'd be saved after the people died. I would be recording the songs, but then people would start talking about their lives, so I'd record that too. I didn't have a clue about oral history, I just got absorbed listening to them. Later, at university, I was trained in folklore, and Michael Stavely, who was a cultural geographer, hired me to do some formal interviews with people who'd survived the tidal wave of 1929. Then I worked for a while with the Newfoundland Inshore Fisheries Association, collecting information on the different cod traps that people used. But I was never a radio-type interviewer, where you direct the conversation to your own ends. Whatever people wanted to talk about, I would listen."

I ask her how she found the songs, and the singers. "I would go to places I knew," she replies, "and I would ask who sings the old songs. My initial purpose was really functional, not academic, I wanted to learn the songs myself, so they wouldn't go out of use. When

Genevieve Lear and I put some of the songs into a book, *Come and I Will Sing You*, what we really wanted was for other people to learn the songs and to sing them too. We didn't want them gathering dust in an archive somewhere. We wanted to keep them alive."

One of Anita's spurs was the colonial attitude she'd encountered in school and university. "When I started at university in the '60s, believe it or not, there were speech classes for rural Newfoundlanders where they were taught to speak with a 'standard' accent. It was at the same time that women were not allowed to wear slacks, only skirts, all that bullshit of the time. People were made to feel ridiculous for speaking with a Bonavista or a Placentia Bay accent. They were actually trained out of it, and this by people with the biggest, heaviest Scottish accents you ever heard! It was horrifying, disastrous – the humiliation of being pointed at, laughed at. Lots of students, really bright people, dropped out, they just couldn't face it. I'd lived in St John's long enough to acquire standard English, more or less, but still I felt such a rage on behalf of people who were treated like that."

PAMELA MORGAN

In 1991 Anita collaborated with Pamela Morgan to produce *The Colour of Amber*, a CD of Newfoundland songs. Northern Journey Online, the Canadian folk music website, calls it "one of the most haunting and beautiful Canadian traditional folk albums ever recorded."

Born in 1957, Pamela Morgan was born into music. "My mother was a piano teacher, so I grew up studying classical music," she says. "Then in high school I was taught literature and drama by a person who'd been resettled from the southwest coast of Newfoundland – he was very angry about it, and he conveyed his sense of injustice to us. This was in the early '70s, when there was a growing movement among artists, writers, and musicians to rebel against the Third World image of Newfoundland – you must have heard the Newfie jokes – and not to have our accents hammered out of us in school. Since music was my main passion, naturally I gravitated to the music of Newfoundland.

And somehow I knew instinctively that there was more to it than the second-rate Irish drinking songs that were popular at the time. So I made it my business to find out what else there was. I started by learning some of the old ballads that Kenneth Peacock had recorded or transcribed in the '50s and '60s."

When Noel Dinn heard her sing one of these ballads in a school play, he asked her to join his new band, Figgy Duff. After leading a successful rock band in the late '60s, Noel had come home to work with the music of Newfoundland. "He played me music from American, English, and Irish bands," Pamela recalls, "people like Jethro Tull who were combining old songs with modern instruments to bring this music to a wider audience. One of the great things here was that the tradition was still alive, people were actually still singing these songs. So we went around and sought them out. We would literally go knocking on people's doors – 'Could you tell us where the best singer is around here?'" She chuckles at the memory.

When people talk about "collecting" songs, it sounds like archeology to me, digging up musical bones. "It wasn't," says Pamela. "In fact, we never did collect in the true sense of the word. When I hear 'collect,' I think of a folklore student going in with a bottle of rum, they stick a mike in somebody's face and they say, 'Okay, skipper, start singing.' I know their intentions aren't bad, but that's not me. I always wanted an exchange, to give something back. They'd sing a song, I'd sing a song, it was a song-circle kind of thing. We'd spend time with people and get to know them, until people were comfortable enough to sing the songs they kept only for themselves."

With her musical training, Pamela was asked to transcribe the songs that Genevieve Lear and Anita had collected for *Come and I Will Sing You*. "I'd listen to their recordings and I'd write down the melodies," she says. "There had been other collections before this, but our book was the first one where all of the songs are locally composed. It's out of print now, but that's a really great collection." (University of Toronto Press reissued the book late in 2003. It lives!)

I ask her about the origin and nature of the ballads. "Traditional ballads are always about something that happened," she says. "They're a bit like oral history set to music. Some of them are hundreds of years old. One song I learned on Fogo Island is about the Saracens, the Crusades. I don't know if it actually originated then, but it was old enough to recall events of that time. Some of the ballads are like soap operas, they've got everything – sex, betrayal, intrigue. It's like a whole year of *As the World Turns*! It's hard to fathom in today's world but as recently as twenty-five years ago, that's how people entertained themselves: they'd get together and sing the old songs, to while away a winter night. They were the radio and the TV. A lot of the ballads are about honour, human grace really, in the way people conducted their lives. There are sexual references too, but they're always very gracefully put. I wish people lived more like that now."

CHRIS BROOKES

VOICE 1: Well, it was a long time ago and he's died, and I guess it is a good thing to disappear.

KATHRYN WELBOURN: Do you think?

VOICE 1: Well, they weren't good times, you know, why keep bringing up something that was unpleasant? You'd like to remember the pleasant part. You go down the South Road now, very few if anybody are going to say, 'Yes, I knew Pearce Power.' His name is not going to stand out, the people don't know him – I don't think they do anyhow.

KATHRYN WELBOURN: Why isn't Pearce Power in the history books?

VOICE 2: Well, I suppose he was a thorn in the side of the government and the merchants, they didn't want to write him up. But regardless of whether he's in the history books or not, it will be all passed down through oral tales. History can't be denied, whether or not it's there in print, people will remember it.

❉ from *Power of the Unemployed*, a radio documentary by Kathryn Welbourn and Chris Brookes, produced in 1996, with music by Pamela Morgan. It won a 1997 Gold Medal at the International Radio Festival of New York.

The night I visited Chris Brookes at his home and workplace, Battery Radio, the taxi driver passed by twice before finding it. In the slick weather, he was preoccupied with staying on the narrow streets that twist along the rock face of the Outer Battery at the foot of Signal Hill. Battery Radio faces onto a narrow neck of water between the St John's harbour and the Atlantic Ocean. In the harbour that night, two ice-crusted Japanese shrimp trawlers huddled by an ancient-looking coastal freighter and two red-and-white Canada Coast Guard ships. The day I landed, a Coast Guard helicopter hovered over a Norwegian ship in twenty-foot seas and plucked a sailor with a badly broken leg off its heaving deck.

Born in London during the Second World War, Chris moved to St John's with his English father and Newfoundland mother when he was two. As it was for Pamela Morgan and many other Newfoundlanders, the 1970s was a time of intense liberation for him. "We joined Canada in 1949, and for the next twenty years under Joey Smallwood, there was a very strong pressure to get rid of our identities, to try to be more like Canadians – whatever *that* meant – and generally to mind our Ps and Qs. I remember trying to lose my accent, because I was afraid I'd never get a proper job in Canada. But by the late '60s people were really hungry to see and hear reflections of themselves, *as* Newfound-landers, the way we are. It affected everything, including politics – Brian Peckford got elected as a very nationalistic premier, and he went to court to change the Churchill Falls agreement." (Negotiated in 1966 between the Smallwood government and the province of Quebec, it remains a disaster for Newfoundland.) "With all that ferment going on, that was a lovely time – you felt so connected."

In 1972 Chris co-founded the Mummers Troupe, a theatre company that took its name from the working-class tradition of mummer-ing – acting the fool and asking provocative questions. "When we began doing plays, we saw it as a kind of community development, getting into whatever social issues the community wanted to consider. For example, we'd look at problems people were having with the health agencies in a particular region. We'd go into the community with our tape recorders or notepads, the actors would fan out and talk with everybody they could, and then in the rehearsal hall we'd try to recreate people and moments they'd encountered. And out of that would eventually come a play."

I remember seeing one of their plays in 1978 – *They Club Seals, Don't They?* – in Toronto on its national tour. It argued that the seal hunt was a traditional, essential part of Newfoundland life and livelihood, and it mocked high-profile international anti-seal-hunt activists. I recall that the play sparked fierce debate among the audience, including me, which was precisely the Mummers' mission.

I ask Chris how they chose to do this type of theatre. "For me it started with the Fogo process," he replies. "Fogo is an island here. In the late '60s it was quite poverty stricken, and the people were due to be taken off and resettled somewhere else. Colin Low, a director with the National Film Board, collaborated with a film unit from the university here. They went out to the island and did long, long interviews with people. They shot great whacks of footage. They would edit it down a bit, bring it back, and show it in the community hall. They'd get people's comments, then they'd edit it some more. The process created an opportunity for people to talk through what they really felt about their lives and this place where they lived. Ultimately they decided that they didn't want to move. Fogo still survives today. I was mighty impressed by that process, and I wanted to do something like that in theatre. Hence the Mummers."

Though driven by a similar impulse, Chris's journey into radio production was a little more circuitous. "As a nerdy little kid, I always listened to the CBC," he says. "In the '70s I got a couple of gigs as an actor in radio drama, and when a rift developed in the arts community here – a tempest in a teapot, as it turned out – I sort of drifted out of theatre and more into radio."

Chris heard that in Nicaragua, *campesinos*, peasants, were doing the same kind of theatre as the Mummers. With the Sandinista movement, they had just fought their way free of the U.S.-sponsored Somoza dictatorship, and were remaking their country. Chris learned

Spanish and went to Nicaragua twice, in 1981 and 1983. "The theatre there was very community based," he says, "In tiny villages way out in the middle of nowhere, with no roads, the *campesinos* worked the fields by day, and at night they made plays. It fascinated me, the way they linked theatre and revolution. They'd put on a play – let's say about the need for potable water – in their own community, which might be twenty families, then they'd trek an hour-and-a-half to the next village and do it there. There were no newspapers, and the majority of people couldn't read anyway, so this was how they talked about their lives and issues – with drama."

In 1982 Chris landed a plum radio job, as producer of the CBC afternoon show in St John's. On Sunday of the first week, he met with the assistant producer. "She was great," says Chris, "but neither of us had any idea what we were doing. We just hoped that nothing much would happen, and we'd just wing it. That night, the Ocean Ranger went down." In a fierce winter storm, with waves over twenty metres high, the world's largest oil-drilling platform capsized 315 kilometres east of St John's. All eighty-four men on board were lost, fifty-six of them from Newfoundland. Chris and his colleague learned their new jobs overnight.

During his brief career at the afternoon show, Chris created a daily soap opera that became a CBC legend: *Oil in the Family*. "We discovered that Newfoundlanders weren't listening to the CBC in the afternoon, they were watching the soaps. So we thought why not do a radio soap opera on how the events of the day affected people's lives? Two writers came up with an eight-minute script every morning, based on that day's news, and we put it on the air at 5:20 just before the Fisherman's Broadcast, which was when we had our biggest audience. That was the best fun I ever had."

Oil in the Family turned into a huge hit – until the episode inspired by a Planned Parenthood court case, which raised some prickly questions about what options were available for one of its characters, a pregnant teenager. Newfoundland had the highest rate of teen pregnancy in Canada at the time.

"Immediately there was a huge fuss," says Chris. "We were attacked from the pulpit. Phone calls poured in from priests, the right-to-life lawyer, the archbishop's communication secretary – who was later imprisoned for sexual abuse. After that we had to send each script to the CBC lawyers. We had a few more episodes in the schedule, then the usual summer break. Under pressure from the Catholic church, which was much more powerful then than it is now, the CBC executives killed the show. They did it in a sly way, by cutting funding to the afternoon show by exactly the amount required to produce *Oil*. Still, it was great fun, and I think it was valuable. For me it was another way to explore large political and social issues at a personal and community level."

In 1983 he returned to Nicaragua, and made several radio documentaries for the CBC, which led to work as a producer in Toronto. In 1989, he came home to Newfoundland, and a few years later launched his own documentary studio, Battery Radio. The studio is located at the foot of Signal Hill; at its crest in 1901, Guglielmo Marconi picked up the first transatlantic radio signal.

I ask Chris if he feels his radio work constitutes oral history. "Of course it does," he replies. "Oral history is a central passion for me – people telling their own stories, the events of their lives from their own point of view, how they navigate through life in a particular place and time. A few years ago I made a documentary with Kathryn Welbourn about a character in 1933/34 that hardly anybody had ever heard of, Pearce Power. In 1933 Newfoundland became the only nation in history to voluntarily abandon democracy – in a referendum, the majority handed over power to the English crown. The excuse was that the country was bankrupt. In the official version you get the impression that there was no resistance to this shameful thing, nothing happened, not so much as a fistfight on Water Street. It's not a proud part of our heritage. But things certainly did happen, huge rallies in opposition, and this Pearce Power character was at the centre of it – he'd speak to crowds of 5,000 people! But we only know this because the Newfoundland constabulary recorded every move he made. Kathryn bumped into his story in their archives. He was constantly watched, every speech he ever gave, what cafés he drank coffee in – it's marvellous stuff! Eventually he was jailed and the movement broken. But I think it's important for us to know today that some people said 'This shouldn't be happening, we want to elect our own government.'"

Starting from the archival documents, Kathryn and Chris interviewed people who knew or remembered Pearce Power. "They'd say, 'Oh yes, I remember Pearce, the police, it was terrible,'" says Chris. "Some of them said he was a rabble rouser and got what he deserved, and others remembered him quite fondly. I see this as history illuminated by people who are still living, to provide some balance to the very narrow account in the official record."

HELEN WOODROW

From early in life, Helen Woodrow also took issue with the official view of things. "Growing up a young woman in Newfoundland, it doesn't take you too long to realize the way the world is," she tells me. "For example, I wanted to learn about the fishery, so I took time off from my work at university – I said my summer school will be on the coast of Labrador, I will go fish with a fisherman. People thought this was just a *riot*, they thought I was nuts. But I did it."

After she finished her degree in history and English, Helen went to work at the Memorial University extension department. "I spent a good bit of time in rural Newfoundland and Labrador in those years. I learned a fair amount about how power operates, and how badly people do who produce the goods of the land and the sea."

Work at the extension department was inspired by the "Antigonish model." "It came out of the ideas of Moses Foley," Helen says. "It was based on a recognition that those who have sanctioned power, political and social – such as Moses, who was a priest – should call on the people who don't have that kind of power to challenge the position they find themselves in economically, and to provide the means for them to change some of those realities. For example, let's build a credit union, we'll give a portion of what we earn, we'll do some lending, amass some capital, and eventually we'll be the owners, the decision makers – we'll have the say."

I ask Helen how this background has shaped her oral history work. "Part of what we know of the British empire was that we colonials were never supposed to respect what was just outside our door, down the road, across the bay," she says. "For me, it always felt important to be a part of urging people to notice, and if necessary to challenge, what was right in front of them, and I believed that process would be greatly enriched when people had the opportunity to see that their own lives, their stories, were 'good enough' to be heard."

She continues: "Years ago a teacher told me she had just finished reading Patsy Brown's *Death on the Ice*, a book about the great sealing disaster when so many men died. This teacher said a student had told her, 'I didn't know you could put words like that in books.' That didn't mean bad words, because there were none in the book. It meant the words we use, our own dialect. When you see people who live in places like Newfoundland and Labrador, especially people who earn their living with their hands, when you see them get locked out of a literary tradition, or when all you see are texts where bureaucrats comment on people's lives, then you realize it's time to change some of that around, and let people have their own say."

> We had thousands of fishermen – they weren't on their knees, they were lied down reaching out for somebody to rescue them. They screamed for years. Nobody listened. Government never came and asked us what we knew. What did we know about what was happening to the cod? What do the currents have to do with it? What do you think the temperatures have to do with it? It was no good to tell them. They wouldn't listen anyhow.
>
> ❖ Pat Cabot, in *Sea People: Changing Lives and Times in the Newfoundland and Labrador Fisheries*, edited by Helen Woodrow and Frances Ennis

I ask Helen what characteristics or skills she thinks it takes to do oral history. "Listening and respect," she says. "Well, maybe it's the same thing. You don't want to do anything that might harm people. When you push or challenge a person, sometimes it can be very uncomfortable, just as when people push us – oh, the hairs start to go up on your arms, you think who in the fuck are you, we were supposed to be having a nice chat, and here you're turning into this villain, just get the hell out of my house! When I'm doing an oral history, the agreement is that I want to document your story and honour your experience, I don't want to shake you up, or have you shake up the world, other than in the way you normally would. I don't often see my role as being much more than a conduit. There has to be a kind of gentleness for us to get any of this work done – not just oral history but any of it. People are so bloody turned off by so many situations where they feel they've been done in. It happens to all of us – someone you thought was a how-do-you-do kind of person and it turns out your back's bleeding from the knife!" She laughs.

For Helen, respect doesn't end when the tape recorder is turned off. In their introduction to *Strong as the Ocean*, she and Frances Ennis describe the intricate collaborative process of creating the book. "After each interview, the tapes were transcribed. The transcripts often consisted of forty-five pages of text, and we had planned for an average of nine pages per story. It was always a challenge to pare down the pages. . . . We were guided by our belief that each story belonged to the storyteller; it was her voice. . . . At each stage – first draft, edited version, and chapter galley proof – the women were asked if they wished to make any changes. This process gave them control over their texts."

Why does she feel it's crucial for narrators to have this much control? "I think I can safely say for both of us that it came from a recognition that the world doesn't often provide a free space for people's voices. On the contrary, it makes it quite clear whether or not it's okay to say what you want to say, and often what you really want to say will get remanufactured to please somebody else. So for us it was the notion 'how could anybody dare take somebody else's words and manipulate them, unless that was part of the process you'd agreed upon?' There was a lot of going back and forth in the editing process, talking about why we wanted to keep this part of the story, or why somebody might want to think about leaving that part out – some things are safer left in the conversation, not in the text. This was our way of honouring and taking care of people."

One thing she and Frances honoured with particular care was the way their narrators expressed themselves. Helen recalls, "This one guy said to me, 'Geez, I sounds so bad when it gets down in print.' I answered him, 'It don't have to be that way. Maybe we misunderstood you, maybe we picked it up wrong from the transcript' – of course we hadn't – 'so we'll change it if you want, we won't print a word until everybody is happy. Personally I think the way you talk is beautiful, but that's because I honour dialect in a way that many of us can't, we have so many bad memories of being criticized for it.' Well, God love him, he said to me on the phone, 'And why would I want to change who I am?'"

AGNES WALSH

MARY ANNE: *(sits down)* A cup of tea would be
   grand. My, but it's some sweltering warm out
   there. They say that drinking hot tea is the best thing for you in
   the heat. Do you think that's true?

ROSIE: Hot tea is good for anything my dear. Anything that ails
   you, and it stimulates the brain. I read that in the Reader's Digest.

JOHNNY: Hot tea! A drop of rum is what stimulates the brain,
   Rosie girl. You must have read that wrong.

ROSIE: You lay off that ole' rum bugger. This woman is here on
   serious business now.

MARY ANNE: Oh, just for a chat, really, and if you don't mind me
   recording our chat . . . *(reaches for her bag with recorder in it)*

ROSIE: No, go on girl. *(Mary Anne takes out recorder and opens
   it, sets it to play)*

JOHNNY: Rosie here tells me you're interested in the history of
the shore . . .

MARY ANNE: That's right sir, I am. I like to record the history and
write plays about it. . . .

In the first of Agnes Walsh's Cape Shore plays, *Just Ask Rosie*, Mary
Anne was played, quite appropriately, by Agnes Walsh. The Cape Shore
is the western coast of the Avalon Peninsula on Placentia Bay. We're
talking not far from the woodstove in Agnes's kitchen, over another
strong cup of tea, in the same St John's blizzard. It's the first time I've
seen snow falling horizontally.

I ask Agnes, a poet and playwright, what drew her to oral history. She replies, "When I was young, I went often to the Cape Shore
with my mother, picking berries. I always thought it was absolutely
beautiful, and I used to do a lot of hiking there. After I came back to
Newfoundland in 1977, I bought a little house out there, and I started
raising the children there in the summers. I was fascinated by the
local stories, and I wanted to learn the history of the area – nothing
was written about it – so I started interviewing the old people. The
Cape Shore never really had a history, at least not one you could ever
get your hands on. At school you learned everybody else's history,
but never a word about the Cape Shore. That diminishes people, it
says their lives don't matter. When you interview them, it brings
their stories to life."

Then her actor friend Paul suggested she do something with the
interviews, maybe write a play about the area. "I got some funding,
wrote *Just Ask Rosie*, and we put it on out there [in Placentia], in an old
one-room school house. It ran for four nights. People went mad for it.
When you write those stories into a play, and get government funding
to produce it, and present it as 'this is about us' – it gives people a
stronger sense of themselves. It was important to me to do that,
because from quite early on, I had to fight for myself."

Agnes was born in 1950, in Placentia, near a large American naval
base built during World War II. Three of her older sisters married

Americans. "I left at seventeen, mostly to get out of school," she says. "I was bored silly. I wanted to learn, but I wasn't learning anything from the nuns – I felt I knew more than they did, except for the Latin. I think from early on I was always questioning the world, mulling things over in my head – I wanted to be a writer, though I didn't really know what that was. I thought only upper-class British people could write. But I started anyway, when I was about ten. In grade eight I said I wanted to start a poetry club, but the nun said, 'Don't be silly, nobody's interested in that.' I said, 'I am.' She said, 'That's not a club.' I said, 'Oh yes, it is!' So I started a poetry club. No one came, but I sat there anyway and I wrote poems. I decided that poetry was the most beautiful thing I had ever seen, and if I stuck at it, surely *something* would happen."

At fifteen Agnes met a young American sailor, Tom. "He was the first male friend I ever had," she says. "As teens we didn't have male friends, it was all flirtations. But he and I hit it off really well. He'd come to our house – that was a no-no in those days, fathers didn't want their daughters going out with the Americans. But Tom was allowed in our house because he talked to our parents. He was my salvation. He'd copy out poems in longhand from books in the base library. He introduced me to the Beat poets, and writers like Steinbeck, I went through them like crazy. When I went to the States a couple of years later, I looked him up, and he told me he was gay. We had a great chat about it. After that I lost track of him. It's too bad, he was a dear guy." Her recent book of poems, *In the Old Country of My Heart,* is dedicated to Tom.

Agnes interrupts our conversation to negotiate Internet time with Simone, her daughter – the snowstorm has closed the schools. "All right," she says, "you can go on for ten minutes. But not a second more." She's waiting to hear from Patrick, her son, to be sure he's safely installed at a friend's house.

At seventeen Agnes headed south to Connecticut, where her sister lived, and where she met a man. "He was after me to marry him, and my sister said if you don't, you can't stay in the country. It lasted

only a year – he was a nice enough person, but I knew it wasn't for me."
For the next few years she travelled, visiting other sisters in Florida
and Idaho. "My first job was in a truck-stop diner in New Jersey. Oh
my, what an introduction to American life! I never knew any Jewish
people before, and I had hardly ever seen any black people, except for
some servicemen at the base. That was the first time I ever saw a guy
in drag. He came in, he asked me for match, I said, 'You're a guy!' He
said, 'Yeah, honey.' I said, 'This is incredible, I've never seen anything
like you!' He thought I was nuts. My naiveté was wonderful. I was wide
open to everything."

Agnes went off to university in Georgia and studied folklore. "We
went around interviewing people. You'd hear these wonderful stories,
but then you'd come back and they'd put it all away in boxes. What a terrible waste, I thought, so I said 'Shag it,' and came home. My father was
getting quite ill, and I was getting pretty fed up with the United States."

Nirvana is pounding away in the next room, demanding our
attention. Agnes calls out, "You'll have to turn that down, Simone . . .
way down . . . way down. . . ."

Agnes came home to the mid-'70s Newfoundland renaissance. She
wrote poems and plays, started a modern dance company, met a
Québecois poet and translator, moved to Montreal, gave birth to
Patrick and Simone, came home again, and rediscovered the Cape
Shore. At about the same time, she settled into her own sexuality.
"When I was growing up, no other thought about sexuality was possible. At twelve or thirteen – I think about this a lot now – when it
seemed that all the other girls were interested in boys, I remember
thinking, gee, I'm not really that interested, but I just didn't know anything else. I do remember falling in love with a girl my own age. It just
happened, then it unhappened and I was going out with a boy. Now I
wonder how come I didn't think anything about that? Through all of
it, the first marriage, I was keenly interested in women, but I guess I
must have intellectualized it somehow. It wasn't until after I'd married
again and had two kids that I finally realized I'm definitely more interested in women! Funny how that happens, eh?"

I ask Agnes how she finds people to interview. "I just went up and down the shore," she says. "I'd hear about somebody who'd been a school teacher, and I'd go ask them, 'What was it like?' People really wanted to talk. A lot of them said, 'Oh, there's nothing to my story,' but I kept saying, 'That's not true, there's a lot to it.' And one person would lead to another. You don't have to ask a lot of questions, people just get gabbing. Especially the older people, which is mostly who I interview – they have the history, and I wanted to go back as far as I could. A lot of older people don't get that much opportunity to talk, so they love having a chat. Sometimes I'd find it disturbing – I knew they had opened up a lot, and I'd worry about them being lonely when I left, especially the ones in homes, with nothing but their memories. So I tried to come back the next day, just to check on them and see how they were doing. Often they'd want to start talking all over again!"

One of her sources became a close friend. "I met Mike McGrath by knocking on his door one day. I was out for a hike and saw smoke at his chimney. I asked who owned the next house, he said, 'It's mine.' 'Would you sell?' I asked. 'No,' he said, 'but do you want to come in?' We hit it off, just like that. I visited him every day for years, we shared many meals, sang many songs, and drank many glasses of rum together. He always felt like a father to me. He's eighty-three now, and he's one of my dearest friends in the world. My kids love him too."

Mike McGrath also turned out to be her finest source. "That man has so much information in his head! He'd say, 'I've got five hundred years of history up here.' He could go back to hearing his father, his grandfather, his *great*-grandfather talk about the first settler in Patrick's Cove, 1797. That kind of information is only kept alive in oral history, there are no records. So people like Mike are an absolute gold mine for my kind of work. I'd bring out the tape recorder, especially when he got singing – I knew he had songs in him that no one else knew – I'd say, 'My memory isn't as good as yours, Mike, so I'd like to tape this.' He'd say no problem. I've been out there with Pam [Pamela Morgan], we'd sit around with Mike until two and three in the morning, drinking rum, and Pam would dig up songs out of his memory that even he didn't know were still there. Anita [Best] has been out too. She knows Mike. The man is a wonder."

LET A LONG
ANGEL PASS

What still draws Pamela Morgan to collect the old songs? "When I started, my mission was to get the songs before they died," she says. "There was a real sense they could disappear in this whole wired world we've got. I don't have that impulse so much anymore, but I still believe they're some of best songs around. Bad songs don't last that long, but good songs do, because they have a lot of life's truths in them. And the melodies are fantastic – when I write songs, I aspire to that level of lyricism. The original songs were all sung *a capella*, so when you're arranging them for voice and instruments, the challenge is to pull out the melody and then to accompany it with instrumentation that doesn't drown it or change it. That seems to come naturally to me, so I just keep doing it. There's a ton of songs, so many beautiful songs, I'll never get to all the ones I'd like to do."

To my central-Canadian ear – and perhaps to my Irish genes – the ways of speaking here have a beauty that is never far from song. Anita Best has collected both, songs and voices of Newfoundlanders. I ask Anita what drives her. "Lots of times I've recorded people who have no other outlet for their voice," she says. "Sometimes it's the only way they can have a say. What if you can't write, or even if you can, you don't feel comfortable enough to write a letter to the paper or to your MHA [Member of the House of Assembly, the Newfoundland legislature]? That's why open-line shows are so popular – you can have your say without having to worry about getting the grammar or the spelling right. Even within a particular group you'll always find a range of views. Maybe ninety out of a hundred people feel a certain way about what happened, but the other ten might see it quite differently, so if you want to get a complete picture, you need to hear what they think too."

For Chris Brookes, the quality of an interviewer is measured in the listening. "From working so long in radio, I know that different people develop quite different ways of interviewing. What I find best is to be a good listener and to not ask many questions, especially follow-up questions. Journalists are taught to ask follow-up questions, to chase the story, but that's not the right way to gather oral history. If you just wait, and let a long angel pass, they may add not only the kind of detail you always hope for but things that are quite unexpected too, unexpected and marvellous."

For one of his favourite radio documentaries, Chris let some long angels pass in the company of two Newfoundland fishermen. "One day I saw an auction ad for a boat, thirty-foot, wooden, built in 1980. It was probably the name that caught my attention – the *Lifetime Struggle*." He found the owners at Beaumont, a fishing village nestled between high cliffs on the Atlantic coast of St Mary's Bay.

> That spring, it was 1980, we decided that we'd build a thirty-foot boat, so that spring we went in the woods and we cut timber, planks for the keel, sternpost, stem, transom – you've got to get the right trees, we cut the keel right over there. We cut it up there in March, the last of March I think, we were up there the whole mornings. They thought you was somebody, because you was working in the woods.
>
> ❁ from *The Lifetime Struggle*, radio documentary
> produced by Chris Brookes in 1995

"They're two brothers," says Chris, "the most honest, down-to-earth Newfoundlanders you could ever meet, and poor. I followed the whole story, start to finish. They built the *Lifetime Struggle* with their own hands. Toward the end of the '80s, they decided to raise the gunnels and get a new engine, and they borrowed about $10,000 from the Fisheries Loan Board to do it. The government of the day encouraged fishermen to take out these loans so they could upgrade their boats and equipment. The deal was, you paid off your loan with 10 per cent of the value of your annual catch. But then came the cod moratorium, 1992, and fishermen were no longer allowed to fish. No catch meant no money to pay off your loan. One by one the boats were repossessed and put up for auction. The *Lifetime Struggle* sold for a couple of thousand dollars – nobody wanted the boats by then – and it was scrapped. The Loan Board said the two brothers were still on the hook for the rest of the loan.

"It's such an outrage, enormously sad. The official history says fishermen were compensated for their losses after the cod moratorium, but the real history – on the ground, seen from the bottom up – is a very different story. That's what oral history does. I thought the story needed to be told, and I hoped it might change the policy. Of course it didn't."

At one point in our conversation Chris refers to himself as "a grumpy old man." That's not my impression of him, but if it is true, I ask, why does he keep doing this kind of work, which seems inherently optimistic? "Because I don't know how to do anything else," he says, with a wry laugh. "I suppose I do it because I still think there's potential for change. Official history is often misleading, or too cryptic, or sometimes just plain wrong. To my mind, there isn't much value in gathering these stories if you're only going to stick them away in a vault. I think anyone who collects oral history has a responsibility to hold it up to the light of day, to let people see it, hear it, consider how it resonates in the present. Come to think of it, I don't like the name oral history all that much – it seems imported. To me it's a matter of asking people what they really think. Like the Fogo folks – everybody was supposed to move, but when they had a chance to talk about it with each other, they concluded that no, they wanted to stay right where they were, thank you very much."

When he takes several hours of conversation and edits it into a documentary lasting an hour or less, does he experience a tension between the two functions, listener and cutter? "Oh, yeah. That's why I don't want to do ten-minute pieces. I was listening to a radio documentary from South Africa with Steve Wadhams [a CBC radio producer]. He said he enjoyed it, and he learned some things from it, but he felt like a person walking down a street where at each house you meet a new person, which is great, but at the end of the street, you realize that nobody has ever invited you in. I tend to shy away from passing the mike around to all available suspects. I'd rather focus on one or two people, and set their stories in a larger context that resonates with listeners, so it doesn't just go in one ear and out the other."

RESONANCE

YOUNG BRIDE: One time I was in to Millers in Placentia, the store there you know, and I was
looking for a new pair of men's pants for meself – because see I
wore the men's pants too. That was the time the shorts came
out. You know the short underwear . . . before that we all had
wooly bloomers. So anyhow everyone was buying the shorts so
I went into Millers and bought four or five pairs. Spring come,
and anyhow Patsy never wore 'em before. This time he took off
the long johns and I said to him I said I'm after buying you
some shorts. You start wearing 'em now. Yes I will he said to
me. Yes I will. That's how he used to talk. So he got up in the
morning to go to work with the railway in Argentia and . . . .
Patsy never knew the difference in my bloomers and the shorts
so what did he do only haul on my bloomers. I didn't know. So
he went off to work in Argentia with my bloomers on him.
Uncle Dave Coffey down in Angle's Cove he was there and he
told us. He said Patsy went to go to the bathroom and Uncle
Dave heard him cursing. What's wrong Patsy, Dave asked and
Patsy said, Ah Jesus bye, he said, there's no fork in them shorts.
Dave yelled out to him, Ah God there are bye. There must be.
There's not, he yelled back. Dave said, Come here til I have a
look. What's wrong with you bye, what's wrong with you? But
Dave knew see, he was after seeing them sticking up in the
back. Look, Patsy said, there's no fork. And Dave said how can
there be bye, they're Bride's bloomers!

❧ from *A Man You Don't Meet Everyday*
by Agnes Walsh (2001)

I ask Agnes how she moves the voices she gathers from tape to stage. "While I'm doing the interviews, the story is the big thing, and some are more interesting than others, but I transcribe everything because I'm very interested in the rhythms of speech," she says. "It takes forever – that's my winter months – but I love the process. While I'm doing it, I make notes: 'Sure she hadn't a clue' – I love the way that's said, and some of these rhythms and figures of speech are almost lost, so I have to fit them in somewhere, in this story or that."

How faithful is she to the original? "I like writing about real people," she replies. "If I'd interviewed you and you went to see the play, you'd see yourself, or bits of you, though maybe under another name – I'd ask in the first place if I could use your name. When I wrote *A Man You Don't Meet Everyday*, the play about Patsy and Bride Judge, both of them were dead. I interviewed the family, I said, 'I really want this to be their story,' and they said fine. One person said to me when they saw the play, 'You really painted Bride like she was a saint, but my God, she was the crossest old bitch on the face of the earth!' 'Well, I knew her too,' I said right back, 'and this is what I saw. You can write a play about her being a bitch if you want, but I didn't see it.' That shut 'em up!"

CONVERSATIONS
IN YOUR KITCHEN

Talking with Pamela Morgan, I draw an analogy between archives and zoos as repositories where living things that should be free are held captive. (This is before I explore any archives and encounter people who sustain them.) "Absolutely," she agrees. "When Figgy Duff started, we ran up against a lot of shit, people saying the music shouldn't be tampered with by using drums, guitars, rock instruments. They said it should be put away for safekeeping. The folklorists were outraged – these were people going around in rubber boots pretending to be baymen – they hated us, we were tampering with their precious heritage. God knows we didn't look like folklorists, the boys had hair down to here, beards, the whole bit. We looked like a bunch of hippies. But look, you have to do whatever it takes to keep the music alive, and that includes breathing new life into it, that's how it survives. You can't just put it in a jar, call it special, and then forget about it. Look at Irish music, they stole the fiddle from the Italians, the bouzouki from the Greeks, and now they're all considered Irish instruments – that's evolution, it keeps the oral tradition alive."

Are there limits, things you cannot do to a song without corrupting it? "Oh, yes," Pamela says. "The worst thing I've seen is where you have very well meaning kids changing the melody of a song to fit into three chords on the guitar, so they can play it and sing along. I suppose that's better than no interest at all, but the melodies get flattened out. You can make a song ordinary by doing that. I'd like to see chords created to fit the songs, not the other way round. You have to be very careful to enhance, not diminish, the intrinsic value of the song."

For Anita Best, keeping the music and stories alive includes teaching – folk music at Memorial University, and workshops on oral history. "Recently I did one with a crowd of community health workers," she says. "They were going to interview retired doctors, nurses, midwives, to get a sense of the history of community medicine in Newfoundland. They wanted basic training – how to think about the project, how to plan it, how much will it cost, how do you select equipment, prepare your questions, and what are you going to do with it afterwards? People don't realize how much there is to think about until someone goes through the process with them. I'm not technically minded, so I can't talk about how a tape recorder works, and most people aren't interested in that anyway. I talk to them about why they're doing what they're doing, some of the ethical issues, how will it be made available?"

She continues, "I think there should be training for teachers who set interview assignments. Some of them will ask the youngsters to go out and collect folklore, without understanding themselves what that really means, or giving any preparation on what to do and what to expect. People think you can just go to your grandfather with a tape recorder and say, 'Okay, Pop, tell me about your life.' So much is lost that way. If they had a bit of training, they'd end up with a better document. Also, it would be more respectful. For example, I think you have an obligation to keep people abreast of what's going on with the stuff – it's their stuff. I still know people I interviewed or collected songs from years ago, the ones who are still living, I even know some of their grandchildren. That's partly why I don't do a big pile of collecting – you just can't have all that many people in your life."

The last time I talk to Chris Brookes, he is preparing to make a radio documentary on kids and their video games, for American radio. "I don't want to," he says, "but they pay a decent wage, in U.S. dollars. I can't survive on Canadian documentaries. There just isn't enough funding for them anymore. I'm a regionalist, I care about this particular place. If you're not part of a culture, if you're not swimming in the listeners' world, it's that much more difficult to speak to them. There are conversations you have in your kitchen, and others you have in a hall with a PA system. The CBC has just about killed any chance for the province and the region to have that first kind of conversation among ourselves. They've replaced it with a pipeline from Toronto. I still want to talk to Canadians about Canadian subjects. I also want to talk to Newfoundlanders about Newfoundland subjects – that's what I most want to do. But how, where, are you going to air it? It's infuriating – some of my best work will only be heard outside Canada, not by the people I most care about but by complete strangers."

My parting question to Chris: "This place you care about so much, what is it exactly? Is it physical, geographic, or – ?" If I were writing a radio play, I'd convey his response like this:

CHRIS BROOKES (softly, with yearning): No, it's an imaginary place. I know the place I live in, I care passionately about it, and I mourn for its passing every day – its survival is probably more in the mind than out there. I suppose that's what it is, really, a state of mind. That's another documentary I'd love to make – if I could find a broadcaster for it.

I ask Helen Woodrow what's next for her. "One project I feel very strongly about will look at recycling," she says: "– what do we understand that to mean, and what kinds of things have people been doing about it for a long, long time? It's really about how do we get out of this whole crazy mess of consumption we're in. We keep buying all these things we don't need, and it's going to kill us. I already have about a dozen interviews, some of them transcribed – for instance there's one on a form of mat-making where you made canvas mats out of old sails, from the boats that used to sail up to Labrador. It's a way of reclaiming – recycling, you might say – a piece of our past. Somebody told me the other day about the one sewing needle that people used to have – if it fell to the floor, which can easily happen, everybody would have to go on a hunt for that one needle, because if you didn't find it, grandma or mother wouldn't be able to do their sewing work, and then where would we be? This person said to me, 'I can't get that image out of my head, now every time I see a needle, I have to rush to make sure it's safe!'"

Along the way in writing this book, I've asked many people, and now Helen, "What it is that sustains you?" She pauses. It's a big question.

"Ultimately I suppose it's knowing that there's often only very small spaces we can operate in, but we have to identify those spaces, move into them, and do what we can. That may be very little – it ain't necessarily going to be powerful enough to stop the shit from coming down, or any number of tyrants from getting elected to high office – but in the long term it may contribute a little toward some kind of dynamic renewal of the democratic voice amongst people. To my mind, the whole notion of citizenship has to be revived, before it disappears entirely. So it's the belief that there are spaces where we can work with creativity and imagination, not necessarily to shake the world, but ultimately maybe to do a little of that. It's all you can do, really, isn't it?"

CHAPTER 7

THE WHOLE TRUTH

My mother disappeared when I was twelve years old. The following day I went to the police station to find her and they told me that they had not taken her there. I cried a lot, all night, but I had to be strong for my brother. We went so frequently to the police station that we made friends with the man there, the same one that tortured our mother, and it was him that told us that yes, they had brought my mother there . . .

I want to know where to place flowers for my mother . . . Sometimes I leave the door open because I still hope that she will return, but no, she will not return but I still cannot accept it.

Everyone in Ayacucho goes to the cemetery on the Day of the Dead, I don't know where to go. I need to be happy, I want to be happy.

✿ Liz Marcela Rojas Valdez, testimony to the Truth and Reconciliation Commission, Peru, 2002

This is the kind of wrenching story that Diana Avila heard, and felt, at the public hearing on crimes and political violence against women. "There were all these women from the different parts of Peru," she says. "You could see the hall was full of the colours of their clothes, their colourful skirts. There were tears, a lot of emotion, while these women were talking about the terrible things they had experienced. It was very touching. Not only for the women that went through these things but for me too, it was very, very powerful."

As executive director of the Project Counselling Service (PCS) in Lima, the capital of Peru, Diana Avila directed the program that supported – or accompanied, as she says – indigenous women in the difficult, dangerous process of testifying before the Truth and Reconciliation Commission. It was a rare chance for them to tell the people of Peru about the horrors they suffered through two decades of armed conflict in the poorest, most isolated regions of the country.

At fifty-three, a mother of three children, Diana has worked a long time on this path. She grew up in Lima, attended convent school – as most middle-class Peruvian girls did – and then the Catholic University, the largest in Lima. Before she joined PCS, she worked as a journalist. "I used to travel to the regions, to try to build the real history, the real dynamics of the violence. In the media you would read always that Sendero Luminoso killed people – and it's true, they did kill many people in really horrible ways. It's also true that the army killed and massacred many people in these regions. But you wouldn't find that in the media, because of self-censorship, the 'war against terror' that we have been living here for many years before the towers came down in New York. Those were the years of worst violence in Peru."

Until the 1980s the majority of Peruvians and the rest of the world knew the people of the Andes only as *National Geographic* figures in native garb who carried luggage or sold crafts along the road to Machu Picchu, the legendary "lost city'" of the Incas on an Andean ridge eight thousand feet above the Urubamba River. Otherwise, the indigenous people of Peru were irrelevant, invisible and silent.

As it has been for centuries, the Peruvian economy in the twenty-first century is still based on fishing, agriculture, and especially mining. In 2001 the country ranked eighth in the world in the production of gold, second in silver, fifth in copper, and third in zinc and tin. But

more than half of the resulting wealth is held by only one-fifth of Peruvians, most of them in Lima, while 54 per cent of Peruvians live in
poverty. In this grotesque pyramid, indigenous people continue to
form the base. A recent government survey found that of six thousand
indigenous communities, in only twenty-six do the majority of inhabitants live above the poverty line; more than half of all the indigenous
communities endure extreme poverty. In the rural department of
Huancavelica, close to 90 per cent of the people live in poverty.

This pervasive, enduring misery offered fertile ground for rebellion, especially among young Quechua-speaking people in the Andean
highlands. Through the 1970s, the Communist Party of Peru began to
win recruits in the rural department of Ayacucho. Under the leadership of a charismatic philosophy professor, Abimael Guzmán Reinoso
– or Chairman Gonzalo, as he came to be known – the party named
itself Sendero Luminoso, the Shining Path, based on the Maoist model
in China. Chairman Gonzalo proclaimed that a long history of failed
uprisings in Peru proved that the only possible path to liberation was
through prolonged armed struggle, to be led by the peasants.

In May 1980, during the first national elections after twelve years
of military rule, a small group of young guerrillas raided the
polling station in the rural town of Chuschi and burned the ballots.
With this gesture they launched the People's War against the state of
Peru. Elections, they declared, only served to maintain the corrupt
rule of the colonial elite in Lima. During the following years, the Shining Path recruited several thousand guerrillas. Senderistas attacked
police stations to seize weapons, dynamited bridges and power lines to
sever links between town and country, and orchestrated "armed
strikes" in various towns in and around Ayacucho. Peasant and community leaders who openly resisted the insurgents were executed.

In 1982 President Belaúnde sent troops to restore state control in
the poorest departments of Peru: Ayacucho, Apurímac, and Huancavelica. Through the 1980s and '90s, a series of governments in Lima
reacted to rapid advances by the Shining Path, and to deepening economic chaos, with ever-increasing militarization, especially in the rural

areas. U.S.-trained counter-guerrilla forces (Sinchis) and death squads escalated violence against the poorest, most marginalized people of Peru. In 1992, with support from the armed forces, President Alberto Fujimori shut down the Congress and the courts, suspended the constitution, and set up a new legislature filled with his supporters.

By 1993, one-third of Peru was under direct military rule. By government decree, state security forces were guaranteed impunity from legal prosecution. Indigenous people of the Andes endured continuous attacks by security forces, Shining Path reprisals against suspected collaborators, forced recruitment into both the Shining Path and army-controlled peasant Civil Defence groups, and "scorched earth" counter-insurgency practices that forcibly displaced more than 250,000 people.

Wherever they found themselves from moment to moment, women did what they could to sustain what was left of their families, setting up people's kitchens, mothers' clubs, and a variety of women's organizations for mutual support. The leaders of these became targets for assassination by both the security forces and the Shining Path.

These were the years when Diana Avila travelled through the rural areas, trying to document the real history of the violence. "I would hear people's stories, and look at what was happening to the social organizations," she says, "because in many cases when the women's organizations, the peasant organizations, the organizations in the shanty towns didn't want to follow the army or Sendero, they would be attacked by both of them. So I would write about these things. That was my job as a journalist, to let Peruvians know what was really happening."

These were also the years of gravest danger for journalists in Peru. In 1983 eight reporters went to the remote town of Uchuraccay to investigate army claims that several Senderistas had been killed by local *campesinos* – peasants. The reporters were stoned to death, their bodies mutilated and dumped in a mass grave. The authorities claimed that they had been killed by peasants who mistook them for terrorists and their cameras for guns. This was proof, said the army, that the *campesinos* opposed the subversives. Though most were afraid to say so at the time, many local people blamed the Sinchis, the counter-insurgency police. Two *campesinos* were eventually convicted and imprisoned. But the message was clear: journalists, especially ones who questioned the official version, could expect to be targets.

In 1991, Diana joined the Project Counselling Service as executive director. The mandate of PCS, a north-south consortium of five international agencies, is to support local NGOs in assisting refugees, internally displaced people, and returnees throughout Latin America. As the violence continued, she went looking for people in the regions most affected by it who could help in rebuilding the devastated social structure.

"I talked to people, and I listened," she says. "I looked to see where the kind of support we could give was most needed. In this way we chose to work in Huancavelica, the poorest department, and very far from Lima. It takes about twelve hours by car, the roads are bad, and if you want to visit the small communities, that means four or five more hours of very bad roads. Even national human rights and international co-operation organizations don't go there very often, so the people are very isolated and excluded. I also had to do a lot of counselling work, talking to local authorities and people in the regions – they were frightened even to talk about what happened, and we knew they would need help to go a step further in the role they should play in rebuilding their communities."

By now Diana was a target twice over, as a journalist and as someone who worked openly with victims of the continuing war. I ask her how she managed the risks. "I always listened to the local voices on where to go, when, and how to get there," she replies. "They are the ones who know what is happening. During the worst years of the war, I remember I would travel with a journalist card in one hand, and somewhere else, with my clothes, another card of the human rights organization, thinking that I might meet situations where one or the other could be useful. Of course both could also make you an enemy in the eyes of someone! The tension in those years, the end of the '80s and beginning of the '90s, it was very bad."

In my community we were all badly treated . . . farmers . . . families . . . They killed my father, my mother and my brother. They took my husband . . . If I had lost him I don't know where I would have gone . . . I was made into an orphan. My father and my mother brought me up with love, and I have not found that same love since, the loving care of a family.

We had to escape after the community was burned down by the military, we lost all our animals. We lost everything.

I don't have a home. I go from house to house, and my husband has to work as a casual labourer.

I came here thinking that I would be happy. It was nice before, but things have changed. Everything is different. . . .

❉ Fidelia Sucantaype Oscco, testimony to the Truth and
Reconciliation Commission, 2002

When Fidelia Sucantaype Oscco says, "they killed . . . ," she describes the nightmarish crossfire that indigenous people faced. "They" includes the Shining Path guerrillas who kidnapped her brother, the soldiers or the guerrillas who murdered her mother, the soldiers who detained and tortured Fidelia herself when she went looking for her mother, and the soldiers who took her father in 1990. To date, his whereabouts remain unknown.

BREAKING THE SILENCE

This is the kind of horror that the Peruvian Comisión de la Verdad y Reconciliación, the Truth and Reconciliation Commission, set out to unearth in June 2001. After the collapse of the corrupt, authoritarian Fujimori regime in 2000, the transitional government had bowed to widespread public pressure for an independent inquiry into what really happened during two decades of unprecedented violence and repression in their country.

In a 2002 speech, Commission president Dr Salomón Lerner described its role: "The Truth and Reconciliation Commission is the most serious effort made to date to face up to the factors which made the violence possible, the consequences of destruction, and physical and moral suffering, especially in the most humble and impoverished sectors of Peruvian society. Thus, the Truth and Reconciliation Commission is to be understood as a unique time for the restoration of justice in our country, in the broad sense of the word; and at the same time, as a presence that will encourage deep reflection on the faults of the Peruvian society, which will contribute to the consolidation of democracy, lost in Peru on so many occasions in the past."

The latest in a series of truth commissions in several countries, Peru's would be the first in Latin America to incorporate public hearings as an essential component in its process. But which of the victims would be willing to testify? No one in power had ever listened to them before. Why would they now? In the past two decades Peruvians had also learned the high cost of speaking out. In 1989 a nurse, Marta Crisostomo Garcia, was shot to death in her apartment. Witnesses identified members of the army as her murderers, but a police investigation turned up no clues. Marta Crisostomo had spoken out publicly about a massacre she had witnessed in 1988, when thirty farmers were murdered by soldiers in Cayara, Ayacucho. She was the ninth witness of the massacre to be murdered or "disappeared."

In addition, under anti-terrorism laws enacted by the Fujimori regime, thousands of Peruvians had been imprisoned in secret military courts under dangerously vague charges such as "affecting international relations," "provoking anxiety," and "justifying terrorism," all of which were widely used to silence opposition. Those laws are still in force. How would the authorities react now to public testimony about atrocities committed by the national police or the armed forces?

Diana confirms that it wasn't easy to find people willing to testify. "At first, people had very little information about the Commission, and we could see that they were not trusting the process. They believed that justice was only for rich people and not for the poorest peasants of Peru. They feared for their children, now grown up, who they said were fooled and betrayed by Sendero Luminoso because they wanted to change the situation of their people, so they took arms and in the end they did very bad things. People said if we speak to this commission now, they are going to put our children in jail, and the generals who were in charge of the dirty war are not going to pay at all. That was their main distrust."

On the other hand, the government in Lima had changed, and whatever it might turn out to be, it was not the much-feared Fujimori regime. When the Commission began to set up regional offices, and Commissioners made it clear that they particularly wanted to hear from the people who had suffered the most, attitudes toward it began to change. "People began to feel more secure," says Diana. "They started to believe that this process might be a possibility for the country to have a better reading of its problems and its opportunities, its historic problems like racial discrimination – which is something you never talk about in Peru. So this Truth Commission could be an opportunity to finally do something about the terrible social problems that led to this war."

Still, given the lingering fear, and the long habit of silence, how were people encouraged to speak in such a public forum? "In the case of the women," says Diana, "we started with encounters in the different regions that would allow them to meet with other women who were also badly affected by the political violence. This created spaces where they could share their own experiences and know that many other women had the same problems, which helped to give them trust and increased their self-confidence. We learned that people from one province didn't know what happened in the next one. The distances are very big, and some people never left – others left, displaced by the war, but some locked themselves in their communities, they were scared of moving around. And as communications are very bad in the rural areas, there was not much contact between the different villages. So we were able to create these spaces for communication among the women, and in this way to understand the whole dynamic of the war in that region."

Many of the women who came to these meetings had never spoken in public before, even in their own villages. Says Diana, "At the beginning they would come to these meetings with the husband or the brother, and the brother would say, 'I'm going to speak for her,' so this woman didn't have a voice. It was a difficult process to support the women, and at the same time to have the brother there. You have to be patient and follow the rhythms of the people, and not clash with the men. Well – " she laughs – "in the end you may clash a little, but you have to be careful to respect their processes and their will. At first there would be men in the room, but as time passed, you could see that women wanted to be on their own. They wouldn't like men to enter the room because they wanted to have a space for themselves to talk about issues that they wouldn't talk about with men there."

Of the 16,885 testimonies eventually heard by the Commission, most were from women. According to Jean Symes, a Canadian colleague of Diana, this pattern is consistent with other truth commissions. "The men, even if they're still alive, are often not able to testify for various reasons," Jean says. "Women tend to be raped but not as often killed as men. So while the men are gone or recovering, the women take over the socially prescribed roles of men. They have to be strong, they learn the role of speaking out for their loved ones, which is really an extension of their usual role, taking care of everybody. Almost always they would talk about what happened to others, their daughter, their husband, their relatives, but hardly ever about their own experience – 'What happened to me is not important, or it may be too shameful to talk about, it's just what happens to women, so it's not important.'"

A key objective at the regional meetings was to elicit the women's own stories. Says Diana, "Part of our work was to insist that they were actors as well, because once the husband had been killed or disappeared, it was they who took over the family. They searched for the husbands and relatives, they denounced human rights violations, and when they had to leave their communities and go to cities, they were in charge of the support, the survival of the family. They were really important actors at every stage, so it was very important for their own experience to be told."

After the regional meetings, the Project Counselling Service and other NGOs organized a national meeting in Lima. Delegations of women came from the regions, and officials from the Truth Commission and the Ministry of Women were invited to hear the stories of the women. By this time some felt ready to participate in the Truth Commission's formal public hearing on crimes and political violence against women.

PCS and other NGO workers accompanied them through the whole ordeal. "Accompanied" is a carefully chosen word, meant to convey a more equal relationship than "support." Diana describes the process: "We would help them build their own stories, to remember the facts they wanted to highlight in the presentation, maybe to put some dates – sometimes it's difficult when these things happened five or even ten years ago. We accompanied them as well in the public hearings. Someone would sit with them, to pass them some water or a hanky, or to hug them, that sort of thing. I was there too, listening to them, congratulating them after the presentation, because they were very brave to say the kinds of things they experienced. We would accompany them after the hearings as well, visit them in their communities, because once they speak, if their testimony is heard by other people in the community who experienced the same situation, they are going to go through the whole process again – not only the person who gives the testimony but the whole group that lived through the same events."

Each person who testified had the opportunity to make a closing comment. Most asked for justice for the crimes they had endured, or in the case of people whose relatives had disappeared, for the remains so they could bury them. Or they asked for reparations, in practical forms like education for the orphans of the dead and disappeared.

Diana vividly remembers one woman who used her moment at the microphone to seek something quite different. "The case was that her sister-in-law and all her children had been killed by one of the peasant civil-defence groups, and this woman felt – all the family felt – that the brother, who was still alive, did nothing to protect his family from being killed. For many years they didn't talk to him because they believed that he was part of this horrible crime. But in the process of the research done by the Truth Commission, it became clear that this poor man could not have done anything to avoid that his wife and all her kids were killed. When she came to the end of her testimony, this woman said, 'Thank you for giving me the opportunity to talk to the country and to tell about the injustices that I suffered, but I also want to say something to my brother. I ask him now to forgive me, because this war has destroyed family ties and relations, even the love we had.' I haven't heard many testimonies go into this kind of personal relations. It was very impressive to hear."

PAIN AND COURAGE

One night the Police arrived . . . and took away my partner. I stayed at home, but they came to arrest me. At the anti-terrorist headquarters they told me that various people had accused me of participating in meetings and terrorist attacks. . . .

Later the so-called interrogations began. I held out through the punches and the near drowning. They wanted me to accept all their accusations. . . . Then later things got worse. The sexual humiliations began that took away my dignity as a woman and a mother. They tied me, completely naked, to a seat by my feet and arms and started to touch sensitive parts of my body, like my breasts and my genital organs, despite my screams and the begging. My eyes were blindfolded. When they began to put their mouths on my nipples, I could not hold out any longer and began to accept everything that they wanted, all the false accusations. . . .

At the end of 1989 I was found innocent of all charges by a court, and I was then absolved of any crime. When I got out of prison I had to find a way to support myself and my daughter, but I could not find work. I had no choice but to sell sweets on the streets . . . On 16 June 1994, as I was selling sweets, I was arrested again. They held me on the same charges of which I had been acquitted. I appeared on television wearing a prison uniform.

The judges at the military court sentenced me to twenty-five years, saying that I was in guilty of collecting funds for the Shining Path in Lima, when I was not even making enough to eat.

❂ Zonia Luz Rosas, testimony to the Truth and
Reconciliation Commission, September 2002

As testimonies began to emerge, the Truth Commission ran into an unexpected barrier – translation. Most of the people who testified spoke Quechua; the Commission spoke Spanish. Diana's colleague Jean Symes works with the Canadian NGO Inter Pares, a partner in the Project Counselling Service. Jean explains, "Spanish was used for the terms of reference and the world view of the TRC. Midway through the process, they discovered that there are no standard translations for concepts such as 'human rights,' 'human rights violation,' words that don't exist in Quechua. And there was confusion about words that refer to things that are not spoken about in these terms in Quechua, such as 'sexual abuse.' They also found that words used commonly in Cuzco to express these ideas were unknown or not used that way in Huancavelica. In a primarily oral language, words are used differently or have distinct connotations in different settings or locations."

Why didn't the Commission anticipate this problem? "Several reasons," says Jean. "Linguistic ethnocentrism – most people believe that other languages are the same as theirs, just with different words. Racism – Quechua, being the language of 'unimportant' people, hasn't been studied in Peru to any great extent, even though a majority of the population speaks it as their maternal language; also for that reason there are relatively few professional Quechua-Spanish translators. And exclusion – Quechua-speaking people were so excluded that those in power didn't realize the majority of people affected by the violence were indigenous and so the majority of testimonies would be given by Quechua speakers." The Commission scrambled to address the issue, with partial success.

During the course of its work, the Commission's impartiality was repeatedly attacked, particularly by politicians of the party in power in the late 1980s, when many of the most serious human rights violations took place. Some called for the Commission to be investigated, even disbanded. The military ignored requests to testify. In September 2002, ex-president Alberto Fujimori, who had fled to Japan, refused to meet the Commission president, who had gone to Tokyo to interview him. Fujimori described the inquiry as a "circus" and claimed that it was trying to persecute him.

Human rights workers also questioned the makeup of the Commission, which included a retired military officer and legislators linked to various parties in power during the worst years of violence. But no one was representing the victims, the unjustly imprisoned, or families of the disappeared.

Even so, many women who testified felt that this was the first time in their lives that official Peru had ever listened to them. I ask Diana what changes she experienced in the women. "They are very proud that they have been brave enough to talk about their experience during the war," she replies. "I think this gives them a sense of relief in a way, which is important for victims of political violence. I have also seen them improve a lot in the way they address issues in public. Now they feel secure enough to stand up and say their own words, and that's very important because this is a very discriminatory place. The people from Andean communities and especially the women are really looked down on in Lima. They know that they don't handle the language very well, so they had to be very brave to speak in that kind of space. After having worked with them for some time, that is very encouraging for me. They have grown as leaders, and now they want to share their experience with other women."

From the beginning the Project Counselling Service and its partner NGOs knew that, regardless of how the Commission turned out, this postwar inquiry offered a rare moment for reflection and opening in Peru. All their activities were geared towards making the most of it. In concert with the public hearing, three hundred delegates from women's organizations in eight rural departments gathered in Lima for the Second National Congress of Women Affected by Violence. They brought with them proposals and demands for how their lives, families, and communities could be rebuilt. Together they formulated a national platform, in which they insisted that in building a new nation, Peru had to redress in practical ways the age-old exclusion of indigenous, rural, and poor people from national life, justice, and economic equality.

Also at the congress, PCS launched "Testimonies of Pain and Courage," an exhibit that combined testimony excerpts with portraits of women who had spoken. The photos were taken by Nelly Plaza, a renowned anthropologist and photographer. Even as the war still raged, she had helped gather stories of victims, children and adolescents, and displaced people in the shantytowns around Lima. Along with the women's words, the photos have a simple, haunting power. The women would not be silenced, and they would no longer be invisible. In one photo, Julia Llacta stands in partial shadow, facing the camera, a lone figure in the doorway of a small house built of rough stones, backed by hard white light of the Andean highlands. Beneath the photo is a fragment of her testimony: "They took me because the subversives took my brother. They kicked me there, stepped on me with their boots . . . My father freed me, he stayed in exchange for me and they beat him too, they tortured him."

After the congress, women took their experience home to meetings throughout the country. "They invited the authorities, the mayor, the people's ombudsman representative, some members of the political parties in the region," says Diana. "The women showed the photographic exhibition. They explained what kind of meetings they had in Lima, and they presented the platform built during the encounter, the expectations related to justice, poverty, reparations, and rebuilding the infrastructure of their communities. They were always saying that reconciliation is only possible if justice is done; otherwise it is impossible. This was very important as a way for people to recognize these women not only as victims but as actors in the whole process, as rebuilders of their own communities."

The powerful impact of "Testimonies of Pain and Courage" led PCS to use it more widely than they had originally planned. "A copy of the exhibit has been shown in the north of Peru in six or seven cities that experienced very little violence," says Diana. "It has also been shown in England, to support Peru solidarity work in London and other cities. Here in Peru, students showed it in human rights week at the Catholic university, and on the 25th of November, a special day to oppose violence against women, relatives of political prisoners put the exhibit in the main part of Lima. About two thousand people went to it that day. I think it has been very, very important to sensitize people in relation to violence against women." The exhibit is also posted on the website of the Canadian NGO Inter Pares, a partner in the PCS consortium.

After two years of intense, wide-ranging research, on August 28, 2003, Salomón Lerner presented the final report of the Truth and Reconciliation Commission to the current president of Peru, Alejandro Toledo. In its twelve volumes and seven appendices, the Commission concluded that "the internal armed conflict experienced by Peru between 1980 and 2000 constituted the most intense, extensive and prolonged episode of violence in the entire history of the Republic."

The TRC found that 69,280 individuals had died in the conflict, more than double the direst previous estimate. It recognized a direct relationship between poverty and the probability of becoming a victim: 85 per cent of the victims had lived in the five poorest departments of Peru; 79 per cent were subsistence farmers.

The report examines in detail the actions and responsibilities of Sendero Luminoso, the Tupac Amaru Revolutionary Movement (a smaller guerrilla group), the peasant Self-Defense Committees, the police, the armed forces, and a succession of national governments. Then it addresses a broader culpability: "The TRC has found, sadly, that the civilian governments were not alone in bowing to the indiscriminate use of force as a means of combating subversion. On the contrary, the proclivity of these governments for a military solution without civilian controls resonated with a considerable sector of Peruvian society . . . that resided far from the epicenter of the conflict. This sector, in the main, watched with indifference or demanded a quick solution, and stood prepared to face the social cost, which was paid by citizens of the rural, poorer regions."

With the release of its report, the Commission came under renewed attack. Peruvian business interests placed advertisements saying that the Commission had "liberated" terrorists. They also offered to pay for the defence of any military official who faced prosecution. A retired general told the press: "I don't regret anything. If I had to use the same anti-subversive strategy again today, I would apply it without hesitation." He had commanded the armed forces in Ayacucho in 1983, when some of the worst army atrocities occurred.

Two days after the report was released, a vice-president of the Peruvian Congress declared on national TV: "I would not hesitate to order collective assassinations in order to eradicate subversion and defend my fatherland. We have to be capable of carrying out heroic actions in order to do away with this scum of terrorism." On the complaint of a Fujimori supporter in the legislature, a Lima prosecutor investigated whether the twelve members of the Commission could be charged with "advocating terrorism."

As it is for all truth commissions, one of the TRC's mandated goals was to reconstruct the nation's historical memory. It quotes the famous adage, "A country that forgets its history is condemned to repeat it." It has a grand and eloquent ring, but in the day-to-day struggle for survival of the Andean peoples, I ask Diana, how much does history really matter?

"I've seen during this process how important it is for people," she replies. "Even my son, who was ten, twelve years old during the worst years of violence, his memories are very weak on that whole time. But living through the Truth Commission process when he was a student at the university made him understand a lot about the problems of Peru. When a photographic exhibit done by the Commission was in Lima two months ago, very many people visited that exhibition, which records what happened during the years of violence. Many schools visited it, which has been very important for school kids, it lets them have their own reflection on the whole process. If you put on top of that the public hearings, reports in the media about the worst years of the war, and the recognition that the Commission gave to the victims, I think this helps very much to integrate this part of our history into the lives of people, especially people who live in the urban areas."

In the rural department of Apurímac, the Project Counselling Service and its partners are supporting a project to establish a museum of historical memory. It will include a monument to the victims, exhibition and meeting rooms, and an archive where people can search through Truth Commission documents for information on those who died or disappeared. "I think that to build these spaces for the relatives and victims is very important for the country," says Diana. "Holding these memories can make people think that you can't live indifferent to what happened in the twenty years that passed – it was that indifference which allowed so many people to be killed and so many unjust things to happen. To avoid this kind of thing happening again, we need to have access to these memories. This is the meaning of the Nunca Más campaign." *Nunca más* means never again.

The final report acknowledged, for the first time ever at such a high level, "the seriousness of ethno-cultural inequalities that still prevail in the country: 75 percent of the victims spoke Quechua or other native languages as their mother tongue. This figure contrasts tellingly with the fact that, according to the 1993 census, on a national level only 16 percent of the Peruvian population shares that characteristic."

Given that one of the central problems of racism is denial on the part of people who practise it, I wonder, how much impact might the TRC's statement have in Peru? Diana believes the report opens a critical debate that would never have happened without it. "This is an opportunity for the country to look at itself, and these kind of issues – the idea of seventy thousand people being killed and so many people didn't care. Of course there have been a lot of reactions, a lot of denials – 'what do they mean, racism? people were killed in every place, Lima too.' But people were killed and tortured and raped much more in Ayacucho or Apurímac than in Lima. Seventy per cent of the killed people are Quechua speakers, 80 per cent rural people, which means they don't have a name. For Peruvians they are just numbers, statistics, so it is important to recognize them as citizens. I think there have been many voices – journalists, intellectuals, progressive people, even people from the right who can be democratic – saying that we must take these problems into account if we want to build a country that doesn't suffer these kind of wars again."

> I asked them why they were taking my son and they told me that he was a witness and that they would release him at the door of the barracks. At that moment I grabbed my son. Damn you, old woman, they said, leave your son. They pushed me, they hit me, they stepped on me. They wanted to shoot me and they took my son away from me to put him in the police car and take him away. I yelled like crazy.
>
> Since that day I wandered aimlessly day and night trying to get my son back and when I arrived at the barracks they told me that they had not taken him there, so I walked fifteen more days like a crazy woman.
>
> It was then that my son had sent me a note from the barracks: Mama, I am here in the barracks, look for a lawyer, look for money to get me out. This is the last memory of my son. This paper is a proof that my son was there.
>
> ✪ testimony by Angelica Mendoza, Huamanga, Ayacucho, 2002.
> She is president of the National Association of Families of
> the Kidnapped, Detained and Disappeared of Peru

Since the collapse of the Fujimori government in 2000, families affected by political violence have been organizing throughout Peru. Diana describes their goals and the obstacles they face: "When people know where their relatives are buried, the places where corpses were thrown by the army – so they know that in this area or under this building that used to be a military base are the bodies of their relatives – people organize and ask the public prosecutor to order the exhumation of the bodies and to open juridical processes against the perpetrators, if they know who they were."

Her colleague Jean Symes tells me that Diana was invited to a meeting of President Toledo with representatives from the association of families of the disappeared. "Each representative was invited directly by the president, and so was Diana," says Jean. "Typically for her, she suggested that it would be better to invite representatives of human rights organizations, but the President's Office said no, you are the person that all these people trust. In the meeting Diana tried hard to refer any questions that came up to the people who were direct victims of the violence. That's exactly why they wanted her to be there. They knew that she wouldn't take over their voice."

As one of its essential functions, the Truth Commission began to investigate several massacre sites. In November 2002, Peruvian, Argentinian, and Guatemalan forensic anthropologists worked with villagers near the town of Lucanamarca to exhume the remains of sixty-two adults and children. After Senderistas killed several peasants here in 1982, a community self-defence group killed ten guerrillas in Lucanamarca's central plaza. Sendero Luminoso retaliated the following month, killing villagers with bullets and machetes.

In August 2002, villagers identified more than ten mass graves near the town of Totos, at an abandoned school the army had converted into a torture and killing centre in 1983. Inhabitants report that helicopters arrived several times a week carrying people who were never seen again. The Truth Commission learned that the military routinely destroyed all personnel files from bases like Totos, which closed in 1988.

Under anti-terrorism laws enacted by the Fujimori regime, many people were jailed by military courts after someone denounced them as a terrorist, or after confessions extracted under torture. Calling themselves "liberated innocents," several hundred of them are now demanding justice. "Some of them spent ten years in jail," says Diana. "Then the Peruvian government said, 'Sorry, we made a mistake, you can go home,' just like that. So now they have made committees to demand reparations for what they suffered while detained."

Torture victims are also organizing, as are relatives of political prisoners sentenced to extremely long prison terms by hooded military judges who became known as the "faceless judges." Diana gives an example: "A poor kid, nineteen years old, was detained because he had some papers in his bag and they said this meant he had links to a terrorist organization – he got twenty years for that. In most cases these people couldn't afford lawyers and they didn't have access to due process, so the relatives get together to demand due process, or to find funds for lawyers to defend their relatives. Very few lawyers can support these people. They are very poor, some of them have been ten years in prison, and for the families to find new lawyers now to take care of the cases – it's a very difficult situation these people face."

In a historic series of rulings, the Inter-American Commission on Human Rights rejected the laws under which civilians could be judged by military courts without due process. Technically, Peru is now required to initiate new trials in civil court for thousands of Peruvians imprisoned by the military courts. Peruvians across the political spectrum are watching these cases closely. "One of the problems is that judges are very scared about dealing with these cases," says Diana. "The media are playing a very bad role in this, with claims all the time that the judges are freeing terrorists." Much is made of the fact that among the prisoners technically eligible for retrial is Abimael Guzmán Reinoso, former leader of the Sendero Luminoso.

"Yesterday I was listening to a woman judge," says Diana. "She was saying that when the judges free someone, it's because they don't have the proof to keep him in jail, but when they have the proof, he stays in jail. This is how courts work in a democracy, no?"

The testimonies and the TRC's research have had other, more direct legal impacts in Peru. When the report was presented, says Diana, "they also presented sixty-five cases to the public prosecutor, with deep research so they can begin to do their own investigations on these cases, which are concerned with murder, torture, and rape. This could mean that some people may be charged for crimes they committed. Everybody knows you can't take all cases to the courts, because many of these things happened years ago and often there is not enough proof. But to have these sixty-five emblematic cases in court and the perpetrators condemned, that dignifies the victims."

The public prosecutor has also received two sets of cases specifically pertaining to sexual violence against women during the war. "Women were massively raped," says Diana. "That was the use of military bases in many regions, soldiers would go out and rape women in the communities just to spend their time. Now army officers have even appeared on television saying, 'But these things happen because those communities have their own customs in relation to women and rape' – as if it was normal for women to be abused! So I think we should put a lot of effort to take the cases to court, to get justice for these women, and to sensitize people about sexual violence against women."

The chances for justice in Peru rose sharply in 2001, when the Inter-American Court declared illegal a blanket amnesty granted by the Fujimori regime in 1995 to all military personnel. Diana explains the implications: "If they were judged at all in the past, military people or policemen were judged only by military courts, which of course found most of them innocent. Now they can be judged again, which opens the possibility for many new trials against perpetrators. That's the case with one of the main paramilitary groups during the Fujimori regime. They've caught almost all of them now, and they're opening a case against them. This is going to be a very important process for justice in Peru."

Within weeks of the Inter-American Court ruling, two retired Peruvian generals were arrested on charges that they led the "Colina group," an army death squad linked to the 1991 killing of fifteen people at a tenement in Lima's Barrios Altos district, and the 1992 "disappearance" of nine students and a professor from La Cantuta University. Also facing trial on crimes against humanity and corruption charges is Vladimiro Montesinos, Alberto Fujimori's closest advisor and de facto head of the National Intelligence Service (SIN), to which the death squads reported. In Japan, Fujimori himself continues to elude prosecution on similar charges, despite international warrants for his arrest.

. . . AND RECONCILIATION

I ask myself with deep pain, how could my son have chosen the most difficult path, already having a secure life, with a future, a family . . . ? He went because of the suffering of others and of his people.

❂ testimony of Nila Rincón, mother of Miguel Rincón Rincón, who was condemned to life in prison as a leader of the Tupac Amaru Revolutionary Movement (MRTA)

One of the most challenging roles of the Truth Commission is embodied in the second part of its title, "Reconciliation." In their final report, the Commissioners made it clear that without effective reparations to the victims, reconciliation would be impossible, or at best, hollow. They write, "For the TRC, reparation means reversing the climate of indifference with acts of solidarity that contribute to overcoming discriminatory approaches and habits that have not been free of racism. Applied even-handedly, reparations must also generate civic trust, re-establishing the damaged relationship between citizens and the State, so that democratic transition and governability are consolidated and new scenarios of violence are prevented."

That is the theory. I ask Diana how it's working out in practice. "There has been some progress," she says. "The president of Peru has apologized on behalf of the state to the tortured people, displaced people, relatives of disappeared persons and others for all the damage that was done to them, and for the lack of protection during the war years. He has also offered some measures of reparation. First, a national registry of victims has to be built – this should allow victims of the violence to have access to health and education programs – the government is in process of creating the mechanisms for that. The president also said the Truth Commission report will be included in the education curriculum for schools, so kids can read in their history books about what happened in those years, and why those things should never happen again. I think that can help in the reconciliation process, the recognition of the victims as citizens. Of course, a lot of political actions will be needed for the government to improve the systems they may offer, and that depends on the strength of the victims' organizations, the human rights movement, and civil society in general. Otherwise they are not going to happen at all."

Another, more direct kind of reconciliation is underway in communities torn by the conflict. "For example, some kids left their communities to join the armed movement," says Diana; "then they came back after and asked to be forgiven and protected by the community. Sometimes the community asks them to work on the roads, or in cleaning the water channels, and to stay in the village under community supervision, then they can become normal community people again. These are small processes that don't happen everywhere. In many regions, public ceremonies of recognition still need to be made about what happened in communities that suffered the violence. There are proposals now from the Ministry of Women and Human Development to do this kind of ceremonies in rural municipalities. I think we will see those kinds of processes in the coming months."

NUNCA MÁS

Much has changed in Peru, but much stays the same. Control of the economy remains in the hands of a small elite based in Lima. At the same time, more than half the population earns less than $US2 a day. The proportion of Peruvians living in poverty continues to rise, from 48 per cent at the end of 2000 to the current 54 per cent. Of these, the lowest earners are the same people who suffered most in the war: the people of the Andes. Life expectancy for rural women is seven years less than for women living in urban areas; the maternal mortality rate in Peru is among the highest in Latin America, especially in the rural areas and Lima shanty-towns of displaced people.

Peru labours under a crushing foreign debt, most of it accumulated by military regimes in the 1970s. In 2002, 17.5 per cent of the government budget went directly to foreign banks, while only 17 per cent was spent on health, and 9.3 per cent on education. The current government is committed to maintaining brutal neo-liberal economic policies imposed by the Fujimori regime and the International Monetary Fund. These ensure deepening gaps in income – the poorest fifth of Peruvians now receive less than 5 per cent of the national income – and continuing privatization of the few national resources still under public control.

In June 2003, eight mayors in southern Peruvian communities went on a hunger strike to protest government proposals to privatize electricity companies, in breach of a campaign promise by Alejandro Toledo, the U.S.-trained economist who eventually won the presidential election. As public protests escalated, the government imposed a thirty-day state of emergency and sent troops into the southern city of Arequipa. Two young people died and 150 people were injured. In a pattern hauntingly reminiscent of the past two decades, the state of emergency was extended in August 2003 to parts of Ayachucho, Apurímac, and Huancavelica.

The national Human Rights Commission reports that, despite having been explicitly outlawed in 1998, torture remains a serious problem in Peru. The Commission documented fifty-three cases involving seventy-seven victims from January 2001 through August 2002. Fifteen of the victims died as a result of torture.

For Diana Avila and the Project Counselling Service, the work goes on. When I spoke with her by phone in December 2003, our call was interrupted twice by crises that she had to deal with in neighbouring Colombia. As it happened in Peru, indigenous people there face a vicious war between guerrilla forces and the Colombian military, assisted by U.S. advisors and troops. At the time of our call, Jean Symes was working with Diana in her Lima office; in the first crisis, Jean told me later, a vehicle had been stolen from one of PCS's partner NGOs. It was transporting construction materials to rebuild houses destroyed in one of the Colombian war zones. PCS staff had to assess whether people had been taken hostage – the usual practice, but this time they were released – and what had become of the vehicle and materials.

In the second crisis, the governments of Panama and Colombia had just announced that they would repatriate indigenous people from Colombia who had fled the violence into Panama. Since they would be forced to return to the place they had fled, still a war zone, the announcement provoked emergency negotiations among PCS, their counterparts in Panama, and – since the Panamanian government was breaking an international convention on the rights of refugees – the United Nations High Commission on Refugees. "In the end," says Jean Symes, "the forced reparations proceeded. The Colombian government gave guarantees that the returning refugees would be protected, but few people expected that the government would either want to or be able to uphold any such guarantees."

For Diana Avila, this was a normal workday.

I ask her what sustains her. Surprised by the question, she repeats it: "What sustains me?" Then she laughs. Like women who testified to the Truth Commission, she doesn't have much time to dwell on her own situation. "The idea that these people are working much harder than I do, and that they deserve respect, and that they should be able to exercise their human rights as other Peruvians do," she says. "To think of a country in the kind of situation that we had, forever, it's impossible. Things have to change so that Peru can survive, and develop, and grow. My youngest kid sometimes says, 'Look at the environment, look at all the wars in the world, there is no future.' I don't want that kind of feeling, the feeling some Peruvians may have that this situation is not going to change at all. I need to have hope in the strength of the people to go on with their struggles. Otherwise it's going to be like hell."

The advances that she looks for are tiny, and enormous. A report that I read mentioned recent progress among local authorities in their awareness of issues facing indigenous women. I ask Diana how she assesses this claim: Is it just the determinedly positive language of such reports, or has she actually observed real evidence of progress?

"Yes, you can see it," she replies. "For instance, you could see it in a congress of women in Huancavelica a few weeks ago. This was a very big meeting, very crowded with about four hundred women from small districts, and very unusual because these organizations tend to be quite small, and in the war areas even smaller because of the violence, the destruction and fear. The women took the lead in talking, half in Spanish, half in Quechua, and all of them were speaking about their own issues, asking for programs they should be getting as peasant women's organizations, and talking about trouble and corruption in some of these programs. And here is something very important: the first day of the congress the president of the Huancavelica region invited the leadership of the peasant women's federation to the office of the regional government, and there they made a ceremony of inauguration for the congress, with him and the mayor and the people's ombudsperson in the national congress. This was a big success for the women."

Diana is not naïve about the capacity of officials to say one thing and to do another. "But you see, before now, these officials would never pay this kind of attention. They would never care about these poor women making their own small thing somewhere. But now the women were there in the capital city, the local press was there – this was an important recognition of these women as citizens, as part of civil society. For me, this shows that it is possible for people to change, and to include other views in their government."

Rofelia Vivanco, a displaced woman in Lima, speaks at the Second National Congress of Women Affected by Political Violence, September, 2002: "Peace is to know what happened and why, and to know that the people who did all this harm recognize their error and contribute to the reparation, to peace for us all."

Behind her floats a huge banner, in Spanish, lettered by hand. Translated, it says: "Truth without the Voice of Women Is Only Half the Truth."

CHAPTER 8

PASSION IN THE ARCHIVES

In his studio at the Gatineau Preservation Centre,
audio conservator Jim McDonnell is cooking tapes,
in a box that looks like a pizza oven.

Until a researcher requested access to a large oral history collection – conversations with Lorraine Monk, formerly of the National Film Board of Canada and the Canadian Museum of Photography – the centre was unaware of disaster looming in their ¼-inch master tapes. Jim explains: "We keep all the masters here at the centre, and we make copies available to the public on request. But until these particular tapes were actually requested, we didn't know that many of our ¼-inch masters had developed a squealing problem. It's caused by hydrolysis, the accumulation of moisture, which makes the binder material ooze through to the surface of the tape, then the oxide and binder agent peels off, the resulting goop collects on the tape guides, and it makes the tape unplayable. If I were to put this tape on the machine, it would play for about five minutes. You'd hear a high-pitched squeal, and then the whole thing would grind to a halt."

The solution: slow cooking in a specially designed oven to drive off the moisture. The process takes a minimum of eight hours, at about 40 degrees Celsius.

In his teens, when Jim played his tapes and records for hours on end, his sister told him he'd never make a living that way. "Look at me now," he says with a grin. He can work with sound recorded on almost any kind of machine, samples of which he demonstrates – a variety of dictation machines, a huge lumbering turntable for radio transcription disks, wax cylinders, and a post-World War II wire recorder, immediate predecessor of the modern tape recorder.

Researching the history of his union local in Hamilton, Ed Thomas found rare 1950 wire recordings of conversations with a former union president (see chapter 11). The only place he could get them transferred to conventional tape for listening was at Jim's lab. "The sound on wire is amazing, but tape is a lot more stable," Jim says. "Wire breaks too easily. I've spent whole afternoons turning the air blue, trying to fix one of these machines after a broken wire jammed it up."

Built improbably on swampland north of the Ottawa River, the centre opened in 1997, an enormous blue glass hangar slung on steel buttresses. On a bright winter day, I've come for a tour. Inside the glittering outer shell, preservation studios and laboratories sit atop a three-story concrete monolith, the vault system. Machines and sensors controlling temperature, humidity, and air quality are located in a connected but separate building, to further isolate the sensitive laboratory and storage functions of the centre.

The labs and studios, housed in what look like greenhouses and Quonset huts, are laid out in street format. In the controlled climates within, some seventy preservation experts restore damaged and decaying audio, video, film, paintings, books, maps, and documents. In the monolith below, fragments of the national story are preserved in forty-eight vaults, each with its own finely tuned climate.

Preservation officer Dale Cameron calls this vault area "our treasure chest." A few years ago in an ice storm, he says, the whole area lost power – "except for us, because of the diesel generators next door. We didn't have enough power for the outer envelope, so we sent the staff home, but the vaults never lost power. This place sort of reminds me of *Metropolis*, the movie. I used to think of it in a negative way, but now I find it dynamic and energizing."

He leads me through a series of vaults, entering each with a security swipe card. Colour film is stored at 17 Celsius and 30 per cent relative humidity, black and white film at 18C and 25 per cent relative humidity. On one custom-designed film storage shelf, I notice a device that looks like plastic tongs. "You got it," says Dale. "It's ideal for pulling out the film cans." He demonstrates: it works beautifully. "It was someone's suggestion. They got an award for it. So here we have a $90 million building, and a $1.50 kitchen implement." In a document vault he tells me that part of the job is pest management. "With textual collections you can get microscopic pests like book lice. They're after the glue."

According to Dale, in 2001 the Gatineau Preservation Centre housed 22 million photographic images, 80,000 video tapes, 225,000 cans of film, 55,000 reels of microfilm, 100,000 audiotapes, and about 140 kilometres – file cabinets, end to end – of textual records, about three-quarters of them originating from the federal government. So much talk!

Across the river in downtown Ottawa, I meet Richard Lochead and Caroline Forcier-Holloway at the National Archives offices. Their building is a leftover from a greyer, more Calvinist era in government architecture. Richard started the oral history collection here about fifteen years ago, but recently he's been "kicked upstairs," as he puts it, to run the Audio-Visual Acquisition and Research section. Caroline, with a background in history and museums, joined the Archives two years ago as audio-visual archivist, and inherited the oral history file from Richard. She's also responsible for the National Film Board archives, the records of several government departments, and French language film, video, and audio.

Chatting about the role of archives in preserving oral history, we begin where civil servants must, with their official mandate. "In theory it's very broad," says Caroline. "We can acquire anything we believe to be of national significance." Richard adds, "But compared to some nations, the oral history part of the Archives tends to be under-resourced. This has to do with how the collection got started. Technically the Archives was responsible for all government film, but since we didn't have the vaults, the NFB kept it by default – until a huge nitrate fire in 1967 destroyed a lot of film there and a decision was made to keep our film heritage in an institution whose mandate is preservation. But that created a situation where the visual media dominates, so it's hard to get resources for audio oral history."

Richard and Caroline also face a continuing debate over whether the Archives should acquire oral history at all. Opponents say the function of archives is to preserve, not create, the historical record; since oral history is a created record, it doesn't qualify for preservation, particularly when there are barely enough resources to acquire existing materials. Opponents also argue that, as historical evidence, oral history is neither as legitimate nor as reliable as written documents.

On the other side of the debate, which includes Richard and Caroline, part of the national archivist's role is to preserve a representative record. Says Richard, "In the official record we tend to get an over-representation of people who have the means to record their own history, and an under-representation of those who don't. Where do we need the least oral history material? Politicians. Where do we have the most oral history?" The two say in unison, with a laugh, "Politicians!" Richard concludes, "If the aim of the archives is to preserve a representative snapshot of society, oral history is one way to do that. From my point of view, it serves to document part of the historical record that isn't well served by other existing avenues."

A third dilemma for the archivists stems from the way oral history has evolved in Canada. "Unlike the United States, where it tends to be valued for its own sake, in this country it's more a technique than a discipline," says Richard. "Film-makers, writers, journalists, academics all tend to use it to get information for some end product of their work. It's almost never generated to end up in an archive. But from the archival point of view, we're very interested in the original materials, what a filmmaker would call the 'outs.' We're interested in the integrity of the whole material."

An example of the dilemma: In the early 1960s the CBC produced an epic thirteen-part series of documentaries on Canada in the First

World War. "They created eight hundred hours of interviews, using a professional historian/interviewer and professional studio facilities," says Richard. "This was a unique oral history project, before oral history was recognized as such. But except for what they used in the thirteen hours, the rest of that material just sat for years in a storage room at the CBC. We have it now. We're working away at cataloguing it."

Caroline adds, "Regardless of the original intent or end use, our first principle here is to preserve material for the public record."

In St John's, Newfoundland, Patricia Fulton, archivist at the Folklore and Language Archive in the Memorial University of Newfoundland and Labrador (known locally as MUNFLA), says her passion for oral history came to her early. "My mum used to say that of the six kids in our family, I was the one who sat at the end of the ironing board and asked her questions about what life was like when she was growing up in the '30s, on a farm in the St Lawrence Valley. I was always interested in the little things, the personal things: what did my mother feel about this or that? I was only five or six, and here I was doing oral history without a tape recorder. Ever since, I've looked for ways to chronicle people's stories. I know that not everything can be captured, and some voices will never be heard, but I believe more will than in the past, now that a wider range of people are able to express themselves, and we can document them. That's really satisfying to me."

As Patricia matured, her sense of time became less expansive. "My mother is gone, my father, my brother, and I never did record any of them. I always meant to, and it makes me angry now that I didn't do it when I had the chance. As you begin to understand what losing people means – the absolute loss – it only gets more poignant, and more urgent."

Now with degrees from Queen's and Dalhousie universities, Patricia can rescue people's stories before they go missing. Her workplace at MUNFLA is a series of small, plain rooms strung along a corridor in the Folklore Department. In one room, a transcriber taps away at her computer. The archive houses over 29,000 audio recordings, several thousand transcripts, 17,000 papers – many of them course assignments prepared by students – a huge collection of Newfoundland songs and commercial recordings, photos and videos, books, and maps. There are also hundreds of CBC Newfoundland programs in the process of being transferred from tape to CD.

The oral history card index fills several file cabinets. Patricia pulls a few cards, each representing an oral history collection: Forest Fire, Placentia Bay, 1968; My Parents in Rocky Harbour; St Bride's College, St John's, 1947–53; Religious Folklore of Outport Newfoundland; Gay Culture; Effects of the Fishery on the Cultural Heritage of Newfoundland. "This is only a tiny fraction of the whole collection," she says. "It's quite impressive to have so many voices represented here when you consider the population of Newfoundland and Labrador [508,075 in 2001]. We have the only recordings of many people who've passed away, which can be of great value for family members. That's part of what we do here – we provide copies of materials to people who, for example, may never have known their grandparents or other relatives. Here they can find their stories and perhaps even some photos. This aspect of our work appeals to me very much, the idea of giving something back to people."

Because the archive grew out of the Folklore Department, which was created in 1968 by American folklorist Herbert Alpert, the bulk of its acquisitions originate in field work and other research done by professors and students at the university, on topics related to life in Newfoundland and Labrador. Others interested in folklore also deposit their materials here; for example, the Law Society of Newfoundland recently donated a collection of oral history tapes. "Folklore is not just about 'old' things," says Patricia. "It touches on all aspects of culture and humanity. For example, there are courses here on belief, on blues and jazz, on vernacular architecture, on language and play, on gender studies, on the music of Ireland – it all depends on who's teaching, and what their areas of interest are. That's how the archive is built."

This passion of hers for preserving the evidence of people's lives: I want to know more about it. "When you realize that each life will never come again, and that a whole range of knowledge passes with each person," she says, "then you come to understand the importance of collecting and preserving that knowledge, the contents of that life. This is the purpose of folklore. In my experience, so much of what we study in school is elitist. It tells us what's important and what is not. It takes us away from our own experience of the world. By taking a keen interest in the small things of daily life, folklore studies honour that experience, the shared experience of humanity.

"It's amazing what the familial or local realm can yield, if you give it proper attention. Folklore looks at how we work – in offices, as nurses, on railroads. It looks at how we sing songs to document events and lost loves, how we tell jokes to relieve stress. All these things are familiar, they're the stuff of our lives, and they're the material of folklore. The specific motive for archiving is to preserve this material and to make it accessible so others can appreciate it, to chronicle as well as we can the lives and the knowledge of people."

In preserving the stuff of people's lives, the lifespan of preservation material becomes a compelling issue. At MUNFLA, fragile reel-to-reel audiotapes, videotapes, and photos are stored in a locked cold room, at a constant 16 degrees Celsius and 38 per cent humidity. "Preservation and access are the two main functions of our mandate," says Patricia. "We have to be very conscientious about physical and environmental conditions. That got to be quite challenging this past summer when we had to move everything around and redesign the rooms. Last year we had a preservation assessment done through the provincial association of archives. We had to fill out a detailed questionnaire with measurements of the rooms, types of raw materials, proximity to motors, and so on. Then a specialist came in to document and videotape the premises. We discovered some things we can do better, and without breaking the budget."

At the National Archives, Richard Lochead also values the lives and stories of the non-famous. After working freelance in history and journalism, he saw his first full-time job in the Archives primarily as a good government job, long-term, manageable, and relatively secure.

"But then, in order to do a reasonable job as an archivist, I found that I wanted to document what all the taxpayers of this country contribute to – a fair representation of the national experience. I didn't think the Archives was doing that, so it became a mission of mine to push for a more representative acquisition policy. Oral history is one way to do that.

"Also, I have the sense that, rather than being second-rate history, oral history material actually complements and enriches the written documents. My job is to ensure that as full an account of history as possible will be here for people researching in the future. You might call it historical equity, or balance – let's say historical affirmative action."

Finding balance turned out to be easier said than done. "Some people donate material to enhance their public profile. For example, in the case of a photographer, a condition might be that we put on an exhibition, which can be a costly proposition. The family of Gratien Gélinas [a Québecois theatre artist] wanted a website." (See http://www.archives.ca/05/0519_e.html.) "That's the ego part, the recognition that being in the National Archives is an acknowledgment of a person's importance. Others see it in monetary terms, for the tax credits they can get with a donation. Oral history, on the other hand, is a refreshing exception – for most donors, what they really want preserved is the subject matter, which nearly always documents someone else's experience! They're an interesting group, the people who do oral history."

But not that easy to recruit as donors. "Many people don't know about the Archives, or they don't know that we do this type of acquisition," says Richard. "Or they're unaware of how important it is to preserve this material. Our challenge is to identify resources before they're lost, and to get them in here. For example, a lot of Native land-claims work is based on oral recollection, but the people who gather this material tend to view it *only* as research for the land claims. They don't usually think of donating it to an archive, particularly a government institution. So there's a lot of oral history material out there that should be finding its way into one archive or another but isn't. Some of it may end up in the Great Plains Research Centre in Saskatchewan. I don't care so much where it is, as long as it's being preserved somewhere."

Caroline Forcier-Holloway adds, "We do have plans to develop a more active acquisition program. Right now it's a bit of a mish-mash, and other institutions are getting records that really should be here. It's quite frustrating."

"It's always a challenge for the Archives to be proactive," Richard says. "We need to do a better job of targeting potential creator sources. For example, *Quill & Quire* [a Canadian magazine about books] puts out an annual list of the books published in Canada, so one thing we could do is look at which ones were based on oral history interviews and go after them. That's just one of various ways to track sources of material."

How to sustain the work with diminishing funds is an enduring challenge at both the Ottawa and St John's archives. Caroline explains, "It's very difficult to generate revenue with oral history. Most of the uses of it are academic or genealogical. But in any case the National Archives has no mechanism to make a profit. Our mandate is service to Canadians. They can come on site to listen to or view materials. If they want copies, and there are no copyright or donor restrictions, we can make copies for them – there is a fee for that, but it's at cost." Richard adds that they used to make the copies on site, but now the work is sent out to a private company.

I can't resist commenting on the magnificent preservation facility I just toured, and its $90 million price tag. "Ah, well, there's always money for buildings," Richard says. Then he adds, "But there's no question we needed a new facility." In other research I came across an example that confirmed his contention: World War II documents that had deteriorated almost beyond recovery in a leaky basement.

When I began to look into the subject of archives, I thought of them as vast caves, dark and dusty, into which history got dumped for the rest of time. Now I know they're not dusty, and they're only dark when the material requires it. But after the archivists have acquired and preserved the material, then what?

Patricia Fulton is clear on the guiding principle: as many people as possible should have access to as much material as possible. "After preservation, our most important function is access," she says. But there are limits: "This is a scholarly archive, and under the terms of our contract with donors, access is understood to mean access by qualified researchers. That leaves it open for the archivist or the director to interpret what 'qualified' means. A lot of people come here looking for information on their families, for example, and we're delighted to accommodate them. But anyone who wants access to material in the archive has to see me first. We discuss the materials, any sensitivities there might be, any restrictions the donors may have imposed for a variety of reasons. If someone is going to publish material they collected, they may not want it released to anyone else until after their own publication date. Or informants may have specified that they don't want any names mentioned."

The law can be another complicating factor. "By copyright law in Canada, technically the material on the recording belongs to the person who put the tape into the machine," says Patricia. "But in folklore the guiding principle is 'from the people, by the people,' so even though informants have signed release forms, in a larger sense the material still belongs to them. Sometimes that can override the collector's rights, and you may have to go directly to the informant for permission. What it comes down to is that we have to look at requests on a case-by-case basis. Of course, this can be quite time consuming, and I'm sure it must be irritating for people with deadlines. But it has to be done – it's the nature of both the discipline and the archives. It's a balancing act between wanting the material to be used and respecting its origins and conditions."

At the same time, Patricia does what she can to promote oral history. "This is a working archive, so we lend out recording equipment for students to do fieldwork. We've also created a series of documents to support that work – release forms and contracts in particular, for official documentation." She also gives oral history workshops, offering practical tips on using a recorder, finding interviewees, planning the interview, establishing rapport, coping with various scenarios in the interview situation, then following up and keeping in touch. "If people are doing oral history for a particular end result, I'll make sure they know how the material will be taken care of here, who gets to see it and how. Informants often require that kind of information before they'll give access to their living rooms."

At the National Archives, Caroline Forcier-Holloway hopes that one of its offshoots, the Canadian Genealogy Centre, will raise interest in oral history. The centre is located in a similar building across the street; Caroline has been working on the virtual equivalent, at http://www.collectionscanada.ca/02/020202/02020206_e.html. It speaks to people searching for continuity in an increasingly virtual, temporary world. I checked out the Getting Started page. "Names, dates and places are the building blocks of compiling a family history," it says. "Ask older family members specific questions about your ancestors. 'What was your grandmother's maiden name?' 'Where did she live as a child?' 'What were her parents' names?' 'When did they come to Canada?' Any clue, no matter how small, may help your search." The site lists twelve genealogical record sources in Canada, including Acadian, immigration, Russian Consular, Métis, military, and the North West Mounted Police.

The Gratien Gélinas website, a first for the National Archives, is also a template for the future. Many Canadian cultural agencies are looking at the web to expand their access points, says Richard, and the main thrust is coming from Canadian Heritage (a department of the federal government). "They're keen that Canadians should connect more with their own stories. The primary target now is youth, so there's a push to package documents on line in ways that catch their interest. These tend to focus mostly on visual stuff, so oral history isn't that much involved – though it wouldn't be that difficult to digitize it and put it on line. Then you'd have to promote it, so people would know it's there. Of course it always comes back to the same old questions: how much, and who's going to pay? We're waiting to see if the current enthusiasm for heritage is backed up by any funding envelopes for oral history."

Knowing from experience that if people can't find the material, they won't use it, Richard and other oral history proponents started working in the mid '70s to produce a guide to publicly accessible oral history collections across Canada. No money was forthcoming from the National Archives, but finally in the early '90s they got a grant from the Social Science and Humanities Research Council. They hired a researcher, Normand Fortier, and in 1993 produced a richly detailed 402-page guide.

Its listings represent the breadth of oral history available in this country: seventeen interviews recorded in 1979 "with senior citizens of Anglo-Saxon origin" in Chilliwack, British Columbia ("sound quality is generally poor to fair"), in the Chilliwack Archives; eleven interviews recorded in 1986 by Patricia Fulton with lighthouse keepers in Newfoundland ("restrictions on publication"), held at MUNFLA; 320 interviews with Shuswap elders, recorded in English and Shuswap ("75 transcriptions available"), held at the Secwepemc Cultural Education Society Archives; twenty-three interviews conducted by Gil Levine (see chapter 11) in 1977–79 with members and former members of the Canadian Union of Public Employees ("some restrictions"), held at the National Archives of Canada.

The guide was published by the Canadian Oral History Association, of which Richard Lochead is a founding member, past president, and past editor. Caroline volunteers as secretary-treasurer. After I heard of COHA by accident from an American oral historian in 2001, I joined, for $20 annual dues. But then it was a challenge to find out what the association actually does. At that point its website hadn't been updated for some time and the last volume of its journal, *Oral History Forum d'histoire orale*, had been published in 2000, on indigenous voices from the Prairies.

I ask Richard and Caroline how COHA is doing. They look at each other and Richard sighs. "Let's just say we're trying to revive it. In the '70s and early '80s it was quite active, but then it got tired."

Caroline adds, "By then oral history was no longer the fad it had been. Now everybody has a video camera. If we get two new members a month, we're doing well."

"South of the border they have a large enough population, and so many more historical commissions, et cetera, that they can easily support an active oral history association," says Richard. "Here the number of people whose jobs are directly connected to oral history – teaching, archives, producing books on a regular basis – is tiny. It's quite ironic, because Canada actually has a stronger oral history tradition than the U.S. – primarily due to the CBC, the NFB, and other institutions – but here it's not recognized as oral history. Most Canadians seem to think it's a U.S. invention."

In 2003, a new issue of *Oral History Forum d'histoire orale* came out, an evident labour of love by editors Ronald Labelle, a folklorist at the Université de Moncton's Centre d'études acadiennes in New Brunswick, and Patricia Skidmore, a historian at Brescia University College in London, Ontario. Last time I looked, the website had been updated by web manager Ken Clavette, of the Ottawa and District Labour Council (see chapter 11).

Richard says they are "trying to revive" COHA. What does he mean? "Earlier on, the Archives put resources into the association, mostly to improve the quality of material we were getting."

No more "sound quality is generally poor to fair"?

"Exactly. We wanted people to at least use decent equipment and the right kind of tape." For Gil Levine's CUPE interviews in the late '70s, the Archives loaned him a professional-quality recorder. "Gil's work is the best example of what we hope for," says Richard. "He knew the topic, he had good contacts, and he knew what questions to ask. That project of his still stands as a model for others. All he needed from us was some decent equipment. Also, since he wanted the tapes to be used, he made sure that the community he'd worked with were aware of them. That resulted in a fair number of requests for the material, more than for most of our holdings.

"I still believe we should be promoting best practices in doing oral history interviews. COHA is a good vehicle for that, especially to exchange information via the website. The association can also lobby for funding, for example to make various holdings across the country more accessible. Of course the more people recognize the value of oral history, the better the chances for funding."

What future do the archivists see for oral history in Canada? In St John's, Patricia Fulton sounds optimistic. "I really like the idea of introducing it more widely in the schools. It's such an epiphany for people to discover that their stories really matter, and when they see the value in studying things that are not generally designated 'important.' The material is so rich, it reveals so much about us – the practical, the spiritual, the emotional, the thoughts – it really gets at the substance of a person, as much as they'll allow. As long as we're around, the need for that is not going to diminish, not one bit."

In the nation's capital, Richard and Caroline sound optimistic too. "I think we'll see a new wave of oral history," says Richard. "Many people whose work requires them to do interviews are going to retire soon. They'll have all these tapes stashed away in their basements, so they'll contact the Archives, just as people do with their more traditional documents. Oral history has been around long enough for that to happen now. Also, as people of my generation retire, they'll have more time to do oral history interviews." He smiles. "Do I believe that?" A little pause, he looks at the ceiling. "Why not?"

"My sense is that everybody has a story to tell," says Caroline. "Oral history is an ideal way to get it out, to make it come alive. I think it's important for people and communities to have access to those stories. How else can we get the whole picture?"

"And if we don't get the whole picture," Richard adds, "how can we ever hope to have real democracy?"

 # 9/11/01

At 2:50 P.M. Vienna time, Tuesday, September 11, 2001, Elisabeth Pozzi-Thanner was sitting in a glass phone booth at the central post office. She was booking interviews for a personal project, to make sense of the complex role her family had played during the Nazi era in Austria.

At the same time in Brooklyn, Karen Malpede and her husband, George Bartenieff, were working in their basement office on an application for a grant to take Karen's latest play to London. *I Will Bear Witness* is adapted from the 1933–45 diaries of Viktor Klemperer, a German Jewish professor of literature. George plays the solo role.

Karen's daughter, twenty-one, was still asleep upstairs. Karen remembers hearing – or feeling, she can't remember which – a low rumble. Lying at their feet, Abby the spaniel began to bark. Abby was inclined to be excitable. "Oh, Abby, don't be silly," said Karen, "it's nothing."

In upper Manhattan, Mary-Marshall Clark had just dropped her son off at school. The taxi turned north on Broadway towards Columbia University, where she was due to teach a class on oral history. She directs the Oral History Research Office at Columbia. Suddenly the driver swerved, nearly colliding with several cars. Mary-Marshall recalls asking him, "Sir, are you ill? If so, please pull over until you're feeling better."

"Didn't you hear?" he said, turning up the radio.

"Hear what?" she asked.

"A plane went into the World Trade Center," the driver said. Then: "Two. Two planes."

"Then it's not an accident," said Mary-Marshall.

From her office she called her son's co-parent, to fetch him home. Then, since the administration had decided that classes would go on, she went to hers.

In the Vienna post office Elisabeth Pozzi-Thanner had just reached a historian in Linz, the city in Upper Austria where she grew up. Her cell phone rang. "Two planes have crashed into the World Trade Center," said her mother, "and another one is headed for Chicago, another for Washington." Elisabeth remembers saying, "It's not possible."

The World Trade Center towered over her New York neighbourhood, near Soho. Her favourite restaurant sat in its shadow, as did a tiny candy shop run by Genny, a Colombian woman, blind for the past ten years. Genny had once been housekeeper and surrogate mother to Elisabeth's stepchildren. Elisabeth tried to call the store, but the line was silent.

Karen Malpede awakened her daughter, who wanted to go immediately to her boyfriend's house on Sixth Avenue, a twenty-minute walk. "Of course I wasn't about to let her go alone," says Karen. The two of them walked towards Park Slope, with its postcard view of the New York skyline. At Flatbush Avenue they encountered people streaming off the Brooklyn Bridge from lower Manhattan. "Refugees," says Karen. "That's the word we both used. Small groups of people, completely silent, covered in white-grey soot – they looked like ghosts."

Karen had shifted into disaster mode, an intense, focused calm. "It's what I do in dangerous situations," she says. The day after Serbian shelling ended in Sarajevo, she had led a workshop on trauma and dreams with students at the city's National Theatre Academy. "Though I had never encountered conflict on that scale before, I had taken a clinical program in trauma work at New York University, and it's what my playwriting is about, the ways people get through and recover from violence – incest, rape, war, various forms of public and private abuse."

The work springs directly from her childhood. "I grew up in a very violent house. There was a lot of denial, both about the suffering of the person who was violent, my father, and the suffering he inflicted on the rest of us. Ostensibly the neighbours didn't know, but of course they did. Often it's said that if you grow up experiencing violence, it's likely you'll grow up to be violent – if you're a guy you'll be an abuser, if you're a woman you'll end up in abusive situations. But the opposite can also be true. You can come out of it strongly opposed to violence as a solution to anything. That was my experience. It has also fuelled my work, which some people call theatre of witness."

Her early years provided basic training in how to behave in violent situations. "One of the ways you get through it is you get very quiet, you try to keep out of the way, you watch and you listen. You don't get hysterical – that's just too dangerous."

Karen left her daughter with the boyfriend. On the way home, a flatbed truck drove past with more refugees, cloaked in chalky dust.

In Vienna, Elisabeth and her mother watched the Twin Towers collapse. "We were glued to the television," she says. "We were paralyzed, we couldn't move." Ironically, before September 11, Elisabeth had been fretting over her daughter Katerina, sixteen, in Beijing on a year-long student exchange, so far away; now suddenly her distance from New York seemed an advantage. Even after hearing that all phone lines in lower Manhattan were dead, Elisabeth kept trying to call the candy store. She dispatched a storm of emails to friends in New York. Nothing came back. She sat with her mother and watched TV.

Karen called the Red Cross to see if she could give blood, but very soon it became clear that none would be required. She offered to do counselling, but the agencies would only accept people with certificates. So she and George sat and watched TV. "It was numbing," says Karen. "Once the buildings had collapsed, there wasn't much more they could tell us. They just kept playing the same images over and over – especially the second plane hitting, that's burned into memory.

It was like a drug. You knew you should turn it off and *do* something, but you just kept sitting there, staring at it."

At Mary-Marshall's oral history class, only one student showed up, an emergency medical technician. Like Mary-Marshall she was flat calm, despite knowing that her best friend was working at the World Trade Center. "It struck both of us right off that however many people were in those towers, it was highly unlikely that many bodies would ever be recovered," Mary-Marshall says. "I began to think that we would need some kind of structured way for people to record the lives that were lost, and somehow to struggle with the meaning of this terrible thing."

When Mary-Marshall acquired her first tape recorder in rural North Carolina, she was ten. "The south is full of storytellers, my father among them," she says. "They specialize in the art of the tall tale, where a strand of untruth is woven into an otherwise true story. As a child I was very shy and would hardly talk to anyone, but I became fascinated with those stories, and trying to detect the hidden strand. That's why I got a tape recorder, so I could listen to them again and again, to figure out what was and wasn't true."

Then she met Albert Baysdon, an elderly man, illiterate, with one tooth in his head, a great lover of people but shunned by practically everyone. "He may have been black, or Indian, I was never sure, but he lived on the edge of the culture. He believed he was the prophet Elijah come back to earth. We agreed to a barter – in exchange for him telling me his stories and visions, I would teach him how to read and write. It was a classic exchange of orality for literacy."

The two sat for hours by the woodstove in her father's insurance office, Albert talking, Mary-Marshall recording. "I had no way to interpret his visions, those nightmares of his that overwhelmed him so – was he crazy, or saner than the rest of us? I know now that I had never met anyone who worked so hard at trying to make sense of the world we live in." By the time they were done – when she went away to college – Albert could read and write and Mary-Marshall had collected more than eighty hours of tape. Without knowing it, she had become an oral historian.

On September 12, 2001, she launched the Columbia September 11 oral history project. "I recognize how privileged I am in having a way to respond immediately to this tragedy that a lot of people didn't have," she says. Within two weeks she got funding to transcribe 300 audio interviews, and 150 people had volunteered to conduct the interviews. She selected about forty whose experience and skills she could trust. "We didn't send anyone into the field who didn't have some kind of background related to oral history or interviewing. This was far too important, too complex, and we had no time for training."

At her first meeting with the interviewers, she outlined the daunting task. The volunteers would record interviews with individuals now, and again in a year or so, to explore how memories of traumatic events are shaped and reshaped over time. As many interviews as possible would be gathered immediately, she said, before personal experience merged with the escalating barrage of media and political interpretations. She asked interviewers to include communities where individuals had been targets of discrimination in the wave of anger and official repression that followed the attacks.

On September 12, a brilliant, unseasonably warm day, Karen went out for a walk on the Brooklyn Promenade. Her daughter had volunteered to take food and materials to rescue workers; Karen was still looking for something to do. Across the East River, in place of the gleaming towers a plume of dark smoke rose, untroubled by wind. People stared at it, hardly speaking.

Karen noticed a young man sitting on the grass, weeping quietly, a motorcycle helmet in his lap. She sat nearby, introduced herself. He was Israeli, had served in the army there, but had to get away from the ever-deepening violence. On September 11, he had parked his motorcycle by the building where he now worked, next door to the Twin Towers. He said he had seen "some weird shit" in Israel, but never anything like this. He saw people plummet from the sky, he watched their bodies explode on the pavement.

He planned to walk over the Brooklyn Bridge, retrieve his motorcycle, and ride to Atlanta where he had relatives and there would be no violence. "I thought this was a very bad plan," says Karen, "so I wanted to sit with him long enough for him to find his way to a more realistic one."

He talked for more than two hours. Karen asked a few questions but mostly listened. Her husband joined them, then a few neighbours they had never met. "Eventually he calmed down a bit," says Karen. "He decided to forget about the motorcycle for a while and instead to go have dinner with his mom, who lives in Queens. We walked him off the promenade, embraced, and said goodbye."

In one of New York's innumerable small worlds, when a close friend gave birth to a son, Karen had provided support; the other supporter at the birth was Mary-Marshall Clark, who would co-parent the boy. Mary-Marshall had seen one of Karen's plays, and later invited her to speak at Columbia on theatre of witness. Now Karen jumped at Mary-Marshall's suggestion that she do interviews for the September 11 history project: "Finally here was something I could *do*, something useful. That impulse to be of use is quite common in reaction to traumatic events, it's a way of holding yourself together. In this case I could use my understanding of trauma and bearing witness, in the sense that it might be helpful for people to talk, to have someone listen to their story. It was also something non-violent I could do in the midst of all the violence rising up around us."

Across the United States, Muslim temples and people taken for Islamic were under attack. George Bush vowed to wage total war on terrorism, a permanent war against any perceived enemy of the United States anywhere in the world – first target, Afghanistan. In Karen's mostly African-American neighbourhood, Clinton Hills, people talked to each other on the street, many for the first time. Karen can't recall a single person who supported a war on Afghanistan. Several quoted Malcolm X's comment on an earlier crisis, "The chickens have come home to roost." One said, "We have been too arrogant, and for too long." But all of this, she recalls, was spoken only in whispers.

In Vienna, stranded by the bankruptcy of Swissair, Elisabeth finally received an email from New York reporting that someone had pulled Genny out of the candy store and got her safely home. A message arrived from the Columbia oral history office: Would Elisabeth do interviews for the September 11 oral history project? "Obviously I said yes."

I met Elisabeth and Mary-Marshall at Columbia's Summer Institute on Oral History in June 2001. Both impressed me as passionate, intelligent people who asked difficult questions of the world. After each day's sessions, Elisabeth and I travelled south together to our respective neighbourhoods, chatting like kids about our day at school. In late November, my partner, Brian, and I flew back to New York for a visit with friends in the East Village. Despite the U.S. Thanksgiving holiday, Elisabeth agreed to an interview at her apartment, and Mary-Marshall at her office. I didn't hear about Karen's work until later; we would meet by phone in December and eventually in person.

At La Guardia airport, soldiers in camouflage patrolled nearly empty corridors with machine guns. Meant to reassure jittery flyers, they had exactly the opposite effect on Brian and me. In Manhattan the Stars and Stripes flew everywhere, unavoidable, from thousands of tiny frayed versions flapping on taxi aerials to a vast eerie shroud that wrapped an entire twelve-storey building in mid-Manhattan.

By Thanksgiving our friends in the East Village were able to get home from work without having to pass through police and military checkpoints. But subway service still stopped well north of Ground Zero. Officials feared that massive retaining walls under the wreckage could collapse and the Hudson River inundate the subway, road, water, and sewage tunnels that run below most of lower Manhattan.

I picked up a discarded copy of the *Daily News*, a New York tabloid. The U.S. government was offering a $25 million reward for Osama bin Laden, dead or alive. George Bush told American troops that the war in Afghanistan was going well. "We cannot know every turn this war will take," he said, "but I'm confident of the outcome." He had just signed the U.S.A. Patriot Act, passed by Congress with virtually no debate and only one dissenting vote. It gave him the tools, Bush said, to defend those freedoms that the terrorists so hated. (Critics called it a licence for dictatorship, but not in the *Daily News*.)

In Connecticut an elderly woman had died of anthrax poisoning, the fifth victim of an apparent bio-terror attack. In Washington, officials at the Federal Emergency Management Agency were questioning whether they had any obligation to reimburse the New York Board of Education for costs incurred in decontaminating schools near Ground Zero.

In New York, Larry Silverstein, the developer who had leased the World Trade Center six weeks before September 11, proposed that instead of trucking debris to the Fresh Kills landfill site on Staten Island, it should be dumped in the Hudson River as the foundation for a memorial. He also proposed replacing the Twin Towers with four shorter buildings, with office space equal to the original.

In its lead editorial, the *Daily News* commented, "The endless reinvention that is New York continues."

We went to Ground Zero the day after Thanksgiving. At dusk, under pink-tinged clouds, tour buses crowded the side streets. People teetered on police barricades, cameras whirring and flashing. At souvenir stands, vendors sold FDNY (New York Fire Department) caps, plastic-laminated photos of the black towers soaring into a luminous sky, and instant coffee table books, *World Trade Center, 1970–2001*. Only a few tattered, ink-blurred notices remained – "Anyone knowing the whereabouts of . . . . ," but nearby walls were crowded with wreaths, flags, and placards: "We Will Not Let Them Break Our Spirit."

Under dazzling movie-set lights, mechanical shovels took deep bites from the mountain of rubble. We recognized a lattice of twisted steel from a tower façade, already an icon. A jagged section of one building still stood, a five-storey skeleton, skin stripped away. Each of its open cells would have once been someone's office.

As soon as Elisabeth could get a flight out of Vienna, she headed home to New York. The timing of Mary-Marshall's invitation was fortuitous. Elisabeth had just finished her work with the Shoah Foundation, conducting more than 150 interviews with Holocaust survivors over the past seven years.

When Steven Spielberg was preparing to film *Schindler's List* in Poland, he recognized that with the passage of time, more than half a century since the end of the Second World War, many Holocaust survivors were dying, and with them went their stories. In 1994 he established Survivors of the Shoah Visual History Foundation to document the experiences of survivors and other witnesses. Since then the foundation has videotaped more than 51,000 testimonies, in thirty-two languages in fifty-seven countries, with 2,300 trained interviewers. Elisabeth was one of a tiny minority of those who were not Jewish.

In 1994 she had landed in a New York sublet with her daughter, Katerina. Her marriage had collapsed, and her last job, with an international children's foundation in Europe, had just wound up. She had no idea what to do next. In the *New York Times* she read that Spielberg had set up his foundation to gather testimonies of Holocaust survivors, and it had opened an office in New York. She called, explaining that she was Austrian, not Jewish, she had worked as a radio and TV journalist for ten years in Austria and Italy, and she would like to do interviews.

When they asked why, she replied that she had two motives. First, her skills and experience could be an asset to the project. Second, this would be a rare opportunity for her to grapple with the big shadow, as she calls it, that has been with her since childhood in Linz. Her grandfather, a Catholic monarchist, opposed the Nazis and died a political prisoner in Dachau. Her father also resisted and was condemned to death for high treason, later commuted to life in prison. But other relatives were high-ranking Nazis. Here was the shadow.

At the New York training course for Shoah interviewers, Elisabeth was the only Gentile. I asked how she had managed to build trust with Holocaust survivors. Did she have to justify herself? "A lot," she replies. "People would always ask 'How did you come to this country, where did you come from?' If you don't look too closely, I could be seen as belonging to the perpetrator side. To overcome that barrier, I said 'I am one who comes from a country that killed your people, but I want to do what I can to show you there are human beings in all situations, both good and bad, sometimes both.' With some people my origin actually turned out to be an asset. Unlike many Jewish interviewers who grew up here in the United States, I know the countryside that we would talk about, tools of that era, foods, familiar smells, certain words. In the end, of all the people I approached for interviews, there was only one who wouldn't talk to me."

Elisabeth and Karen both had the quality of experience and insight that Mary-Marshall sought for the Columbia project.

PUBLIC WITNESS

In the first few days when people were still floundering, before the drive for vengeance went into high gear, politicians and media commentators kept asking, "Why do they hate us?" Often the question was rhetorical, but to Mary-Marshall it was worth asking, and the answer no great mystery. "I suspect that very few Americans have any idea how the rest of the world sees us," she says. "I had the advantage, if you can call it that, of growing up in the highly segregated world of the South, where I couldn't help seeing the schizophrenia and evil in daily life that comes from excluding a whole people from your definition of humanity. It's not hard for me to understand why America might be hated in the world, even enough to do this horrible thing."

As she saw it, September 11 and its aftermath offered oral historians a unique opportunity to work in a radically new way. "Traditionally we're accustomed to responding to things thirty, fifty years after the fact. But here we had to respond in a few days – either that or risk losing people's authentic stories in the media wash. It was instantly clear to me that this is where oral history should be moving, toward something that I would call bearing public witness."

To her, one of oral history's primary missions is to offer people a chance to make sense of the insensible. Clearly September 11 wasn't Pearl Harbor, as many commentators claimed. By its scale it resembled a natural disaster but wasn't. What was it, then? What did it mean? The authorities and media were quick to provide packaged meanings.

Within hours the media coined the catchy term "9/11," and in stoking the fires of perpetual war, George Bush provided a handy answer for the why-do-they-hate-us question: "They hate us for our freedoms." Here was the official version, newly minted and rapidly hardening by endless repetition.

But what did this catastrophe really mean to individual New Yorkers? What did they make of it, how did they cope? Says Mary-Marshall, "If it's properly done, oral history can provide a space where people can grapple with these huge questions, independently of all the journalists, the spokespeople, the official historians. It's part of our job to resist any authority that assumes the right to impose their own meaning on this, any kind of collective interpretation that says we all feel the same about it. Oral history argues that we don't all feel the same. In fact, there may be as many interpretations as there are people. I think that's one of the greatest assertions you can make in defence of humanity."

Later Mary-Marshall would question even the glib presumption of "9/11": "We really ought to be saying 9/11/01," she says, "not to forget that Chile also had a 9/11." September 11, 1973, was the first day of the U.S.-engineered military coup that destroyed the democratically elected socialist government of Chile and led to the torture, murder, and "disappearance" of more than thirty thousand Chileans. "So now suddenly we have an American encounter with something the rest of the world experiences all the time."

In the first few weeks after September 11, 2001, interviewers were asked to seek interviews randomly in the many worlds of New York, starting with public spaces where many people were congregating downtown, primarily in Union Square. They were asked not to go to the piers, where people waited for news of missing relatives or to identify the dead. "We felt it would be a huge violation of their privacy and grief," says Mary-Marshall.

In the first three weeks, some 150 interviews were collected with people from more than thirty countries. "Then we were given money by the Rockefeller Foundation to expand the archive deliberately to seek out Afghani-Americans, Latinos, Muslims, and artists, especially ones who lived downtown," says Mary-Marshall. "We wanted to make sure we included the experience and perspectives of groups who were targeted as terrorists immediately after September 11."

KAREN

Since Karen lives in Brooklyn, it became part of her "beat." The Brooklyn Food Co-op, where she shops, is next door to a firehouse that had lost eleven men at the World Trade Center. "I couldn't imagine barging in there and saying, 'Anyone want to be interviewed?' I didn't want to be invasive in any way," she says. Instead she did what trauma work requires: she watched and listened.

At yoga class her instructor mentioned another fitness teacher who was also a firefighter. "This man happened to take a class I was in, so afterwards I told him about the project and asked if he'd be willing to do an interview. At first he said no, everyone wanted to hear his story, and each time he told it he got more depressed. So that was it, no more. But when he heard that this was for the archives, for the record, and that I could guarantee it wouldn't be used in any way without his permission, he said he'd do it. We talked for a long, long time. It's an amazing story. He ran to Ground Zero from the fitness centre where he was teaching, and because he was off duty, he wasn't suited up, no helmet, no mask, nothing. Both towers came down literally all around him. It's a miracle that he survived."

In a theatre class she teaches, Karen invited students to talk about their experiences, fears, dreams, anything they needed to get out. A young Cuban-American mentioned that he was in the National Guard, and he had seen some rough things. After class he agreed to do an interview. He told Karen he had been assigned to Ground Zero and for the past two nights had been packing body parts into bags. Karen didn't need to ask any more questions. He just talked.

At a social event an African-American man agreed to an interview. He works for a temporary employment agency, and on September 11 he'd been assigned to the Bank of America across the street from the World Trade Center. As the towers fell, he took photos. He'd never told anyone before, he said to Karen, why he developed this passion for photography: If one day his memory were to fail, he would still have the photos, a record of his experience. "As I listened to him, I felt that taking those pictures as the towers came down was his way of protecting himself from the horror of what was happening," Karen says. "It was a kind of protective cocoon. Of course he was terrified, and he had to run for his life, but just for a moment, here was something he could do. He could make memory out of this experience."

As the Bush regime geared up to bomb Afghanistan, she asked the photographer what response he thought would be appropriate to the terrorist attacks. It had come up earlier that he considered himself a conservative, pro-death penalty, anti-choice for women. He thought a moment, then said, "The ones who are guilty should be caught and tried. If Osama was guilty – I haven't seen any evidence of it myself – then he should also be caught and tried. But not war. That won't work. What did the people of Afghanistan ever do to us?"

Karen interviewed an elderly couple and their daughter. The mother is seventy-eight, a retired psychiatrist who lives in Battery Park City, an apartment complex between the Hudson River and the World Trade Center. While crowds fled north, the daughter ran south to get her mother out of the building and put her on a boat to New Jersey. Then she managed to get back uptown – with no subways running, few buses, and most taxis out of commission – to get her own daughter from school. At the same time, her father was driving home from Albany. When he heard on the car radio that the towers had collapsed, he assumed they must have fallen onto Battery Park and his wife must surely be dead.

A few days later, when residents were allowed back into their building to collect pets and essentials, daughter and father, eighty-two, went together to retrieve some medicines. But the emergency services official said the old man looked too frail and he wouldn't allow him to climb the stairs, now the only way to reach their tenth-floor apartment. In separate interviews, father and daughter both told Karen how devastated he was at being denied entry to his home. When the two returned a week later to collect more things, the daughter found a nurse willing to climb the stairs with them. "If my father had died on the stairs," the daughter told Karen, "it couldn't have been much worse than trying to stop him from going in there again."

ELISABETH

Genny, the blind Colombian woman, provided Elisabeth's first interview. Not surprisingly, all her memories of the day were rooted in senses other than sight: sirens, an unearthly roar, screams, the acrid smell and taste of ash and dust, the feel of her rescuer's hand. They had kept in touch. The rescuer agreed to an interview, but each time Elisabeth called to make an appointment, she put it off. "My gut feeling," says Elisabeth, "is that once the total adrenalin high of the emergency has passed, now you have the reality of pain, fear, the nightmares. Under the circumstances, I think I would be careful about talking to a stranger too."

She sought interviews primarily from women who lived just north of the World Trade Center and another group who commuted from outside Manhattan to work in the Financial District south of the Twin Towers. "It was an opportunity to compare those very distinct experiences that emerged from the different geography. Some people who lived three blocks from the towers told me they were glued to the television. They couldn't look out the window to see what was happening right there on the street. Some mothers with children at school in Brooklyn had to arrange for their kids to sleep over at a friend's house. But when I asked them about going to pick up their kids the next day, some of them told me they let the kids find their own way home, some of them by themselves. Since you were not allowed by then to come over the bridge into Manhattan, these kids had to be quite street-smart to get back home. Afterwards these women said they could hardly believe they had done such a thing. These are very careful mothers. I don't think they were even conscious at the time that they acted differently from what they would normally do. It's an indication, I think, of how big their fear was, and how we can react in an extreme situation."

In her Shoah interviews Elisabeth had listened to one account after another of unimaginable cruelty and horror. "I don't remember ever having openly cried in any interview," she says. "I may cry in my heart, but I'm so totally focused on the other person that I'm able to keep my own composure."

One survivor recalled that her train, en route to Bergen-Belsen, stopped for two days on a railway siding. She looked out through the slatted walls of the cattle-car and saw the station, automobiles, people going about their business, ordinary life. She had just turned fourteen. When the woman named the city – Linz – Elisabeth's stomach knotted. "When I was fourteen myself," she says, "I would frequently use that very station to go to Vienna. If I hear something that really cuts into my soul like that, sometimes the pain of it will only surface later, usually in a situation that seems to have no connection at all with the interview. Then suddenly I will start to cry. It can overwhelm me for days."

When Elisabeth and I recorded our interview in November 2001, she was still grappling with a September 11 interview she had conducted a few days before. "L" worked in an office next to the World Trade Center. After the planes hit, employees were told to remain indoors. Through street-level windows they watched bodies hit the pavement and vaporize. Then the towers collapsed, one after the other. L bolted from her building. Apparently she lost consciousness on the sidewalk; when she woke up she couldn't move. She was buried in dust and debris, her leg sliced by a shard of glass still embedded in it. She could hear faint voices, some screaming. Then she became aware that she was lying on another body. After some time – she has no idea how long – she struggled free. She was taken to a hospital and two days later sent home to recover. Co-workers travelled out to Queens to ensure that she had food. Even so, she had continued to feel as she had under the rubble – alone, silent, buried alive.

People working on the Columbia project were urged to open their interviews not with the obvious question, 'Where were you on September 11?' but instead 'Will you tell me something about your life?' This approach originated with Peter Bearman, the Columbia sociologist who co-designed the project with Mary-Marshall. Each person's life story, or whatever of it they chose to impart, would provide a frame in which their experience and reactions could be set, and perhaps understood.

When Elisabeth interviewed people like L that she regarded as particularly fragile, she would invite them to her bright, spacious fourth-floor apartment on the edge of Soho. "As I couldn't do interviews in a neutral place – I don't have a quiet studio, and any café here is much too noisy for digital quality sound – I offered my place, and also jokingly said, 'If you feel it's too much, then you can walk out the door.' I could see that it would be easier for a person to do that than somehow to get me out of their house – that would require much more emotional strength."

L accepted Elisabeth's invitation. "This woman was only here for two or three hours, but I could see right away that she was intelligent, very sensitive, a good person," Elisabeth says. "I also saw a woman in her early fifties who looked at least fifteen years older, not well, beaten down in some way, and quite haunted. Of course I assumed that it was due to the trauma she'd suffered on September 11."

Elisabeth asked the usual opening question: Will you tell me something about your life? L said that her back had been broken in her teens, and since then she'd lived with a scoliosis, a twist in the spine. She had seven siblings but had no contact with any of them now. She had been in an intimate relationship once but fled. She loved children but had none. She screened her calls. "This woman is painfully aware of how she is cutting herself off from life, but she hasn't found any way to get out of the cage that she's building for herself." L hinted at another trauma earlier in life but declined to offer details. "The damaged spine seemed like such a powerful metaphor," says Elisabeth, "This is someone whose ability to stand up for herself has effectively been broken."

No matter how deeply moved interviewers may be by some people's stories, Mary-Marshall had stressed, oral historians aren't therapists. Most aren't trained for it, and in any case, most don't have the time or resources to follow up. Elisabeth understood that, but with L she took an unusual initiative. She called R, the woman who had referred L to her for the interview. Elisabeth knew R as a former Shoah interviewer who would therefore have some experience in dealing with major trauma. Elisabeth asked her to keep a friendly eye on L. "Of course I couldn't tell her any of the details I had heard – confidentiality doesn't permit that – so I just told her how touched I was by L's story and left it at that. I hope I did the right thing."

MARY-MARSHALL

Mary-Marshall also argues that oral history isn't journalism. She worked several years for the *New York Times*, interviewing people the editors had decided were significant. When *The Times* refused to grant any public access to this material, she resigned. Before she left, she conducted a series of interviews with women who had sued senior personnel at the newspaper for sexual harassment. A few years later, a student working in the corporate records department at *The Times* discovered a list of "dangerous women," including one Mary-Marshall Clark. "That was one of great highlights of my career," she says with a mischievous smile.

I ask her what separates the oral historian from the journalist. "We're not after the big public stories," she responds. "Journalists can – and will – give us books on this in thirty days. I don't want to put down their skills, but we're looking for something different. We want to hear people's real experience, not just the heroic, not just the tragic, but the complex, nuanced stories that aren't sexy enough for the press. When you tell people this is going into the archives and they'll have a say in how it's used, you get very different stories from what you'll see in the press. We're hearing about firefighters who ran for their lives and who don't want to be held up now as heroes. We're hearing about people who did not help other people to get out, and now they struggle with guilt. This is exactly the kind of space we want to open up, those silent spaces that are being obliterated by the journalistic accounts – the space to talk about what it's like not to be a hero but a human being, scared out of your wits."

From her own experiences in journalism and oral history, Elisabeth makes a similar distinction. "As a journalist you're pushed by your employer to ask very leading questions, in a very blunt way. A journalist talks with you for maybe twenty minutes, if you're lucky, then he takes two little half sentences out of it that maybe you don't even like. That's how it works, the journalist has to deliver a specific product, packaged in a specific way. Maybe that's why I left journalism. In oral history it's more about being quiet and listening. Instead of pushing a person to say what you want them to say, you help them to navigate through their own story. I tell them, 'This is your story, you're the master of it, and I'm just the person who helps you to tell it.' I love having someone sitting in front of me, and helping them to tell me how they perceive events in their own lives, knowing there is no pressure to explain it or package it. It is what it is."

The same respect for narrators as the owners of their stories pervades the Columbia project. "We know from experience that big institutions like Columbia have a lot more power than individuals do," says Mary-Marshall, "and in fulfilling their institutional missions they often use their power without even thinking about it. We wanted to make sure that the people we interview have as much power over their narratives as possible, and for as long as possible. This is the way I believe oral history ought to work." Each narrator is entitled to see a transcript of the interview and to specify cuts or changes. Narrators consent only to depositing their interviews in the September 11 archive, nothing more.

As a writer I'm distressed to imagine this great wealth of stories disappearing into the vast cavern of an oral history archive. "They won't," says Mary-Marshall. "We're a public archive. Our mission is to disseminate material to the public. Before September 11 our existing collections were already widely used by writers and historians. We get over two thousand researchers a year in here. That whole wall of books – " (she gestures at floor-to-ceiling books in her garret office atop the Columbia library) "all of that is work that came out of these archives, and if we had the space, we could probably fill another five walls."

As soon as permissions are in order, the public will have access to the material, and in theory, no one – no journalist, professor, interviewer, not even Mary-Marshall – will have privileged access over anyone else. "The material is so rich, any number of people will be able to create any number of works out of it," she says. "If we can find the resources, one of these days we may even look at doing a book or a film ourselves. It won't be a blockbuster, just human stories."

For days after September 11, Mary-Marshall walked familiar New York streets and read faces. It's one of her ways to know her city. The people who looked most disturbed to her – in shock, literally – were the young, especially adolescents. Their faces were blank. "I have a theory that in this culture of video and computer simulations, the deaths and battles don't matter because they're not real," she says. "But in this moment, suddenly death became real, absolutely real, and shockingly present. Children I've talked to are struggling with huge, complicated questions: 'How could those buildings just disappear? Why would anyone want to kill themselves in such an awful way, how could hijackers with children do that?' I think children are getting into this in a deeper way than most adults. We adults have so many ways to intellectualize it, to package it and push it away."

Karen Malpede also registered the blank faces. She had seen them before, in Bosnia. "Many children in the United States lead pretty sheltered lives, especially if you compare to places like Afghanistan or Chechnya. For many kids here, this had to be the first big – *huge* – disruption of their safe world."

She interviewed a colleague who teaches at the City University of New York, a little north of Ground Zero. His four-year-old son attended preschool in Building Four, one of the lower buildings in the World Trade Center complex. The father ran south to save the boy, but teachers had already evacuated the children.

A few weeks later the son asked, "When can I go get my pictures from school?" "We can make new pictures," the father replied. He tried to explain what had happened to the school. The boy asked, "Why did they do that to my school?" In the interview with Karen, the father said, "I just started to bawl. I couldn't stop."

Mary-Marshall told me that at the school her son attends, child psychologists were brought in who told the children not to worry, everything would be all right. Her son came home in a rage. "Why do they keep telling us it's not a big deal? Are they *crazy*?" The mother of one boy in his school had worked on the 46th floor of the south tower. When the boy heard that the tower had collapsed, he fainted.

"I think who they're really trying to comfort is themselves," Mary-Marshall told her son, "and the only way they can do that is to pretend it's not a big deal. They're wrong. This is a big deal. It's a really big deal."

"How big a deal is it?" he asked. "Are we in danger?"

"If we were really in danger, we would leave."

"You shouldn't say that," he retorted, upset.

"Why not?"

"Because you're supposed to be impenetrable." That's the word he used; theirs is a wordy household.

"But I'm not impenetrable," said Mary-Marshall. "My body, my life is no more impenetrable than the World Trade Center was. We're vulnerable, all of us. If you're human, you're vulnerable. This is what it means to be human."

 9/11/01 + 2

Two years after September 11, 2001, the debris has been cleared from Ground Zero, to make way for the new World Trade Center.

Local media report continuing feuds between the architect selected to design it, and the developer who leased the original complex a few weeks before the Twin Towers came down. In a major international competition to create a memorial for victims, 5,201 entries were narrowed down to eight finalists. All met widespread disapproval from art critics, journalists, and citizens.

Uptown at the New York Historical Society, an exhibition called "Recovery" has just opened. It documents the enormous, gruesome two-year operation at the Fresh Kills Landfill in Staten Island, to recover human remains, personal objects, and material evidence from the wreckage of the World Trade Center.

In November 2003 I saw few tourists on the viewing platforms at Ground Zero, only men in well-tailored black coats marching purposefully to and from the several smaller towers of the World Financial Center that overlook the empty site. At its northern edge a flight of concrete steps leads upward to nowhere. To the south, a slice of charred cladding is cut away from a third, shorter tower, revealing the frame within and lights on each floor. To the north, the smashed facades of several other buildings are under repair.

State Governor George Pataki has set August 2004 as the deadline for laying the foundation of Phase One, the "Freedom Tower," designed to be 1776 feet tall. Pataki, a Republican, intends to orchestrate the historic event in concert with the Republican National Convention, at which George W. Bush will be crowned the party's candidate for president.

To mark the second anniversary of 9/11 in 2003, Families for Peaceful Tomorrows held a ceremony of quiet remembrance at the site. Founded by relatives of victims, its mission is "to turn our grief into action for peace, to seek effective, nonviolent solutions to terrorism, and to acknowledge our common experience with all people similarly affected by violence throughout the world."

"We are all very weary of Ground Zero, a sacred space where there are still remains of people, being used as a backdrop," said Andrew Rice, whose brother David died at the site. "We want a hands-off policy for any candidate from any political party. This week is a sacred week, and we hope especially next year with the Republican convention that it will not be appropriated by people for their own political gains."

The Columbia University September 11 project has similar goals to that of Families for Peaceful Tomorrows – to honour private memory, and to resist the imposition of public meaning. While I was in New York, I recorded follow-up interviews on the project with Mary-Marshall Clark, director of the Columbia University Oral History Research Office, and two other women who have worked on the project with her, Elisabeth Pozzi-Thanner and Karen Malpede.

A short walk from her office, Mary-Marshall shares a spacious apartment with her son and his co-parent. On a dark afternoon, rain sheets down the tall windows. Mary-Marshall settles herself into the sofa. From what I know of her work life, it seems a rare moment of stillness. I ask her for an update on the project.

"In the first year, we did 431 interviews," she tells me. "Random interviews in public places at first, then we focused in on specific communities. With funding from the Rockefeller Foundation, we were able to do interviews with Afghani-Americans, with Sikhs, with people from several Latin American countries, from Pakistan, Egypt, and other countries. For many of these communities there was a lot of terror immediately after September 11, because they were targeted as the evil 'other.' The people who had actually done this thing were so unknown, so vague for most Americans, and Osama bin Laden so unavailable as a target, many people ended up attaching blame to whole ethnicities and nationalities."

In such a tense climate, how did they find people willing to be interviewed? "Some turned up through existing contacts, but most of them through hard work and patience," she says. "One of our most profoundly gifted interviewers, Gerald Albarelli, went to a mosque in Queens, he was there for six weeks. Eventually he developed so much trust with people, they started coming to him, not only to tell their September 11th stories but also what happened to them in the aftermath, and their life stories, what had brought them to this country, who they were. Because they could sense Gerry's politics and the depth of his interest – he's a writer/filmmaker, and he understood that the event itself could only be dealt with in the context of all that came before and after – he got incredible stories. He asked one man, 'I would like to know about your family history, start anywhere you want.' The man said, 'Well, I have to start four hundred years ago.' Gerald replied, 'I have all the time in the world.' Seven hours later they got to September 11."

The original plan for the project was to gather interviews before people's own impressions were engulfed by the tidal wave of officially imposed meaning, and then to do follow-up interviews in about a year, to explore how people's lives and perceptions had evolved. By November 2003, about 250 follow-up interviews were complete.

"The second interviews have turned out to be harder than the first," says Mary-Marshall. "Many people don't necessarily want to talk about their September 11 experience again. There are all kinds of blocks – people's changing circumstances, the wars. Also, we didn't have as clear a protocol this time on the kinds of questions that people should be asking – there was no way to do that, because even though we're talking about a giant collectivity, there are tremendous differences within it. What the interviewers had to do was craft a distinctive approach for each individual. That's very tough to do. It's a real art form to figure out where to open up the interview, to make it bigger, and where to cut away from one trail to another."

Now that she has begun to read transcripts of the second interviews, she is finding that the more skilled interviewers have been able to trace the shifts, sometimes subtle, in people's experience and thinking about the world two years on. "From the beginning we wanted to focus on how this event has changed people, and the country. You can't ask that explicitly, because most people will say nothing has changed, but then you ask them where they're working, they'll say somewhere different. You ask them what they do in their daily lives, they've converted. You ask them about their family life, they're divorced. Nothing has changed, but everything has changed."

Since September 11, 2001, the Bush regime has invaded two countries. Both have turned into long-term occupations, resulting in incalculable death and suffering for the besieged populations, enormous cost to American taxpayers, and immense profits for corporate interests. The regime has also established a string of military bases around the globe and launched a new high-cost space race. To finance these imperial ventures, it has plunged the country into record debt and accelerated the gutting of its remaining social and environmental programs.

The U.S.A. Patriot Act and its enforcer, the Homeland Security Department, apparently pose such a grave threat to civil liberties – freedoms the Bush regime vows to defend – that by November 2003, 136 communities and three states had passed resolutions opposing the act. At the same time, the regime continues to push aggressively for passage of the Domestic Security Enhancement Act, dubbed Patriot II, which many critics say will move the country even faster towards a police state.

———————————

KAREN

Karen Malpede lives in a stately, faded old house, which she and her husband, George Bartenieff, rent on a tree-lined street in Brooklyn. I was surprised to hear that the roses on their kitchen counter were freshly cut from their garden – at the end of November. As it was in 2001, this autumn has been unusually warm. Abby, their spaniel, wants to play. George takes her for a romp, while Karen and I talk in the sitting room. Books line one whole wall, up to the high ceiling.

In both the first and second rounds, Karen interviewed a young Cuban-American who attended one of her acting classes. As a soldier in the National Guard, he was assigned to Ground Zero immediately after September 11, packing body parts into bags. "It turns out he originally went into the military instead of to jail," says Karen. "His father had worked a deal with the judge. He's from a pretty right-wing Cuban-American business family in Miami and very close to his father and his brother. One of his jobs in the military was to guard Bill Clinton. He was a big fan of Clinton's. After 9/11, he had the choice to re-enlist or not, so he got out. He knows a lot of people who went to Iraq. This is a kid who reads the *New York Post* and watches CNN, that's where he gets most of his information, but he had an instinctual feeling that this war was a very bad idea, and he's a harsh critic of George Bush. He told me that right before the presidential election in 2000 when he was in the army, his battalion were all lined up and told to vote for George Bush. They said if the soldiers wanted pay increases, they should vote for Bush."

Karen tells me about losing contact with one of her first-round interviewees, a Palestinian-American woman. "She was here for dinner not long ago, but when I called her cell phone to set up a second interview, she said she was in the Gulf, but couldn't tell me where. I know she was in Iraq during the invasion in March and April, working for the UN. She was there for part of the bombing, then there was a bit of a lull before the violence heated up again. Because she speaks English and

Arabic, she was in touch with American soldiers and Iraqis. She could also talk to Iraqi women – that's another story, they can hardly go outside now, it's so dangerous. I'm afraid they are not among the 25 million people we're supposed to have liberated! She told me there was no water, no electricity, and she'd seen first-hand some of the birth defects, mental retardation, and cancers caused by depleted uranium bombs that were dropped in Gulf War I – and I'm sure again in this war. When she was here in the early fall, she was being asked to go back to Iraq, not with the UN but with an NGO, and she was weighing whether or not she should go. For all I know, she might be there now."

ELISABETH

Elisabeth Pozzi-Thanner agreed to meet me for our interviews – I had also asked her to interview me for this book (see chapter 12) – in a borrowed apartment upstairs from our hosts' in the East Village. Her daughter was home for Thanksgiving with friends, so her own apartment would be too chaotic for interviews.

Since September 2001, as well as doing two rounds of interviews for the Columbia project, Elisabeth also directed the North American component of an international oral history project with survivors of Mauthausen concentration camp in Austria. Based on her extensive work with the Shoah Foundation and the September 11 project, she was recommended for the job by Mary-Marshall and by Jessica Wiederhorn, now associate director at the Columbia Oral History Office, who had also done Shoah interviews. "It also happened that I grew up ten miles away from that camp," says Elisabeth. Between August 8, 1938, and May 5, 1945, some 195,000 men and women were imprisoned at Mauthausen, a network of camps near the town of Linz. More than half the prisoners were killed outright, or worked to death in rock quarries nearby.

Elisabeth's job was to find a team of interviewers in the United States and Canada, bring them to Austria for preparatory workshops and a visit to Mauthausen, produce eighty-five interviews by the end of February 2003, and keep her part of the project within its limited regional budget. The most urgent task was to locate survivors. "The youngest I found was seventy-five, and the oldest in her nineties," says Elisabeth. "Every week a few more of them are gone." She recruited most of the interviewees herself through survivor networks and conducted a portion of the interviews.

When the digital tapes were ready, and photos taken of people who agreed to put a face with their voice, Elisabeth sent copies of everything to Vienna – tapes, photos, and any documents or artifacts that people had donated to the project. The university kept a copy for its own archives, and master copies are stored at the Mauthausen Memorial Museum, where they will be incorporated into educational exhibits. "When I was that age, I went only because my father brought me there," says Elisabeth. "But if you're a school kid now in Austria, you go at least once to Mauthausen. It's part of the history curriculum."

After she completed work on that project, Elisabeth went "into hibernation" for a while, before resuming work on the September 11 project. By the time we met in New York, she had completed sixteen of her second-round interviews. "This time I would not say to people, 'Please tell me your life story' – we had covered that in the first interviews. Now I would ask them, 'How has your life changed since September 11?' and I would shut up and let them talk. Then the whole thing would start to unfold naturally."

Since the goal was to look for changes, what kinds did she observe? "For me, the most obvious change was that the large majority of women told me, on or off tape, that they are now on anti-depressants," she says. Only one person she interviewed immediately after September 11 had mentioned anti-depressant use. "One woman was so depressed and had put on so much weight I almost didn't recognize her. In the first months after, we all had this urge to talk about it, to analyze it, to share our stories with each other. This adrenalin was jumping so much in all of us, the real effects were not so obvious. Now they are."

One woman she interviewed lived and worked in Tribeca, her office three blocks from the World Trade Center site, her home five minutes away by foot. "In the first interview I got the impression that this woman was well connected in her neighbourhood, but she also liked to go to the opera, to exhibitions, to all kinds of things uptown," Elisabeth says. "When I asked her in the second interview if she goes out, if she travels, she told me that now she hardly ever ventures north of 14th Street, and then only when she absolutely has to. This woman was among the first people who sneaked back into that area when the police had evacuated everybody and it was still totally closed off. Then she became very active in making people aware of contamination in the air, and sound contamination when they had, day and night for four months, constant machines and trucks loading debris under their windows. But now she has become trapped in this place, in this paradox that home is the only place where you can feel safe. Until she spoke these things out loud with me in the interview, she was completely unaware of it. For me this is a powerful indication of trauma."

She adds, "I also interviewed two other women who are very good friends with that person. Those other two told me, 'Isn't our friend remarkable, nothing can shake her, what a rock in the ocean she is, how much strength we get from her!' This is the role she can play with them, so that neither they nor she have to realize how traumatized she is herself."

I ask her about "L," a woman she interviewed in the first round who had been buried in rubble when the towers collapsed, and cruelly isolated afterwards, buried again. "Ah," says Elisabeth, "now that's the flip side. When I saw her the second time, and we also had dinner afterwards, I found that she is much better. Before, she was so incredibly severe to herself, not allowing herself any kind of pleasure, but now suddenly she started talking about how she had invited her old friend from school to come to New York. They went to movies, to the theatre together. She told me, 'I know I don't have much money, but I have just one life, and why shouldn't I have a little joy?' She does go to see her brother who is dying, but she also says, 'I have five other siblings, I can't always be the one to do that. They should do their part too.' I think she will never be somebody who goes out a lot or has a large following of people, but to the extent that she can reach out, she now does. She seems so much more serene now than the first time we talked. That was really fabulous to see."

I ask Elisabeth the same question she and other interviewers asked their narrators: How has your life changed since September 11, 2001? She hesitates, takes a breath. "Strange as it may sound, though I wasn't here at the moment it happened, I'm grateful to have had the opportunity to live, witness, feel the aftermath a few days later – otherwise it remains theory. By having had this closeness to the horror, living in the neighbourhood, smelling, seeing it, being with people deeply affected by it, I think it has also helped me in a spiritual way, but also in the body, to understand – no, that's too much – to come a little closer to understanding some of the trauma stories that I've heard from sixty years ago. I can see how such horror manifests in a person sixty years later, and how it's being transmitted to the children, and the grandchildren, but I had never experienced such an event so directly myself before September 11."

Earlier in the day she accompanied a friend, another September 11 interviewer, to the "Recovery" exhibit at the New York Historical Society. "As well as the three thousand people that died," says Elisabeth, "the exhibit told us that what they were buried in was two million tons of debris – *two million tons*! My mind cannot grasp that, it's too much – I stood on top of these buildings, I walked underneath them – so I need somehow to reduce it to a scale I can comprehend. I find that quite often now I think of an anthill. I think about what happens if a nasty boy comes to an anthill and destroys it, what happens to the ants. At first it seems like utter chaos, but very quickly it reorganizes itself from within. Each group has its own tasks – one rescues, another transports debris, another takes care of the eggs, the children. It's strange, but this is the only way I can even begin to envision the enormity of what happened that day."

It strikes me that Elisabeth's response addresses the impact on her work but not on her own life. I ask again, how has her life changed? She nods, "yes," gathers herself. "Somehow it has made me more fatalistic about my own safety, in the sense that I'm very little afraid now about what might happen to me – if something happens, it happens, that's what the world is. But it has also made me far more vulnerable in thinking of people that I love, my friends. I feel their pain so much more, and worry so much more about their well-being than I did before." That must be quite a burden, I say.

"Very much," Elisabeth replies. "Before September 11, I was in a good period of my life, I thought somehow that anything positive was possible. Now that has reversed itself: now I think almost anything negative, frightening, hurtful, or hateful is possible, and imminent around me. I'm in an age group now where every parent of friends, if they're not dead yet, at least they start to say goodbye. Even child-hood friends of my own age are starting to drop dead, from heart attacks, breast cancer. All of this would happen anyway, but after September 11 somehow the impact on me becomes much stronger. Some-times I would love to totally shut myself in my own little world. Then maybe I would be able to protect myself better, which now I have a hard time to do."

KAREN

When I speak with Karen Malpede in late Novem-ber, she tells me she has been putting off her last four interviews. For several months, writing a novel has absorbed all her energy and left her exhausted. But also, she tells me, "I get over-whelmed with the violence, and the threat of more violence. As soon as you relax for a moment, you get thwacked again. If you read the paper or watch the news, hardly a day goes by that you don't see some other building in rubble. This has become an iconic image these past two years. Of course these things happened before, Israelis blowing up Palestinian houses, other acts of terrorism, but now it seems so much more pronounced and constant. Iraqi insurgents fire rockets at the Palestinian Hotel, the U.S. bombs a street of houses. The way terror is being used, it's like being battered all the time. Homeland Security keeps warning us there's going to be another attack, it's just a matter of time."

The day we spoke, the Homeland Security threat advisory level was yellow: "Significant Risk of Terrorist Attacks." From time to time the level goes to orange, but so far it has never dropped below yellow into the more tranquil green or blue zones. Under a billow of stars and stripes, the Homeland Security website opens with the slogan: "Terrorism forces us to make a choice. Don't be afraid . . . Be Ready." It offers advice on what to do in case of biological threat, chemical threat, explosions, nuclear blast, and radiation threat.

Says Karen, "Always in the back of my mind is Indian Point, a nuclear reactor about thirty miles out of New York, which I and others spent a lot of time trying to shut down in the '70s. It's an ideal target. They say this all the time now – cargo planes are going to fly into nuclear plants. Of course if there were to be a major disaster at Indian Point, they have these evacuation plans – basically we're supposed to get on the highway and drive. It's absurd! But you do get this cumulative sense of being battered all the time with threats and warnings. It's awfully wearing."

MARY-MARSHALL

In the second year of the September 11 project, Mary-Marshall Clark retained a psychologist to work, as needed, with both interviewees and interviewers. "I'd been warned by a psychiatrist friend about the potential for trauma damage to both, and in particular the risk of secondary trauma for interviewers," she says. "For interviewees it can be a liberation to talk, but over time the people listening to all that experience of trauma can be in trouble themselves. My interviewers were incredibly strong people, and most of them worked quite independently. But I also began to get a lot of late-night and weekend phone calls, and desperate emails from interviewers worrying about their own mental health. After a while I was beginning to question my capacity to direct the whole project, do my own interviews, listen to and read all the other interviews, and take care of people at the same time. My worry got very profound when one of people we were interviewing became suicidal. By that point I couldn't sleep at night, so it made sense to look for some help."

Mary-Marshall retained Marylene Cloitre, former director of the Paine-Whitney Trauma Unit, who specialized in counselling survivors of sexual abuse. "She also has degrees in neuropsychology and political psychology," Mary-Marshall says, "which meant we could study how memory functions, something I've always wanted to do. We have so many arid theoretical debates in oral history about the differences between individual and collective memory, but they all have so little meaning because when you're going back thirty, forty years, we don't have any empirical way to watch how memory is made. That's why I've always wanted this project to be a case where we can watch the formation of the collective memory, or at least a memory that has public meaning."

One of Marylene Cloitre's first tasks was to explain the role that sensory destruction plays in trauma. Says Mary-Marshall, "One of the theories about post-traumatic stress disorder (PTSD) is that at the time of a disaster, senses that normally work together get separated. The power of the event actually strips the mind of its capacity to categorize and order the sensory experience – this is what I saw, smelled, heard, and tasted – which is why some people could only remember what they saw on September 11, not what they heard, or vice versa. Until you can bring those senses back together in a narrative, the trauma gets stuck in a part of the brain responsible for that particular sensory function. This was very helpful for us to understand. In the first year we were looking for people's life stories, but Marylene reminded us that what people really needed was simply to narrate what had happened to them, to make sense of it, literally to re-order the senses, to say 'This is what I heard, what I saw, what I smelled, what I tasted.' Once people were able to do that, and to put it in the context of their life stories, it may have helped prevent some PTSD. That's exactly Marylene's area of research."

Two years later, the effects still reverberate. Recently Mary-Marshall received emails from two people she knows, one an editor at the *Wall Street Journal*, the other a student who lost her fiancé in the September 11 attacks. "Both these people are losing their memory," she says. "The editor is about to lose his job because he can't remember how to spell words."

Over time, Marylene Cloitre noticed that the highest incidence of PTSD seemed to have occurred in people for whom smell was the governing sense. "Apparently their whole sensory mechanism was invaded and overwhelmed by the dust, the ash, the smell," says Mary-Marshall. "All of us knew in our gut that this was also going to be a real health problem at the site and in the surrounding neighbourhoods. I don't think people were nearly quick enough to get down there and do epidemiological studies. I know that one was done with pregnant women, but I haven't heard of any others."

I mention having read that in the immediate aftermath of September 11, the U.S. Environmental Protection Agency blocked the release of information to the public on air quality in the area, allegedly for reasons of national security. Mary-Marshall nods. "It's outrageous. It's really outrageous." In October 2003, the *New York Daily News* reported that doctors at Mount Sinai Hospital had told a congressional panel that one-third of the seven thousand workers at the cleanup now suffer from a variety of serious respiratory ailments. These are believed to have been caused by inhaling what workers called "the crud" – the toxic plume of dust, ash, fumes from burning plastic, pulverized concrete, and vaporized human remains. Of the affected workers, the doctors testified, one-third are currently unemployed and 40 per cent have no health insurance. Two years after the cleanup began, federal funds promised for illnesses resulting from it had not been disbursed.

Aside from the job stresses she mentioned, I wonder what effects Mary-Marshall has experienced in doing interviews herself. Any secondary trauma? "Never in doing the interviews," she replies, "because it was such a relief to get out from behind the desk! My traumatization was *not* being able to do the work, but managing it, watching everybody else do it. In doing interviews I was doing what I love to do, and I could feel I was helping someone. I was like a freed bird, so ready for whatever people might say – I had read over a hundred interviews by then so I knew what had happened down there. It didn't have the shock effect it might have for interviewers going out for the first time. Plus, I love building this relationship with another human being who's a stranger to me, a really deep encounter, which is what oral history does. Even if I never see the person again – what a gift!"

No trauma in doing the interviews, she says. Does that imply trouble elsewhere in the process? "I think it has finally hit me in the last three months," she says. "Reading through four hundred interviews, listening to them, trying to make meaning from them, to go into the deepest, most horrible experiences that people had, that's been really tough. Now I don't sleep well, I have nightmares, and when I hear a helicopter I think it's another attack. That never happened to me in the first two years. I'm a battleship, I have such a good defence structure, I'm just kind of resistant. As a child I was an athlete and a daredevil. As a youth I travelled around the world, I raised wild stallions. I'm a risk-taker, and I have a lot of confidence in my ability to withstand things. But now I have all this knowledge in my head, this sensory knowledge of what happened, and how people felt. I know how it affected Afghans, Muslims, mothers who were so terrified out of their minds that they forgot their children at daycare centres, cops who had complicated reactions to their Muslim brothers on the force, priests who had to decide whether they were going to bless body parts because they didn't have the bodies, schoolteachers, psychiatrists, doctors in hospitals who didn't have any live bodies to work on, nurses in the burn unit. After a while, all of that has a cumulative effect."

Her strategy is consistent with her self-description – the battleship steams ahead. "The challenge I'm facing now is how to disseminate these interviews in a way that won't retraumatize other people, in a way that does some good."

In our first interview, Mary-Marshall said, "It's part our job to resist any authority that assumes the right to impose their own meaning on this, any kind of collective interpretation that says we all feel the same about it. Oral history argues that we don't all feel the same. In fact there may be as many interpretations as there are people. I think that's one of the greatest assertions you can make in defence of humanity."

Two years later, I ask her if she still feels the same. "I feel that more than ever," she replies. "We all know that the meaning of September 11 has been hijacked by the government for its own purposes. That is completely obvious. But when people get a chance to read the interviews, they'll find – for example – an Afghan-American journalist who had to report non-stop for ten days, fifteen hours a day, in a newsroom where people were saying to her, 'Your people did this to us.' When she was interviewed in December 2001, she said, 'I'm very sorry for all the people who've been killed in the United States, but I can't get it out of my head that now five thousand civilians have been killed in Afghanistan.'

"You can find hardly a single interview where a person who saw the incredible violence that day calls for revenge. The things people saw – human bodies as bombs, jumpers coming out of windows killing people when they landed, legs falling, hands falling, people pushing each other down in the streets to get away, all the things that happened in the catastrophe that you never want to remember again – when you've lived through, when you've witnessed that, you don't ever want to imagine that any other person could go through what you went through. We don't find vengeance narratives in the interviews; we find people searching for solace, searching for peace, people saying over and over, 'Please God, don't let this happen to anyone else.' Even when people said they wanted to attack Afghanistan, you'll find a few minutes later that they say, 'No, I don't really mean that.' Some people actually say, 'I'm afraid that our experiences will be used to promote a war of retaliation.' I think that these stories will affect people powerfully. They'll serve as a reminder that the public meaning the United States government has imposed on 9/11 was hardly representative."

Earlier she mentioned her desire "to watch the formation of the collective memory." Why? "It's not individual memory I'm interested in, but to really look for the social meaning," she says: " – how it was experienced at the time, and how that experience is shaped over time by the media, by writing, films, and stories formalizing what happened after 9/11 in the city of New York. Everybody was telling these stories, it was a human need, and we were lucky enough to know that we should capture them. Already there are people who want to claim, 'This is the real meaning of September 11,' but now we have all this testimony from individuals at the time the event happened. If you listen to the interviews, you really can't claim any one meaning, because we've heard so many different meanings from so many different voices. If you're writing the 'definitive' book on 9/11, it will only be your own take on it, nothing more. Omniscience is necessarily narrow. It's a fabrication by someone claiming their interpretation *is* the real experience. I want to complicate that, I want to make it messier than that. I think that from this archive will come many books in the future, on the experience of the many people who were there, which is far more complex, less predictable, and more interesting than anything we see in the media."

This passion for multiple voices goes to the heart of why Mary-Marshall believes in, and does, oral history. "I think it can lead to democratization, to real dialogue about real things. It breaks down falseness, and silences, and fears – such as the fear that many Americans have of knowing how the rest of the world feels about us. This was a chance when we could know."

I comment that it still is. "It is," she agrees, "although I think that, sadly, many of us have not chosen to go that route. Some of the people we interviewed said, 'How tragic – for a moment the wall between the United States and the rest of world was torn down, we could have kept that alive and started to learn. But instead we built another wall.'"

When I spoke with her in November 2003, none of the interviews were available yet to the public. "I want them to be open as soon as possible," she says, "but it's very labour-intensive work. We've got some first-year transcripts back from people who've signed a legal release, about fifty of them by now. But many people have been taking a long time to think about their transcripts, which of course is their right. After we get the releases, we have to prepare the interviews, make copies, index them, and put the originals into the rare book and manuscript archive for proper preservation. If we had a bigger staff, that would all be done by now. As soon as we have a hundred or so ready, we'll open those to the public so anybody can come and use them. Eventually I want all of them to be fully accessible, so we'll have to see how that can be done. We're a public archive, but hardly anybody knows that, because Columbia is a private university. One thing I've always wanted to do is donate the interviews to a September 11 memorial museum, once such a thing is developed. These interviews need to be in a very public space. They belong to the people of New York."

In the meantime, Columbia University Press has invited Mary-Marshall and Peter Bearman, co-originator of the project, to create a book of interviews. "I thought we'd wait longer," she says, "maybe five years from now we'd do a different kind of book. But they want us to do something more quickly, and we're considering that."

I wonder if it might help to get the weight of all those interviews out of her head. "I certainly hope so," she says with a laugh. "I feel as if I have a sort of composite image in my head by now, an aerial view of what happened from all those different perspectives – I can circle around, I can see it from Vesey Street, from Trinity Church, from below the World Trade Center, from near the river – all of that is in my head. But now my danger is to walk around thinking I'm the 9/11 archive! These experiences don't belong to me, they belong to the world. So I have to be disciplined and put it all back out there."

KAREN

Karen Malpede is putting it back out there in the ways she customarily does – teaching, making connections, writing. She teaches writing to adults at the City University of New York, and describes her students' work with obvious delight – the retired police officer working on his first novel, the

Hungarian émigré in her seventies writing a memoir about going back to the town where she was born, the young woman who writes "wonderful edgy, beautifully written lesbian sexual stories."

One of the people Karen interviewed in Brooklyn is an African-American performance artist. "The first time I interviewed her, she had just moved to the city, she was hanging on by a thread economically, and she was very frightened about what this would do to her future," Karen recalls. "It happens that I have a friend who teaches at Paul Robeson High School in Brooklyn. Virtually everyone who goes there is below the poverty line. It's an amazing school, where the principal and the teachers all work extremely hard to create a cohesive community. I introduced Kimbali to my teacher friend, who's involved in creating an arts program there – with no official money of course, but they raise money wherever they can. Now she's the artist-in-residence there. She's doing wonderful work with the kids, video and theatre, and everybody loves her. It's a source of steady income for her, and pride. In the second interview she wept, but this time it was tears of joy."

The primary way that Karen expresses herself is through writing – more than a dozen plays produced, screenplays, essays, short stories, and novels. One of her recent short stories was inspired by a man she interviewed, a former firefighter and yoga teacher. On September 11, 2001, he was at a fitness centre near the World Trade Center. "He ran to Ground Zero," says Karen, "Because he was off duty, he wasn't suited up, no helmet, no mask, nothing. Both towers came down literally all around him. It's a miracle that he survived."

In the first interview it was apparent to her that this man had a lot of animosity towards the New York Fire Department, but the reasons for it were not yet clear to him. Since then, he has left the department on medical retirement due to lung damage. He underwent an intense detoxification program at an ashram in India and now teaches yoga full-time in New York. On the first night after 9/11, he sought refuge at the home of another yoga teacher. They've been together since. "They've had to work through a lot, but they seem quite happy and committed," says Karen. "She's a pretty independent woman, and she told me she wasn't really looking for a relationship. She said it was the pain, what the day had done to him, that opened her heart and allowed her to enter a relationship with him."

In his second interview with Karen, the grounds for his rage at the Fire Department emerged. "One of the sources was that it's so grossly macho and homophobic," says Karen. Is he gay? "No," she says, "but as far as they were concerned, he might as well have been. As a yoga teacher, a vegetarian, and a gentle man, he was constantly having to defend his non-macho stance against the steak-eaters and the football fans. I think there's another layer to it as well. Firemen were used as heroes for a while, but then he felt not cared for at all, not understood on many levels. He's Italian, his father was a firefighter, and growing up in Bensonhurst the deal is, you join the Fire Department, you get married, you have kids, you buy a little house in Bensonhurst, and you hang out with other Italian Catholic firefighters. His journey didn't go quite like that. He did join the Fire Department, but then he divorced from his wife, he became a vegetarian and a yoga teacher, he got involved in this whole other world that he can't explain to anyone. In his case, 9/11 brought all of this to a crisis point." He has begun to write a memoir, and Karen has agreed to help.

In the way that she faces and interprets her world, another interview provided the catalyst for a project that absorbed her for most of a year, a novel. The man had worked in computers at the World Trade Center, on the floor where the first plane hit. By chance, he was late for work that day and watched the collapse from the Brooklyn Bridge. "Afterwards he became obsessed with the Internet," says Karen. "He'd search for hours, day after day, learning everything he could about oil, the back story on Halliburton flying Taliban people into Houston. When I met him the first time, and pretty much the second time too, he couldn't make eye contact. He seemed so alone. He said he hadn't talked to anybody about this, so the interviews were really helpful. But I also felt with him a kind of deep isolation that interviews couldn't solve. There was this moment when he could speak, but after that – what? This man's story isn't the story of the novel, but it is the impulse behind it."

As all of Karen's work does, her novel explores how people deal with the effects of violence. It also looks at the ambiguous potential of the Internet. "It's almost a character in the novel," she says. "It can isolate us, and by barraging us with all this information we don't know what to do with, it can make us feel more and more powerless, more and more hopeless. On the other hand, depending on how we use it, it can also connect us, and by connecting us it can even humanize us."

Responses to the novel were enthusiastic from several trusted first readers. Her goal was to get it out into the world by September 11, 2004. "It's a fictional representation of an alternative way to look at current events. I really want this book to contribute to a dialogue we desperately need to have in this country between now and the next election. The book suggests, or offers, that even in this moment, there is the possibility of opening to others, and in the quality of those connections, the possibility of sustenance that's counter to all the destruction. When you bomb somebody, you just annihilate them, that's the end of it. But when you hear them, when you look at them, something else can happen."

In the ten days before we spoke, Karen had got rejection letters from seven agents and publishers. "The way I read them," she says, "they're saying this novel doesn't matter, it won't matter, I don't want it. I'm sort of reeling. I had a lot of hopes attached to this book, I thought it was a good book. Now it's even hard to hold onto that idea."

As a fellow writer, I remind her of two things: good work is rejected every minute by gatekeepers, and especially in a country like hers, where the dominant voices were already so loud and pervasive, but now since 9/11 many degrees more so, the space for alternate views shrinks by the day. Paradoxically, I mean to be encouraging. She nods. "I do think there's a whole other story in the novel, of what people really feel about what happened, that isn't allowed to be heard. Or maybe the gatekeepers just don't know how to accept it. Maybe it's so different from what they believe that all they can say, as one agent did, is that it's not realistic."

To write my own book I've talked with many people, including Karen, about how oral history can help silenced people to be heard.

"One of the ironies for me is that what I'm left with right now is the sense that my own truth isn't being heard," she says. "This book, where I put my deepest truth about what's happened in the past two years, and the human response to it – as long as I can't get it published, it won't be heard. That's where I am now. It's enormously painful."

Another theme of my book is the ability of human beings to find meaning that affirms life, even in the most apparently meaningless violence. It is a theme that also runs through Karen's work. Her play, *I Will Bear Witness*, details Viktor Klemperer's experience of life in Germany before and during the Second World War. Part 1 covers the prewar years, 1933–38, when the Nazis were consolidating their hold on the country, and beyond. "It's chilling when people see it now," she says. "It's so much like the present in this country – the slow, carefully paced erosion of freedoms – it's too eerie. Which is not to say we're going into a repeat of German fascism, because we're not. We're going into something entirely new and unimaginably awful."

One of the major attractions for her of Viktor Klemperer's diaries was their clear-eyed candour in the face of horror. "This was a man who, by facing his own fear, and rage, and helplessness, and cowardliness – every aspect of himself – actually grew as a person through this horrible time. At one point he writes, 'The days begin like this: First Eva is hysterical, then I am hysterical, then we are both hysterical.' But he kept himself sane, and he was able to help other people be sane. He did it by making meaning of things he valued most in life – home, relationships, friends. There's a wonderful moment in *I Will Bear Witness*: as the Holocaust heats up, Klemperer talks about the need to find pleasure in something every day, even if it's only the minute growth of a philodendron leaf."

I ask Karen how she makes meaning herself, day to day. "It becomes a little tricky at this point, doesn't it?" she replies. "I mean, are the people in power literally going to destroy the world? We seem awfully close to the edge." I comment on the roses in the kitchen, cut from the garden, improbably, at the end of November. Just that morning, she wrote a poem about them. "What could be more lovely than having roses at Thanksgiving?" She adds after a moment, "On the other hand, what do they tell us about global warming?"

ELISABETH

Elisabeth Pozzi-Thanner also has anxious questions rooted in the past. She grew up in Austria shortly after the Second World War, and she has documented the life experience of more than 150 Holocaust survivors. "I keep thinking, why, why, why couldn't the United States, or the people who lead it, see what happened on September 11 as I and so many other people see it, as an act of terrorism? Why did they need to immediately declare it an act of war, with everything that has followed?"

Earlier in the day she visited an exhibit on the recovery of materials and human remains from Ground Zero. "When I got out of the subway," she says, "suddenly in front of me were about a hundred school kids, maybe ten to fourteen years old, most of them black, and all of them in camouflage uniforms. This older guy, also in camouflage, he ordered them around like a paramilitary group – 'Get into line, put your right hand on the right shoulder of the one in front!' he was shouting at them, then they would shout something back to him. I got so scared, I thought, 'Oh my God, what is going on here?' I don't think I would have been that scared before September 11, and everything that has happened since."

She reiterates her new-found sense of fatalism. "I tell myself I need to be ready any moment, that things can suddenly be over, finished. The fragility of life is very obvious to me now. It's why I really love the good moments, why I search for them – good people, certain smells, anything to do with the senses, and beauty. All the things I enjoy in life and in other people, I cherish those more now than I ever did before."

She is about to move on to a new task. The Henri Nouwen Institute, at the University of Toronto in Canada, has asked her to set up an oral history project on the life and work of the famous Dutch priest, to complement their extensive collection of his papers and other materials. "He was a very colourful, very controversial man," she says, "a theologian who wrote forty books, a teacher at Harvard and Yale who gave lectures around the world. He also lived and worked with the indigenous people in South America for a few years, and in the last ten years of his life he worked at a village for severely mentally and physically challenged people. And he was gay. All these things make my heart rejoice, but different people experience them quite differently!" She laughs.

"I have to admit, I'm really looking forward to working on the first project in quite a few years that doesn't have any huge traumas involved! Of course, I could be surprised. You never know."

MARY-MARSHALL

In conversation with Mary-Marshall, I comment on my difficulty in comprehending current events, so many of which seem to defy any kind of reason that I can fathom. "I think you're describing the condition that many of us are in," she replies. "It's one reason that people – Americans born here, that is – had trouble comprehending 9/11/01. In so many interviews, we heard that people who immigrated here from violent countries or situations, especially the elders, were able to make meaning of this event very quickly. They weren't so surprised because they'd seen it before, and they knew the kind of global police power that the United States exercises in the rest of the world. But many people who grew up here have been protected all of their lives from these larger realities. We've reached a point of such overwhelming nationalism that we can no longer see reality as it's experienced in other countries. What happens to people in Iraq or Afghanistan simply isn't real to us."

I describe to her a conversation at dinner the night before, where most of the guests were American citizens. We got to talking about September 11, 2001, and its aftermath. I referred to some of the questions that have emerged about the attacks. For example: In the months preceding the attacks, the Bush regime shut down five different FBI investigations into bin Laden and Al-Qaeda, and immediately after 9/11, promoted the FBI official who shut them down. Over the preceding year, U.S. Air Force fighter planes had been routinely scrambled on the northeast coast sixty-seven times, and for lesser threats, yet on the morning of September 11, not a single plane was ordered into the air until it was too late to intervene; all standard operating procedures were inexplicably shut down. A string of such questions hangs hauntingly over the event. Did the Bush regime know in advance, and allow the attacks to go ahead? Was it involved?

One woman at the table said she didn't know how to cope with the possibility that the government of her country could have killed, or knowingly allowed to be killing, so many of its own people. To me the idea is deeply disturbing, but in the context of history, not such a big leap.

I mention to Mary-Marshall the rising alarm I feel as a Canadian watching the United States, and its faithful servants in Canada. Witnesses I trust who were in Miami at the November 2003 protests against the Free Trade in the Americas summit described the massive, heavily militarized police operation as "a dress rehearsal for a police state." At about the same time, the man who directed U.S. propaganda operations in Qatar during the invasion of Iraq moved to New York to direct media strategy for the Republican National Convention in August 2004. In a secret report, "Nuclear Posture Review for 2002," the Bush regime outlined its readiness to use nuclear weapons on a first-strike basis against North Korea, Syria, Iran, and China.

"These are scary times, aren't they?" I say. It's the kind of leading question that oral historians are never supposed to ask. "I think it's the scariest time I've ever lived through in this country," Mary-Marshall replies, "and I was witness to the end of segregation in North Carolina, where my parents were civil rights activists, so I've seen some really nasty stuff. But what's happening now is more terrifying than anything I've ever seen, or even thought about before."

In November 2001, Mary-Marshall described the faces of children she'd noticed on New York streets immediately after September 11. They were blank, devoid of animation, which she read as a sign of shock. In our first interview she observed that whereas adults found ways to intellectualize what happened, the children she'd talked to were struggling with huge, complicated questions: "How could those buildings just disappear? Why would anyone want to kill themselves in such an awful way?"

It was one of her dreams, she said then, "to work with children, to use oral history as a way of helping them to come to terms with catastrophic events like September 11." In co-operation with Marylene Cloitre, now in child studies at New York University, she has begun to realize her dream. "Together we've got a grant to work in four middle schools in Chinatown, teaching students how to use oral history to understand and interpret events like September 11. We've already done two pilot programs, one in Chinatown and one in Brooklyn, as part of the Telling Lives project I created the summer after September 11. Our intention is to help build community and strengthen resilience through public oral history."

Chinatown is a short walk from the World Trade Center, and heavily dependent on restaurant traffic. After the disaster, thousands of jobs disappeared, 10 per cent of all the jobs lost in New York City. Given a long history of survival under adverse, sometimes hostile conditions, it's a community well suited to a project on resilience.

"We heard about a teacher at Middle School 131 in Chinatown who had already done an oral history project without knowing about oral history," Mary-Marshall says. "After September 11, all the teachers were told by the Board of Education not to talk to anyone about it, which was crazy because people really needed somebody to talk to. This woman defied the order, took her students out, and they interviewed people who had lost their jobs. We asked her if she'd like us to do a pilot project in her school, and fortunately she agreed."

The oral history club at the Dr Sun Yat Sen Middle School met weekly from January to June 2003, gathering stories of elders who had survived war, migration and other hardships. The project worked so well that the principal at the school asked the teacher to lead a full-time course in oral history.

Selections from the students' interviews are on display in *Living Through History: Chinatown Stories*, a multimedia exhibit at the Museum of Chinese in the Americas, upstairs in a former school on

Mulberry Street. "It's a wonderful place," says Mary-Marshall. "It's so nice to know that oral history is going to end up in a public place with creative curators who know how to make it come alive. As oral historians we're just good at getting down the stories, but then we really don't know what to do with them. So why not work with other experts who can figure out that part of the puzzle?"

In January 2004, two of the September 11 project's most seasoned interviewers, Gerald Albarelli and Amy Starcheski, began work in four middle schools in Chinatown.

"They'll be teaching the children how to use tape recorders and cameras, how to write a journal, and how to interview elders who've lived through other difficult historical events," says Mary-Marshall. "Ultimately we hope the students will learn how to place themselves as active participants in history, by creating and expressing themselves, becoming the ones who are making meaning, instead of being kids that no one listens to."

Not long after the attacks on the World Trade Center, Mary-Marshall asked her son, who was eleven at the time, "Are you surprised by this?" "Of course," he replied, "but then don't you remember the USS *Cole*?" (In October 2000, two suicide bombers in a rubber dinghy attacked and nearly sank the American destroyer in the Yemen port of Aden). "And look what's happening in Israel and Palestine. These things go on everywhere in the world, all the time."

"These things are more real to lots of kids than they are to many American adults," says Mary-Marshall. "This is why I'm so eager to work with kids. They're the future, they're going to be in charge before long. Right now I think we have a unique opportunity to help deepen their understanding of the role they can play in our country, and the role that our country plays in the world. Between the two extremes of retreating into narrow isolationism or charging out in this crazy kind of rogue aggression, hell-bent on global domination, there is something in between. It is actually possible to use your head, your analytic powers, to figure out what the heck is happening around you, and then try to do something about it. That's about the only hope we have, don't you think?"

CHAPTER 11

History on the Floor

The cops must have got a tip that something was going to happen because the whole city police force was guarding the Hill, going around in a circle, backwards and forwards and around. And we came up within four feet of the police line. Inspector Burroughs who was in charge of the outfit was right in front of me. And he knew me. And he wanted to know who were the leaders of all this. We said, "There's no leaders, we're all the same. We're all the same."

✿ Pat Lenihan, interviewed by Gil Levine, 1977

I ask Gil Levine about the first time he used a tape recorder. He replies, "In the 1950s and '60s, before the union was in a legal position to strike in Ontario, they'd have to meet with a provincial conciliation officer, and if that didn't work it would go to a three-person board. When I came on the scene, I started writing the briefs they'd take to these boards. I would always meet first with the executive of the local – they knew the issues a lot better than I did, and the brief needed to be in their words, but they didn't know how to put them down on paper. We happened to have bought this Grundig machine to tape the proceedings at our conventions, and I had learned how to operate it. So I would lug this thing – it weighed over twenty pounds – into meetings with local executives. Then I'd put together the brief out of what I'd heard from them. That's how I started."

We're talking in the living room of the townhouse Gil Levine shares with his wife, Helen, on a gardened courtyard near downtown Ottawa. His vividly coloured t-shirt comes from San Miguel de Allende, a mountain town in central Mexico where they spend their winters. The town, established in 1542, is named for a Catholic saint and for Ignacio Allende, a freedom fighter in the early nineteenth-century Mexican War of Independence.

Gil turned eighty this year. Almost half a century ago, after a brief stint in social work, he applied for a job doing research with the newly formed National Union of Public Employees. "I wasn't any good at social work," he says, "but this was my dream, to work in the labour movement."

He grew up in Toronto, in a family of Jewish immigrants from Eastern Europe. "My parents sent me to a Jewish school to learn Yiddish and socialism, so I got both at an early age," he says, with a comfortable laugh. After high school, and two-and-a-half years in the army, his politics moved further left. "In my first year at university I joined the Communist Party. In those days there were strong connections between the party and the labour movement. We would do things like provide picket support for local strikes. So when this opening came up for a research job in the union I belonged to – as a municipal employee in Toronto – I grabbed it."

Easier said than done. After he applied, more than a month passed before he was summoned to an interview at the King Edward Hotel. "It wasn't a fancy hotel in those days. Lots of union meetings happened there," Gil says. By the end of the interview, he was offered the job. "But then I was tormented," he says. "I had a young family to support. My job in Toronto was shitty, but at least it was a job. What if we moved to Ottawa, then I got found out as a Red? This is when the anti-communist witchhunts were at their peak in the labour movement. I decided to tell NUPE that I'd been a member of the party. The three guys who'd interviewed me called me in again. One of them, a conservative, said flat out, 'We can't hire him.' The second, an English-man with a sense of fair play, said, 'Well, he told us, so he's honest.' The third man was Pat Lenihan, president of the union and a former CP official in Alberta. He said, 'So what?' It was two to one, so they hired me. We moved to Ottawa in December 1956."

In 1963, NUPE merged with the smaller NUPSE (National Union of Public Service Employees) to form the Canadian Union of Public Employees. "They had to decide who would get what job," says Gil. "The other union also had a research director, who had only three years experience compared to my seven. But the NUPSE president was viciously anti-communist, and he said, 'No way we're going to have a communist as research director.' My guys stood with me. The merger almost fell apart over the issue, but the NUPSE president was so anx-ious for the merger to go through – they had agreed that he'd be first president of the new union – that he swallowed his opposition. As long as he was president, until 1975, there was always political tension between us. Several times he would have fired me if he could, never over questions about my work, only the political differences. Things came to a head during the Vietnam War, when I was active on a local anti-war committee, and he accused me of using union money for the committee's work, which of course was total nonsense. It turned out this guy was working with the RCMP! Fortunately he was pretty incom-petent, so the stuff he came up with on me was really off the wall. About ten years ago I got my file through Freedom of Information, but so much of it was blanked out, I couldn't make much sense of it."

One of Gil's first tasks was to gather data on wages and working conditions in public service jobs across Canada and to make sure the information got shared among the locals. After a while he concluded that the lack of co-ordinated bargaining was costing workers. "Even after NUPE formed, all these independent locals still had a lot of auton-omy. I felt that bargaining in a co-ordinated way with employers in each field – municipal, hospital, and so on – would be a lot more pow-erful. For years I met all kinds of resistance from local executives pro-tecting their turf, but I just kept pushing it. Now it's a given, and it's made a huge difference. In the hospital sector, for example, virtually every province has some form of province-wide bargaining."

How did he go looking for data, and what did he find? "Like you," he says, "I asked a lot of questions. What I found is that the media, and the general public who rely on it, misunderstand what unions do and why people join them. The media always focus on wages, but that's rarely the major issue. When people organize, usually it's out of frustration at being treated like shit. That's the issue that moves people into unionizing – dignity. Wages are part of it, but I kept hearing that what people really want is to be treated with respect. The problem is, how do you negotiate that into a collective agreement? You can put things like wages and benefits in writing, so they can be enforced, but how do you negotiate respect from managers to workers?"

One way to increase respect for workers within their own union was to ensure that members were informed. "I was getting a lot of requests from locals to evaluate their collective agreements, to see how they were doing," says Gil. "The only way I could see how to do this was to come up with some kind of ideal agreement as a basis for comparison. I read every collective agreement we had, extracted the best clauses – vacation, seniority, sick leave – and put them together into what we called the CUPE standard agreement. Until then, all the agreements were written by lawyers, which meant only they could understand them, but I wrote the standard agreement in plain language, so it would be comprehensible to every member of the union."

Next step was to convince the union reps that they should include the standard agreement in the package they provided to new locals. "A lot of them would say, 'No, just send it to me and I'll interpret it to the locals.' What they were really saying was, 'Don't let the membership see the ideal agreement, because maybe I won't be able to meet those standards.' It was a way for the staff reps to hold more power – 'If the members know more than I do, I'm in trouble.'" Gil kept pushing.

How did he get from collective agreements to oral history? "The first impulse for me was my mother," he says. "She had a fabulous memory, and lovely stories about growing up in a little town in eastern

Europe, so I decided I had to get some of that on tape. That got me going on family history."

In 1977, the CUPE staff union negotiated that one person each year would get a sabbatical leave to do independent, union-related work. Gil was the first to qualify. "I decided to travel the country and collect the stories of people who helped to build the union. They were in their sixties and seventies by then, so the clock was ticking." He travelled for several weeks and conducted twenty-three interviews, most of them two to three hours in length.

In Calgary, Gil planned to spend a day or so exploring Patrick Lenihan's story. "But I got so intrigued, I ended up staying at his house for ten days, and recorded about twenty hours of tape! Pat was involved in the Irish rebellion [1916], so he had to get out of there. He came to Canada, got involved with the Wobblies [Industrial Workers of the World, a militant labour movement in early twentieth-century North America] in the '20s, went to Calgary in the Depression years, where he led the unemployed workers' movement, which became so large and powerful that Calgary ended up with the highest relief rates [precursor of unemployment insurance] anywhere in Canada. In 1938 he was elected to city council as a communist, and because the party opposed the war in its early stages, he spent a couple of years in jail. After that he returned to Calgary, got work as a parks labourer, built up the Calgary municipal local, reached out to other Alberta locals, and eventually set up a provincial council, which provided the basis for forming the national union. It's quite a story!"

Originally, as with his mother, Gil's goal was to capture irreplaceable stories while the narrators were still alive, and in this case, to deposit them for preservation in the National Archives. But in 1998, twenty years after he recorded the interviews, the Canadian Committee on Labour History published *Patrick Lenihan: From Irish Rebel to Founder of Canadian Public Sector Unionism*, edited by Gil Levine. "Even after I realized what a powerful story this was it was hard to give it time while I was still working," Gil says. "I wanted to catch the flavour of his language – he's a wonderful Irish storyteller – but still have the proper grammar, not to make him sound stupid. Also I discovered that some incidents from thirty, forty years before weren't always accurate in terms of names, times, and places, so I had to check all that out too. And of course he didn't tell it in a neat chronological order. It was a huge editing job. It took eight revisions – *before* I had a word-processor!"

Given the work he put into it, Gil is quite modest about his role. In the introduction he writes: "When the Sound Archives of the National Archives of Canada are asked for examples or instructions on how to do oral labour history, they invariably refer to the Lenihan tapes as one of their best examples. Most of the credit for that goes to the interviewee, not the interviewer. Lenihan was not only a great story teller, he also had a great memory for the words of songs of the Irish rebellion, of the Wobblies, of the hoboes, and of the On-to-Ottawa Trek, all of which he sang beautifully on tape."

The interviewer/editor is also candid about his subject's less heroic side. "There is much to admire about Pat Lenihan. But he was not always a nice man . . . or a good man. He drank too much. When he did, he lost control and became a different person. He inflicted his rage on the people closest to him – his wife and children – and at the same time demanded their loyalty to his cause. Were I to have the chance to talk to Pat again, I would ask him about these things. I don't. But I feel strongly that that part of the truth needs to be on the record."

Gil Levine has regrets about both his oral history projects. "With my mother," he says, "I wanted to know her story, and I want my kids and grandchildren to know it too – it can give them a better appreciation of where they came from, the rich history that preceded them. Well, it turns out my two grandkids in Ottawa, who are eighteen and twenty-one, don't give a shit about *my* history, let alone my mother's! Karen [his daughter in Toronto] has a nine-year old son, and he's got a more curious mind, so maybe he'll be interested, who knows."

When he deposited the union tapes at the National Archives, he intended that they be used, and made it known to the labour movement that they were available. "But they've hardly been consulted at all," he says. "People have asked why don't I write a history of CUPE. I gathered the material, let someone else write the history. A young woman told me she was going to do it for her doctoral thesis at York University. I said, 'Why don't you listen to those tapes?' I don't think she ever did."

As it happens, I had just been to the National Archives (see chapter 8) and was delighted to inform Gil that Richard Lochead, head of the Audio-Visual Acquisition and Research Section, told me the Gil Levine tapes were some of the most requested in their entire oral history collection. "That interview he did with Pat Lenihan," said Richard, "I think we've had more requests for it than for any other interview."

Gil chuckles. "That's good. That's good to hear."

KEN CLAVETTE

That same week in Ottawa I talk with another workers' oral historian of a later generation. Ken Clavette regards Gil as a pioneer. "He keeps saying, over and over, 'Don't just do oral history twenty years after the fact, do it while it's happening," says Ken. "People go through all kinds of battles in the union movement, but when you ask them years later what it was like, they'll say, 'Oh, it's water under the bridge.' They lose the passion of the moment. You can't help it, you let go of these things and you move on. Gil says if you want to know how people feel during a strike, interview them during the strike, or right after. If you don't, that's it, you've lost the passion of the moment. By the way, we're still not doing that."

Ken loves history, and he loves talking about it. At forty-five, in addition to his job at Ottawa Labour-Community Services, he's also chair of the Ottawa Heritage Advisory Committee, a member of the local Workers Heritage Committee and of the outreach committee at the Workers Arts and Heritage Centre in Hamilton, as well as past chair of the Canadian Oral History Association. "When you understand the past," he says, "it helps you make sense of the present. Look at all the moves to privatize hydro. There was a reason why a small-town Tory alderman decided eighty years ago that we had to take over the private power companies in the '20s – electricity was becoming essential, but because it was under private control, most people couldn't afford it. Now here we are today, same struggle all over again. They just hope we'll forget why it happened in the first place."

We're talking amid the rubble of work-in-progress in his small, crowded office at Labour-Community Services. As co-ordinator of the joint labour movement/United Way project, he supports labour volunteers involved in the United Way, runs a peer counselling program to help workers grapple with social issues, and serves as a liaison between organized labour and social justice movements in Ottawa, so each can better understand and appreciate the other.

I ask him for an example. "Right now we're working with the Women's Committee of the Labour Council to set up a bursary program for Ottawa women to go to post-secondary education, as a practical memorial to the women who were murdered at the Polytechnique in Montreal," he says. "We look at how we can link the labour movement into issues like violence against women, or pay equity, or funding cuts, and also how can I get some of these issues that affect workers to be recognized more effectively at the agencies."

In a capital and university city where most people come from away, Ken considers himself part of a small minority who call themselves locals. "I was born in Buckingham in the Ottawa Valley, my dad in Glengarry County, my mother in the Pontiac on the Quebec side. My grandfather worked in the lumber camps, he was a log driver on the river. My wife was born in Ottawa. So there's a strong sense of local and regional history, unlike, say, for someone from Vancouver who comes here to work as an economist for the federal government. People come and go. Ottawa has one of the highest turnover rates of any city in Canada."

He worked for several years in the federal civil service, starting at age nineteen as a clerk in the Department of National Defence. It's where he began to learn his politics. "Around 1980, I remember being taken down to this room where we were shown a film about the Cold War and how the Soviets were building more missiles than the Americans and so on. When the credits came up, I was probably the only one in the audience who noticed that AFL-CIO [the largest American labour body] had helped produce it. I was outraged! I kept telling my co-workers that with all the military installations around here, we're ground zero, so we ought to be peaceniks for our own security. Even though most of them were older men with military backgrounds, we actually got along pretty well." Listening to Ken, I sense that getting along is one of his talents.

In 1982, he walked his first picket line, in a nation-wide strike of forty thousand federal clerical workers, most of them women. The next year, at twenty-five, he was elected the youngest president ever of the Ottawa Labour Council.

I ask him how he found his way into oral history. "In the final days of the NDP government, in '93–'94," he tells me, "they made $100,000 available to the Ontario Heritage Foundation for workers and unions to do histories of workplaces that were disappearing due to technological change. Some of us in the Ottawa Labour Council had been talking about the need to look at industries that used to be here before all the high-tech stuff – particularly Ottawa Car and Aircraft, where they used to make streetcars four blocks from the Parliament Buildings, and the Beech Foundry that produced stoves, furnaces and refrigerators. We thought we should try to get the stories of people who'd worked there." They applied to the Heritage Foundation and got a grant.

"None of us had a clue about how to do oral history," Ken says. "We got the Labour Council to buy a VHS camcorder, and we brought in some union people who worked in broadcasting, to give us tips on how to use it. We set up working groups and we trained thirty-four people. Two people would go do the interviews, an interviewer and a camera operator. Some of the people they interviewed got so absorbed, they forgot that the camera and a second person were even there."

How did they find people to interview? "Once we started looking, it was amazing how many turned up. A librarian at the public library said, 'Oh, my father worked at Ottawa Car and Aircraft,' and a woman who works in the building here told me her dad worked there, she remembers the strike in 1948. Then Dave Brown [a widely read local columnist] wrote a paragraph about the project in one of his columns – "Lunch Bucket History," he called it. The next three days my phone rang off the hook! And word of mouth. It turned out we didn't have enough French interviewers, so I called every francophone I knew in the labour movement around here, and they did a few interviews each."

Since the owners' history, the official version, had already been documented, the goal of the project was to elicit how workers felt about their experience: what was it like to work where they did, what did they recall of the war years, how did they support their families, how did they get through the 1948 strike. "We worked with Don Bouzek [a producer, now living in Saskatchewan] on the two videos we made," says Ken. "He would look at the raw footage as it came in, to see how we were doing. Some people would put the camera right across the room, which might give you a good idea of the person's living room, but it makes it kind of hard to edit! Sometimes people would miss a question that seems obvious to me – for example, two people meet on the assembly line and get married, but the interviewer didn't think to ask *how* they met under those conditions, how they managed a courtship. He just went on to the next question. There's a story there! That's one of the problems with minimal training – you don't really have time to develop interactive listening skills."

GOD, IT WAS COLD!

In 1946, the owners of Ottawa Car and Aircraft announced that they would reduce their workforce from two thousand workers to three hundred. While the owners claimed they were losing money, they continued to pay dividends to their shareholders.

> We went out on strike in February. Cold – God, it was cold! You gotta be in a picket line, seven in the morning until six at night. For two or three weeks they didn't have no scabs, then they

brought the scabs in – that's when they had the fight with the policemen, because the policemen had to bring the scabs in. The first day they came with their billysticks, but the strikers took away their billysticks and beat them with them. The next day they came back at us. The first row, they didn't have billysticks, but the ones behind, they had billysticks. You know, getting hit on the side of the head with a billystick, that's not funny.

❁ Wilfrid Cire, metalworker, in the video *On All Fronts*

A strong impulse in Ken's pursuit of oral history is the tenuous nature of life. "We had people on our list who passed away before we could get to them. I felt really bad about losing those stories – who knows, maybe we lost some gems. One gentleman we interviewed, Mr Cire, who broke pig iron [an essential step in making steel at the time], figures in both the videos we made. We had set up that everyone would get copies of both the finished video and their own tape, but Mr Cire didn't have a VCR, and we hadn't sorted out what to do about that. Then one day I saw his death notice in the paper. I phoned his home, gave my name, and his grandson, a man in his sixties, called me back. I asked if he'd like a copy of his grandfather's tape. Yes! It warms my heart to be able to give people back a part of their history like that."

He and his co-workers documented the closure of the Canadian Forces Uplands base – a major employer in Ottawa – and a daycare workers' strike in the late 1970s. He wanted to document Lebreton Flats, a working-class neighbourhood on the Ottawa River that had been sacrificed to "urban renewal" in the late '60s. He called a local writer, Phil Jenkins, for leads; Jenkins happened to have a dozen interview tapes on the subject in his desk. "He's a writer," says Ken. "He's not thinking about oral history, but then by serendipity he bumps into me, so those full interviews are now preserved in the city archives, not just the bits he used in his book."

Ken heard that a researcher, Steve High, was going to interview workers around the Great Lakes basin on the closure of their industries. "I asked him what he planned to do with the tapes. He hadn't thought about it. So I said, 'Why not see if local archives or museums are interested, anywhere you go?' He did leave copies of the tapes in each place, so that gives back a piece of their own history to these communities."

Ken is a tireless sleuth. "We tracked down a past president of the United Auto Workers for an interview, and it turned out he kept all his records in the basement, near the sump pump. They were pretty mouldy, but we found some wonderful photos of a strike here, taken by a professional photographer – it turned out these were the only existing copies! Now they're in the city archives. If we hadn't done oral history with this guy, we would never have found any of that other stuff. It would have just died in a dumpster somewhere."

I wonder what drives Ken to record the human voice. "In our society there's a huge bias towards documents," he says. "In the U.S., even oral historians seem to put a lot of emphasis on the transcript. For them the written word is the Bible. Well, it seems to me Enron, World.com, and the rest of them ought to have shown us by now that the written word isn't exactly reliable! Every document has its own bias. My bias is towards the workers' point of view. Well, guess whose story doesn't get recorded in the documents? If I'm doing a workers' history – let's say a paper on workers in the 1870s – I'll put a footnote at the beginning to say that I'm limited by the published sources, which all carry their own biases, and it's hardly ever in favour of the workers. When I look at documents, I always want to know the story behind them. So much of it isn't there. Look at minutes – they only record motions. There's no account of the struggles that went on behind those motions. I want to know what really happened, what forces were at play, what kind of pressures did the employer bring to bear, how did the workers resist. I want to get people to reminisce about these things."

In the absence of documents, oral history may be the only historical source. Ken cites the Canadian Seamen's Union as an example. The CSU was famous – or notorious, depending on the bias – as a radical union that fought for decent wages and living conditions for its members working on Canada's merchant fleet. In the late 1940s and early '50s, the RCMP worked with a known mobster, Hal Banks, to destroy the union and replace it with the more compliant U.S.-based Seafarers' International Union.

"You can't find any records on the CSU anywhere in Canada," says Ken. "Either they were deliberately destroyed or they just vanished through neglect. So you have this important left nationalist group of mostly illiterate workers taking on the corporate world, and when Green goes to write his book, what has he got to work with? [Vancouver dock-worker, union organizer, and anti-poverty activist Jim Green published *Against the Tide: The Story of the Canadian Seamen's Union* in 1986.] Basically he's got some heavily slanted newspaper reports, and the RCMP files – I always say if you want to save our history, put it in an envelope and mail it to the RCMP or CSIS, they'll file it somewhere! But aside from that, what are his sources? The workers' own voices. Oral history."

Ken's determination to promote the voices and experience of workers extends into more physical realms, even the naming of city streets. When the former provincial government forced Ottawa and the surrounding municipalities to amalgamate, advisory committees were set up to foster the illusion of a democratic transition. Ken pressed the Ottawa Labour Council to nominate workers to these com-mittees. "In the 1910s and '20s the labour council always used to appoint people to city committees – the voice of the working man was actually considered important enough to include. They even had city councillors that were workers, people active in their unions. So we nominated people to various committees, and I picked heritage. When they chose a chair, they put me in, I guess because I was a little younger than most and I had some political fire. But the other people are open enough that union heritage doesn't conflict with the genealogy of French Canadians, or the Bytown Museum that glorifies Colonel By but also the people who actually built the canal. Our common interest is to promote heritage in Ottawa."

One of their advisory functions was to come up with names for streets in the newly amalgamated city. "We chose to promote Daniel

O'Donoghue. He was an amazing guy – came here from Ireland, helped found the first printer's union, the first labour council, and the first national trade union organization in Canada, the Canadian Labour Union. Then in 1874 the workers put him up as their candidate in a provincial by-election, and he won. He was the first independently elected trade unionist in the British Empire. So we said, 'Let's name a street after him.' A municipal councillor from one of the suburban wards, a pretty right-wing guy, said, 'Look, this O'Donoghue is important, why just name a street after him? Why not a park, and we'll put up a plaque or a statue so people will take notice.' So the motion was amended to say street and/or park. The city planners chose a park out in Kanata Lakes – in the last census, that was the second wealthiest area in Ottawa, after Rockcliffe Park! The planner said to me, 'Would he not be happy out there?' I said, '*They* would not be happy.' So Daniel O'Donoghue will probably get a street in the new Lebreton Flats, which is supposed to be built sometime in the next few years."

Ken's next project is to create a workers' museum in the former city of Vanier, a small working-class community now surrounded by Ottawa. In the chaotic process of amalgamation, the city ended up owning an 1870s worker's house, and now municipal property managers are questioning why they are paying for heat on a vacant house. "The city manager, who grew up in Vanier, approached us about turning it into a workers' museum," says Ken. "It's a wonderful house, a little under twelve hundred square feet. We're looking into how we might create a museum – it could be something like the tenement museum in New York City – and how we could use the space to promote workers' culture."

And he's off. "We could use the upstairs as a meeting room and library. The ground floor could house displays. We could bring in exhibits, for example from the Workers Arts and Heritage Centre in Hamilton. It has a great yard, we could do heritage gardens – make a partnership with local gardeners. We could work with other museums in town that don't have enough space, if they came up with exhibits that reflect workers history. And it could be a resource centre where students come to do research. I'm talking to a prof at the University of Ottawa who's written about working-class women in Lower Town and Lebreton Flats – we could get students to help develop curriculum on working class issues like that. We'll get workers in, say three electricians plus a few other volunteers to pull wire for them, take a day and rewire the whole building, bring it up to code. Or build a wheelchair ramp. Maybe all this will help the bureaucracy types who want to save the house from developers that want to turn everything into condos. This is how my activism works. I'd have loved this as a kid. I would have volunteered all kinds of Saturdays to do this stuff!"

THE WORKERS ARTS AND HERITAGE CENTRE

Second stop on the Workers' City walking tour in Hamilton's East End is Woodlands Park. In the 1930s it was a six-acre wooded area where workers could play baseball, debate politics, or relax on hot summer evenings.

When people on the walking tour turn on their cassette guides at Woodlands Park, they hear a local man explain why his father always hated firemen:

> One time when I was about thirty we were sitting on the verandah, and I asked him, "How come you don't like firemen?" Then he told me this story: In the 1930s the government was so afraid of communism that any time there was a gathering, they sent in some kind of force to break it up. My father went down to hear Tim Buck [head of the Communist Party of Canada], I guess it was May 1st, and there were quite a few unemployed people gathered in the park. All of sudden a bunch of firemen came in, and they had the nozzles of the hoses – there's a handle on the front so you can pull the hose, or at least there was in those days – and they whaled into this crowd with these things and drove them out of Woodlands Park, because that's the way they handled things in those days.

The walking tour guide-book describes how the park became a key organizing site for the United Electrical Workers in the 1940s. It quotes Local 504 president Alf Kelly: "It was nothing to see two or three thousand out there on a noon hour . . . we would talk about what the union means. And the men got bolder. At first they used to listen, all hiding behind trees so the boss wouldn't see them. Then they came out from behind the trees." In 1947, the book goes on, the city cut down most of the trees, demolished the bandstand, and flattened and sodded the land. The workers lost their park.

"Our Workers' City walking tours use a lot of oral history," says Renee Johnston, executive director of the Workers Arts and Heritage Centre (WAHC) in downtown Hamilton. "People take the cassettes with them on the tour, or they'll listen to them in the car. Parts of them have been played on the CBC and other radio stations. We have quite a good oral history collection here. It's been built up through various projects, like the interviews we did with women on trying to make ends meet during the 1930s Depression. I just got a tape that a local man made about the old neighbourhoods around the bay – he used pieces from some of our oral history interviews for that."

WAHC emerged from discussions in the 1980s among artists, labour historians, and activists in Toronto who saw a need to preserve and celebrate the history and culture of working people. On a warm day in June, I tour the centre with a friend, Myrna Wood, a library worker and union activist in Hamilton until she retired to Picton a few years ago. She introduces me to some of her friends and allies here. The centre's home on Stuart Street in Hamilton's North End is an imposing three-storey stone building. The first two floors are renovated; the third awaits further funding. Built in 1860 as a custom house where civil servants checked goods coming in by train, it has served since as a community centre for working-class families, a public school, a YWCA, temporary housing for victims of economic depression and for recent immigrants, a vinegar factory, a yarn factory, a macaroni factory, a martial arts academy, and finally in 1995, the Workers Arts and Heritage Centre. A board member refers casually to ghosts in residence upstairs. There seem to be four of them, and for ghosts, they seem reasonably content.

I settle down to talk with Renee in the resource centre, a square, high-ceilinged room on the ground floor. My first question: How does she define the centre's purpose? "I'd say it allows space for a populist approach to art, culture, and history. It allows all of these to blend together," she replies. "What I hope we're doing here is interpreting culture in a new way to counter a built-in bias against the lives and culture of workers. I believe art and history can both be powerful transformative tools for social change. They can also break down all kinds of barriers, including barriers between artists and activists. This is a participatory organization, meaning that all our projects involve groups working together, which has the potential to break down economic, social, racial and other kinds of barriers between people."

It sounds impressive but a bit theoretical. I ask for an example. "Recently we did an exhibit on *maquilla* sector [low-wage sweatshops producing goods for export] workers in Guatemala," she says. "We worked with a black artist in Hamilton, to transform their images into the exhibit – so in this case people of two different cultural backgrounds worked together to create a new vision. Institutional art galleries tend to compartmentalize people, so you'll get the window-dressing of a black history exhibit in Black History Month, but people aren't brought in to become part of the organizing process. We want to break down preconceived notions of who people are, where they come from, how they live, what they believe."

I'm curious to know how an executive director manages "a participatory organization." Renee laughs. "Sometimes it's like trying to herd cats!" She sees her role as catalyst. "It's my job to identify communities, bring them together, and then to identify resources – people, money, ideas – that can hold that nucleus together until it's ready to grow on its own. Then my role becomes supporter/trouble-shooter, to stand back and watch. Because I have a little distance from the process, I can help solve problems in a fairly neutral way. Right now I'm working on 'And Still I Rise,' an exhibit on African-Canadian workers in Ontario. I'm the only white woman in the group. It took two-and-a-half years to get this group together, formulate ideas, and get the project moving. In the early stages I was the driving voice, getting people together to talk out what they want to do. Now I have a supporting role, I'm outside the circle. If there's a question about design or text, I'm there to help, to remind people of their first principles, which I have them draft when they're starting, so they can return to that when they're getting lost."

How did Renee, who is an artist, get involved in this kind of work? She replies: "Both as a spiritual and political person, I believe that not everyone has been given a fair shake. As the only girl in a family with six boys, I know something about what it's like to be the one on the outside. The good side of that is that I've hung out with every kind of guy imaginable, my brothers and their friends – in other words, what you might call a male-dominated culture – which certainly helps me to work in the union movement! Also I went to a Dutch Reform Christian school, where I was an oddball, the only artist, so again I know what it's like to be on the outside looking in."

Kathryn Petersen, co-chair of the centre, is a library worker and union activist in the Hamilton Public Library. She describes the vision that drives the centre. "When you go to school or university, when you see movies and TV, you may learn something about your country, but you certainly don't get much about 'ordinary' people, all of us that work and make our country what it is. This centre is part of a larger movement to give voice and vision to what people do – not the famous leaders, the corporations, but what's *our* role, how do we live, work, fight – and how do we party? One of our early exhibits, 'As We Go Marching, Marching,' looked at events like May Day, Labour Day, International Women's Day, the ways that working people celebrate, and promote the good things of our lives."

Kathryn grew up in a politically engaged Jewish family. "For me, Judaism is a story of liberation," she says. "It's the struggle of a people to preserve who they are in the face of centuries of oppression, ghettoization, inquisitions, and pogroms. That came through to me very strongly from my parents, the obligation to defend, protect, and advocate. On a temple that my grandparents founded, there's an inscription, 'Do Justice, Love Mercy, Walk Humbly' – I'll leave out the 'with God' part," she adds with a smile.

"Education and culture were both valued highly, as ways to make sense of the world, to be part of the world. In my home there was always art and music, books, and I'd go to museums, art galleries. The art always seemed beautiful to me, but flat somehow, all those images of leaders, famous people, flowers, and waterfalls. When I saw "Guernica" in a gallery in Chicago, that was a pivotal moment for me – art as life! Now as a unionist, it's important to me that our stories take forms that people can see, have access to, and feel validated by. I want my kids to have that. The art of the elite is out there, lots of it, it costs tons of money, but this is something else. It's unique and it's ours."

Kathryn learned early the steep cost of doing justice. Her parents moved from Canada to the U.S. when she was a child, and she lived near Chicago until she was a young adult. "The parents of all the kids in my youth group were either socialist or communist. In the '50s, with McCarthy there and the RCMP here, I saw people going to jail, suicides, lives shattered, families broken up. It wasn't surprising that people retreated. My parents' generation never again played much of a role in the movement for political change, not in the way they did when they were young. But they did create these youth groups, so their ideas and dreams weren't entirely lost. I went to university, got into the anti-war movement, and when I came back to Canada, the women's movement, socialist organizations, and the daycare movement in particular."

In current North America, Kathryn hears clear echoes from her youth. "I have a friend who fully believes that the state is benevolent. She's sure it will maintain social programs, we'll be protected in our old age, and so on. I don't feel at all secure, probably because I'm Jewish. When one of my daughters was twelve, she asked me, 'Do you ever think about it happening again, the Holocaust?' I said, 'Yeah, sometimes.' She said, 'I'm just trying to figure out which of my friends would rat me out.' I was stunned. But as a Jew I do believe it could happen, and as a socialist I believe it could happen. The U.S. already has concentration camps – they're called maximum security prisons – and when they want more, they can throw them up in no time at all."

It's a rather grim prospect. Why does she keep fighting? "I don't think we have much choice," she replies. "The more people who do fight, the harder it is to get all of us. That's one of the basic principles of union organizing. And despite what I've said, in the long run I'm really an optimist. There's the Marx thing – either we'll have socialism or we'll have barbarism. I don't accept the inevitability of barbarism, so I have to keep pushing the other way."

For her, the Workers Arts and Heritage Centre plays a crucial role in pushing the other way. "This place is definitely part of the fight-back. It helps us to make sense of what's happening, and what's at stake in the broader context. When I was teaching a course on women's studies, I was amazed to read primary sources from the suffragette movement and to find that they had said the same things we're saying now! How many times do we have to reinvent the wheel? Doesn't it make more sense to preserve and protect what we've already learned? When you have to fight back, you're so much stronger when you can see your own situation in a broader context. It gives you grounding and validity so you can speak with more authority on the issues. That's why we need to keep places like this alive and active."

To visit one of the centre's current shows, "Punching the Clock," we enter through a gate, and punch in on a functioning time-clock – the first time I've had to do that since I worked many years ago in a supermarket. A notice explains why the clocks were introduced – another step in turning workers into disposable parts for the industrial machine – and how workers resisted.

Renee Johnston has just completed a certificate in museum studies. To prepare the exhibit, she took the design team through a working factory. "I wanted them to experience the atmosphere: Does it happen on overhead pulleys? How's the pace of work? What kind of sounds do you hear? How much light is there in the place? Then we tried to simulate some of those conditions in our exhibit. Instead of the typical museum setup behind rope or glass, or a gallery where art is something on a wall, we want people to walk through the exhibit, to experience it, to touch it and smell it."

She spins a large roulette wheel, at child-height. "Before the union came along, whether you got work or not was a huge gamble. You'd line up outside the factory very early in the morning, and the foreman would decide who got the available jobs that day. You were completely at their mercy."

Inside a locker, I press a button. A recorded voice tells me that if I offer a bottle of booze to the foreman, or if I say it's okay for him to pinch my wife's butt, maybe I'll get lucky the next day. "Really, it was that bad," says Renee. "That's taken from an interview we did for one of our oral history projects."

In the next room, we see a video simulation of a child's sixteen-hour working day in a garment factory. We hear a young girl and a woman compare notes on the experience. "We dramatized that from actual interviews that we've done," Renee says. "It would have been too difficult to edit down the original tapes. We also used testimony from government hearings when they were first developing the Factory Act."

The last section of "Punching the Clock" invites people to run a toy car along a chain that snakes through the display; they've got forty-three seconds to do it. "That's how long it takes a car to come off the line," says Renee. "It's a way of illustrating acceleration in the industrial process, and the demands that makes on workers. We've actually developed a school program out of this exhibit, working with teachers, and we're about to market it. This program is designed to connect to the business and technology units in the curriculum – we talk about the impacts that these processes have on people. With the education system so business-oriented right now, you have to be quite inventive in making the links."

A few years ago, Kathryn's local, CUPE 932, did an oral history project at the library with help from the centre. It was part of a wider project on public sector workers, called "Can I Help You? Canadian Workers at Your Service." "We partnered with a local writer, Bernadette Rule," says Kathryn. "She set up workshops so we could tell our stories – what it's like to work in a library, some of the funny, scary, validating, and awful things that happen. The interviews were transcribed, and we made them into a book."

For the sake of devil's advocacy, I ask her why it matters that workers' stories be told. "Because it's how we make sense of the world," she replies. "The media tells us who are the bad guys, what we should fear, who we should trust. That's not the real story, it's only the story of a few people who own the media. If you read Grisham, Steele and so on, you get the stories of rich, powerful characters in crisis – those are not our stories. Nobody in Hollywood is telling our stories. Oral history is our chance to tell our own versions – I say 'versions,' in the plural, because I don't believe there's only one. When we published the book about our experience as librarians, people said it put what we do in the bigger context of our commitment to the public. It made us all walk taller. That's ennobling, it makes people proud, and stronger. People can hear these stories, they can come into the resource centre here and see their union banners, read their charters, or a book that somebody wrote about their industry or service, and they can say, 'That's me, these are my people.'"

In another WAHC program Renee, with the help of cultural interpreters, worked with immigrant women from five countries to draw out their stories. "Essentially we asked the women one question, in two parts: Why are you here, and how are you doing? Many of them had never been asked this before, unless it was hostile, like 'What the hell are doing here, why don't you go back where you came from?' Some of them wept. They said, 'Nobody's ever cared enough to ask me that before.' They realized that no matter where they'd come from, they had shared experiences of persecution, war, dislocation, and worries about their children.

"Once they'd got their stories out, next they figured out what they wanted to do with them. In the end they produced four exhibits, working with local artists – a garden, a tapestry, an installation, and a sculpture. One weekend the whole group went camping. Some of them had been forced to live in camps before, but this was a very different experience – they were here by choice. Sitting at the campfire, eating, they became quite a spectacle in the campground. People there weren't used to seeing such a diverse group of women, and with no male partners. But they were able to get up, to sing and dance, and the whole campground ended up in a big circle around them, clapping. It was a wonderful homecoming experience. After that, some of the women took computer courses, which is something they would never have done before. Others felt brave enough to talk to politicians about getting other family members here. I know it's a bit of a cliché, but I really do think the project helped them find their voices. And the starting point was to say, 'Your story matters.'"

As for any organization that exists for reasons other than profit, survival is an open question at WAHC. I asked Renee how they get by. "We get some funding from unions," she says, "but then of course unions across the country are under siege these days, so their resources are limited. We get some revenue from renting space to three tenants, and we do fund-raising, for example, from foundations. The current [Conservative, when we spoke] provincial government hasn't given us any money. We're not a big-sell operation, we try to maintain our dignity and not get into the desperate scrambling that some institutions do. I believe that if we have a good product, we'll get funded." The week I visited, the centre was waiting to hear results back from two major funding applications. "As we say in non-profit, we could be gone next week. But if that happens, at least we won't go out in an undignified way."

In the meantime, the centre continues to develop innovative programs. Kathryn describes a recent project that's about as close to cost-free as possible. "It's called 'Working Family Treasures.' We worked with grade school kids to identify some object of great value or meaning to the family. The students interviewed family members about why this object is important to them, why it's a treasure, then they wrote it up, they took some family photos, brought in the object, and together we made an exhibit. Opening day was great – the kids came, their relatives, teachers, the media. The kids were incredibly pumped to have their stories seen like that. And the grade eight teacher who worked with us on the project said it covered eight of ten curriculum requirements. Now we hope to develop it as an Internet template, so any community can use it to talk about their heritage, their identity, and their struggles."

ED THOMAS

On the day we tour the centre, a room in it is given over to polling booths for CUPE local elections. One of the candidates for Local 5167 recording secretary is Ed Thomas. He's also a past co-chair and currently a member of the board at WAHC. Later on at the CUPE office I ask him why he thought he'd make a good candidate.

"In twenty-two years I've learned a lot about the day-to-day affairs of the local," he replies. "I think I'm honest and sincere. I believe in what I'm doing, and I like to help people. Over the years, people come to trust you. Most of them know that if they ask me something, either I'll have an answer for them or I'll get it. Some people use union jobs as stepping stones to advance themselves into management. People know that's not my intent." Myrna Wood nods enthusiastically; she knows Ed from years of working together on union health and safety campaigns.

I know of him from his work as an oral historian and the author of three books; this is the first time we've met. He's solid, soft-spoken, and a little shy. My second question: On one of his books he's credited as Fast Eddie Thomas. How come? He laughs. "Many years ago I used to be in a bike club, the Black Rebels. If you belong to a club, you have to give it your all, but I couldn't – I was working afternoons and nights at the post office – that's why I left the club. I still have the bike. It's collecting rust in the back yard." He laughs.

First time around at school, he flunked a few times, repeated grades, got pushed ahead, flunked again. Eventually he quit. For a few years he did odd jobs, then worked at the post office for seven years. He tried the local adult education centre, the community college, then was accepted as a mature student at McMaster University. "They needed people like me to get funding for adult education," he says. "I went for a year, but I was way out of my league. Kids in class were just out of grade thirteen, I was twenty-six. They'd say words I didn't know what they meant."

In 1977 he started working as a labourer for the city, and after a few years, tractor driver. "There's two things I enjoy about it," he says. "First, if the job screws up, they know who to blame. If you're the head of a crew and other people aren't getting the job done, they still come to you. But if you're on a tractor, there's only the one person who can screw up. Also, when I'm by myself, it's an opportunity to think. In the three to four hours it takes to cut a field, you can think a lot. I like that. It's a chance to hash around projects I'm working on, to figure out different approaches. It can also drive you nuts. The mind can really get you." He smiles.

In 1989, Ed's union local was selected for a pilot project on literacy in the workplace, organized by the Workers' Education Centre and the Hamilton District Labour Council. Ed signed up. "I was vice-president of the union at the time. I was fairly effective in my local, but my spelling stank, and my vocabulary wasn't much good either. There were still words I couldn't understand. The literacy instructor came in, we talked a bit, then I said, 'So what's involved?' He told me that the way the course is structured, there's no set formula. You do what interests you."

He had convinced his local to buy a computer, an Epson with a twenty-megabyte hard-drive, state of the art at the time. "I took some night courses on how to work it, DOS and that kind of thing, but when I got back to the office I could never remember what they'd said. So we figured I could learn to use the thing and learn to spell at the same time for this literacy program. Meanwhile, a retired union member happened to donate some old photos to the union. I started looking at them, and anyone who was around would start trying to identify who the people were. So I got to thinking, our local's got a bit of a history. For my literacy project I decided to write a leaflet, nothing too big, just to give people an idea of what the union was about."

Why? "Most of what's written about unions is written by academics," he says. "There's hardly anything written by working people. But who can tell it better than us? I used to think pretty much like everyone else – we're just workers, who cares about our stories? But then I started to realize we're just as important as John A. Macdonald. Workers have shaped this country. You see plaques everywhere, such-and-such a great man built this city. But what about all the poor suckers who poured the cement and hammered the nails, where are they? Unions are organizations just like governments. They've won all kinds of positive changes that we all benefit from – it was unions that gave us the weekend! That's why these stories matter, and it's why we need to make sure they don't get lost."

I take a breath to ask my next question, but Ed isn't done yet. "You know, history gives you a sense of where you've come from, and that helps you to know where you should be going. If workers don't know about the struggles of the past, they're going to have the Mike Harrises [former Premier of Ontario, right-wing, anti-union] walking all over them. When union members say 'What does the union do for me?' I say 'Look at the safety boots, look at the extra statutory holidays, look at the paid vacation,' and don't think the employers gave these to us because they wanted to – other people have struggled long and hard to win these things. And none of them are guaranteed, we could lose them – " he snaps his fingers " – just like that."

Ed started his historical search by looking for documents. He raided people's attics and basements, rummaged through union offices, local archives and libraries, then plunged into the National Archives in Ottawa and the Labour Canada library in Hull. At the Archives he waded through thirty-eight boxes of old union files and RCMP files only recently opened to the public. "The files were collected during the early

1900s and related to the RCMP's activities centred around the monitoring – that's what they called it, but basically it was spying – on labour activists and radicals." At York University in Toronto he found rare wire recordings of a former union president. They could only be played and transferred to tape on an equally rare machine at the Sound and Moving Images Archives in Ottawa (see chapter 7).

In addition to the mountain of documents and photos he collected, Ed also went to the living sources – people who had built and sustained his local. As an oral historian, he started from scratch. "The first people I interviewed, I was like an idiot. I would tell them what I thought about things, then I'd go home and listen to the tape, and I'd hear more of me on there than them! After that I learned to just sit there and keep my mouth shut. I discovered that some of the older members knew a lot of people, so I started calling them, and then they would lead to somebody else. I have to say, some people really didn't remember all that much, so I'd try to tweak their memory a little – 'Isn't this what happened?' – then they'd say, 'Oh yeah, that's what happened.' Problem is, was it them telling it or was it me?"

He was writing a history. Did he ever worry about the accuracy of his narrators? "Sometimes," he replies. "Sometimes the interesting story isn't necessarily the most factual, but when you're writing a history you have to be as factual as you can. I would try to get other people to substantiate what actually happened, but then people remember things differently. Or I'd check it against the documents, especially for places and dates. If I couldn't substantiate something, but it was a good story, I would include it and say this is how so-and-so sees it. It's factual to that person – not deliberately fabricated. After that, readers can choose to believe it or not."

Along the way, he learned to listen between the lines. "One time at work, this guy said I should talk to Albert Page, he worked for the city from 1920 to 1933. I did. But when I asked him if he knew anything about the union, he just kept talking about his own job, how terrible the working conditions were and that kind of thing. I shut it out, I didn't think it would be any use. But then I started thinking about it – what he was really talking about was why we needed a union in the first place! So I asked him if we could talk again. But the second time I didn't get him on tape, I just wrote a lot of notes. He came up with some fantastic stuff."

There were also stories that got away. "One person I never got to was Frank Rogers, the Local 5 recording secretary for thirty-three years," says Ed. "I wrote him a few letters asking to talk to him, but he never got back to me. I found out later that he'd wanted to talk to me, but by then he couldn't, his health was failing. Then he died. A few months later, his wife dropped off some photos at the union office. She mentioned that her son had thrown out three filing cabinets of his dad's papers – just personal stuff, she said, like letters about union business! Stupid me! It still bugs me today. Why didn't I talk to his son – he's a supervisor with the city, management, we would never have even said 'hi' to each other, but for this it would have been so easy. Or why didn't I just go and get the stuff myself? Now it's gone. A major part of our history, gone."

By the time Ed was done, six years after he began, he had interviewed over sixty people, he had learned to spell, and his pamphlet had turned into a book, *The Crest of the Mountain: The Rise of CUPE Local Five in Hamilton*, published in 1995. Production and printing costs were covered by a grant from the Ontario Ministry of Labour during the NDP government, by a CUPE-organized fund-raising appeal, and by the city of Hamilton which provided a small grant, funded a student researcher for three months, and bought one hundred advance copies. Ed did all the research and writing on his own time. "I'm not Pierre Berton – I couldn't just lock myself in a cottage and write," he says. "I still had my job, my family, and my regular union work to take care of."

His second book, *A Worker's Guide to Doing a Local Union's History*, was published in 1999 by CUPE and the Workers Arts and Heritage Centre. "Workers should not be afraid to tell their own stories, to say it in their own words," he writes. "The time to write your union history is now! The longer you delay, the more difficult the process becomes. Memories become foggy, members die, documents are destroyed or lost forever. So why not start right now?"

The book is a distillation of everything Ed Thomas learned in researching and writing *The Crest of the Mountain*. In the "How to Conduct an Interview" section, he advises: "One key thing to remember when interviewing is to keep your mouth shut. Don't offer people what you think the answers should be. Sometimes you may have to sit on your hands and bite your tongue because you are dying to say something. The purpose of the interview is to hear what the person is saying. If you really want to hear yourself talk, you can go home and interview yourself."

In his third book, *Dead but Not Forgotten*, Ed turned his attention to the millions of workers who die on the job or as a result of it, and the worldwide movement to honour their lives. He quotes statistics from the International Confederation of Free Trade Unions (ICFTU): 335,000 deaths a year from occupational accidents, 12,000 of which involve children; 325,000 deaths a year from occupational diseases, as well as unionists murdered, attacked, arrested, and fired for their trade union activities.

How did the book come to pass? "In 1984, CUPE became the first union in the world to recognize April 28th as a day of mourning for workers killed on the job," he says. "Then in 1991 a private member's bill got assent in Parliament, and Canada became the first country to officially recognize April 28. So I got the idea, why not write a book about this whole movement? I mentioned it to a few people, and by the end of the day people had told me about five different monuments."

I saw one of them in Hamilton, in a park next to the City Hall: a tall panel of rusted steel – this is the Steel City – slightly tilted, with a figure dangling off it, barely holding on by both hands to the top edge. The figure is damaged, corroded, its head torn off, the neck a twist of metallic tissue.

Ed began to lobby unions and governments to raise funds and support for his project. "One day I got a call from the ICFTU in Brussels inviting me to a health and safety meeting over there, but they told me I would have to get my own funding. Myrna [Wood]'s local paid for my air fare, CUPE Ontario paid for accommodation, and some individuals threw in some money as well. Anything left over from the trip went into the book." At the ICFTU's request, Ed co-ordinated two international union delegations to lobby country representatives at the UN to support the day of mourning. "At last count trade unions in 120 countries have recognized it and about ten governments."

I ask him what's next on his agenda. "Well, I've got this idea floating around," he says, "to write something about ordinary people that made a difference in their community. Maybe they saved somebody's life in a fire, maybe they coach kids in trouble, that kind of thing – not famous people, just everyday people, the kind that if you read about them in the paper, in a week you wouldn't remember them. I'd like to get a sense of why they did it and where they are now. There's that, and – oh, about six other ideas floating around in my head. That's what you get when you drive a tractor!"

It's late in the day. I'm packing up my recorder and tapes. Ed and Myrna chat about old times and the union election. Then Ed says, "You know what oral history is? It's passing it on. That's how I think of it – passing it on."

His parting shot reminds me of something Ken Clavette said in Ottawa, also at the end of our interview. (There's a lesson here: it's not over until it's over.) Ken said, "If someone shares their story with you, you have a responsibility to share something back. Let's say you make a union video, and you interview thirty people, you end up with maybe sixty hours of tape – for a one-hour documentary. Where does the rest of the story go? You've got the story of that union there. If you don't preserve it, if you record over the tapes so you can use them again, you lose the full picture. All you've got in your documentary is the highlights. Can you imagine just watching the highlights of a soccer game? This is my sense of oral history: It doesn't belong to any one of us, it belongs to all of us. The Dead Sea scrolls, Einstein's brain, the genome sequence – these things don't belong to two or three researchers, they belong to humanity. That's especially true of oral history, it belongs to all of us. Oral history is community."

CHAPTER 12

TURNING THE TABLES

When a friend read *Eating Fire*, my book on queer relationships, she was bothered by a controversial chapter about a man who spent a third of his life in prison for having sex with males in their teens. "You say what he thought, and you say what other people thought of him," she commented, "but you never say what *you* think of him. I want to know that." I argued that she was really asking me to make a judgment on the man, and that wasn't my job; very likely, neither did she know what I thought about any of the other people in the book. She wasn't satisfied. And the exchange left me wondering: Is it possible that I hide behind the oral-historian mask, to avoid showing my own writer's face?

This is the kind of question I wanted to explore in looking at my own work. But given the focus of this book – the gathering of people's stories through interviews – it seemed only fair that I should go through the same interview process as others did who agreed to share their stories with me.

Since 2001 I've interviewed Elisabeth Pozzi-Thanner three times about her oral history work (see chapters 9 and 10). More than once she has said, "One of these days I'd love to turn the tables and interview you." In September 2003 I wrote to her, "I'm coming to New York in November. Here's your chance." She agreed to do the interview.

I met Elisabeth in June 2001 at the Columbia University Summer Institute on Oral History. She impressed me with the quality of her questions and comments, which seemed to be informed by compassionate intelligence. One afternoon, she complimented me on my courage for having come out to a group of strangers. "It's why I'm here," I replied. "This work is supposed to be about the freedom for people to tell their stories, and being gay is an essential part of mine." Despite my offhanded response, I did appreciate her active gesture of support. Since then I've come to regard Elisabeth as a friend. I also suspected that her experience as a journalist would be an asset in interviewing me.

I approached our encounter in New York with a familiar, escalating anxiety. When I write, I can sit quietly and compose my thoughts, shaping and refining them until I'm satisfied or, more likely, the deadline arrives. Normally when I give interviews, whether to promote a new book or make points on a political issue that impassions me, I rehearse mentally for days in advance, shaping and refining what needs to be said. Even so, inevitably by the time of the actual event, my tension – performance anxiety, really – has reached fever pitch. So it had when I sat down with Elisabeth. She was surprised when I told her. I've learned to hide the signs, though if we had shaken hands rather than hugged, she couldn't have missed the chill in mine.

Contrary to my usual obsession with getting it right, in this case I doubted my capacity for candour. I told Elisabeth, "As a child I learned that it was dangerous to say what I really thought or felt, so I learned to package it in ways that would be acceptable to others. Sometimes that can be useful, but in doing this interview I worry that I may not be able to resist that kind of packaging, out of habit. I want to answer your questions freely, but I'm not at all sure that I will know how."

"That's for you to judge when you listen to it. I can't judge it." She smiled, graciously. We carried on.

Elisabeth interviewed me face-to-face for three hours in New York. Then I asked her to do a follow-up interview by phone a couple of weeks later, when we talked for another two-and-a-half hours. As I did with the other interviews, I transcribed the results, then shaped them into this chapter. I resisted the strong temptation to rewrite some of my words but did reduce and rearrange them somewhat, as I have done with other interviews. However, I allowed myself a benefit that others didn't have – the comfort of second thoughts. After all, it is my book!

In our first interview Elisabeth asks about my motives for getting into oral history. Since it's probably more accurate to say I fell into it (see chapter 1), I need to begin at the beginning, before oral history, before writing, in the strange garden of my childhood. "When I was growing up, long before I had any sense of being gay, I was an outsider in my family. Sometimes I felt I was from another planet – things I thought, my friends, were all seen as weird by the others in my family. My mother used to say that I was the noisiest baby in the nursery – she'd be joking, but I always knew the subtext was that it was embarrassing for her. Or they'd say, 'There he goes again' – 'agin the government' was my grandmother's expression for me – that's all they could see, this contrary child, regardless of any legitimate reasons I might have had for being at odds with them. That's how they dismissed anything from me that they didn't want to hear – 'You're just contrary, always agin the government.' So I had no way of knowing there could be any justification for what I felt. And though of course I never thought of it this way at the time, that seems to have led me to identify with people who are outsiders, people who are not heard."

Elisabeth asks, "In the '60s when you got those horrible treatments [see chapter 1], that was also a way of trying to silence you, wasn't it?" I reply, "Yes, sure. And the scary thing is, not only did I consent to the electric shocks, I actually sought them out. I had fundamentally absorbed this notion that I didn't fit, so there must be something wrong with me, in which case I had to remake myself somehow. And here was one thing I could do: I could make myself into a heterosexual, which is what you're supposed to be."

Am I rambling, I wonder, is the package getting too bulky? But Elisabeth looks expectant, encouraging – the gift of a good interviewer – which I take as permission to forge ahead. "When I came out and got involved in gay liberation, it wasn't primarily from the point of sexual liberation – that part was always more difficult for me – but as another way of confronting this thing I had been resisting all along, unjust power. Now I would resist consciously and conscientiously. That to me is what this notion of finding voice is about."

"When you use the word 'power,' is it empowering others that you're interested in?" Elisabeth asks. I reply, "In gay liberation, and since, I've understood the fundamental struggle as being about justice, and much more broadly, about the right to live fully, which means you have to identify the ways that people are *not* allowed to live fully – materially of course, in the sense of poverty, or simply being wiped off face of the earth, but all the other, more subtle ways that people are denied the right to live fully. We all have the capacity in one form or another to speak, act, think critically, to make connections, but all those capacities can be contained, denied, and impoverished. So for me, empowering is freeing those capacities to the degree that they can be. Unless they are freed, we can't act in the larger arena. But sadly, instead of trying to find these capacities in ourselves, often we look for them in somebody else, so we continue to elect the Bushes of this world. In the schoolyard it's the bully – if I stand behind him, I'll be okay. Finding those capacities in ourselves – that's the motive for me in doing this kind of work."

Given the two guiding themes I mentioned in the first chapter – finding voice and making sense – there is another formative experience I neglected to mention to Elisabeth: As a child I was punished frequently in various ways, including physical violence, for being Bad. A thoughtful child, I kept trying to figure it out, to make sense – what did it actually *mean*, being Bad? It was important to know. If I knew, maybe I could avoid getting hit. If I got it right, maybe I'd be loved. I never did get it right. But still, I keep trying to make sense. By now it's a habit.

Sometimes it can be useful – for example, in discerning subtext in an interviewee's response, so that a follow-up question can be formed to elicit further detail or depth. Sometimes it can be a nuisance, for example, in an argument with my partner, when pointing out subtext (or worse, internal contradictions) is rarely appreciated.

And sometimes it's no use at all, for example, in trying to figure out why people would choose to vote for leaders who casually support torture and mass murder. It doesn't make sense.

At one point in our first interview, Elisabeth asks, "Have you always used writing as your final goal in your oral history work?" It's a good question, but since the writing came first and the oral history impulse only showed up later, and even then had to be identified by others, I have to turn the question around in my mind, to something like this: How did oral history happen to find its way into my work?

I reply, "Before writing the books, I've made films, videos, and radio documentaries, and without any conscious intent it seemed to come to me that a natural way to understand people's stories was to listen to them, and give them space. One radio documentary I made was with a progressive American Jesuit worker-priest who had been in Chile – under the Pinochet regime, he was arrested, tortured, then expelled. This was a half-hour documentary, just him talking about himself. Most radio producers don't approve of that, you're supposed to insert yourself, but what was I to say about these things? Of course I asked him questions, and edited it down to thirty minutes – that's how I inserted myself. Similarly, in the early '80s I made two of the first videos about AIDS, again with no narrator. They had a specific function, to deal with the panic, but so little was known then and I knew nothing at all. So I talked with nurses, doctors, people working with the blood supply, asking them what they did know, or think they knew. I also talked with the first man in Canada to speak publicly about his experience with AIDS. He died during the making of the videos. This is how I learn: I ask questions."

In some of the interviews I've done for this book, people have commented that being interviewed gave them a rare opportunity to reflect on what it is they actually do in their oral history work. The same is true for me. I continue, "This questioning approach is rooted in the notion that the story is the essential human communicative medium, that in some way people *are* their stories. By conveying that, you somehow convey something essential about the person, their connections to others and to the world, which after all is politics – how we know our place in the world, or refuse our place in the world, and demand a larger or better or safer place. That's the most funda- mental form of politics, the part I think matters the most, rather than the 'big' politics. Especially now – who can make sense of the big poli- tics? So the question is, how do you find in people their own potential to create?"

On the page, it reads a bit like a pamphlet. But that's what I said, and it is what I believe.

Elisabeth asks me if I experience a tension between my two roles, oral historian and writer. "Often," I say. "As a listener, I want to respect the authentic voice of the narrator, but as a writer I want to generate material that's compelling to readers. Sometimes it's a balancing act – you have to weigh something you think will make a strong image, a provocative statement, against the possibility that it might have a neg- ative impact for the narrator."

Recently I asked people to check the profiles I'd written about them for a local newspaper, based on interviews they gave to an oral history class I led. Some of the changes they requested were to correct inaccuracies, but more often people were anxious to avoid being mis- understood or upsetting others in our small rural community. In each case, the person said something along these lines, "That is what I said, but now that I see it written down . . . " The lesson for me: People, especially those not accustomed to packaging their stories for public consumption, are quite capable of trusting an apparently empathetic interviewer far more than they should. I'm uncomfortably aware of how easy it would be to exploit that trust.

I can also experience tension in my role as conduit for other people's realities versus my own point of view, as person and writer, I tell Elisabeth. "When I wrote *The First Stone* [on the battle over homo- sexuality and ministry in the United Church of Canada], I went across the country interviewing hundreds of people who'd played some role in the fight. When I talked to people that I knew hated homosexuals, I didn't tell them I was one. I had qualms about this – not on ethical grounds but from my own sense that coming out is essential to human dignity. But I suspected that if bigots knew, either they wouldn't talk to me or they'd be much more guarded in what they said. If anyone asked, I wouldn't deny my sexuality, but otherwise I would say nothing." To my surprise, no one asked.

"I ended up in some interview situations where people would say to me, 'Homosexuals should be put on a boat, sent out into the ocean, and sunk.' I knew my job as a writer was not to argue, but to say, 'That's interesting. Now why do you think that?' As a child I learned to hide my feelings, so by then I could do it quite well, without apparent effort. But of course I'd come away from situations like that feeling poisoned, and very angry. Then critics said *The First Stone* was a good book because it was so fair! Not only did that 'fairness' cost me dearly, but in retrospect I came to understand that it was also something of a fraud. I did convey exactly what the bigots said, word for word, but of course my interpretation came through in the way the whole book was shaped. It strikes me now as rather hypocritical to have played this 'objective' role when I have such a strong antipathy to the colossal, carefully groomed lie that mainstream journalists are objective and balanced."

After that, in the next three books I've become much more present and engaged as the writer. Even so, when I write about other people I still feel an obligation to be quite careful with what is, after all, the material of their lives. It is this carefulness that led to the argument that opened this chapter.

Next project for me is a novel. There, I imagine, I will have no obligations to anyone but the characters.

In our second interview, Elisabeth asks, "What can you tell me about the value in seeing things from the margins?" I have to confess here: I put her up to asking this and several other questions. In typing the transcript of our first interview, I was amazed at how much I had forgotten to say. It's another sharp lesson from the other end of the microphone. I asked Elisabeth to do a follow-up interview by phone, and with a degree of temerity I now find embarrassing, sent her a list of questions I wanted her to include. People that I interview hardly ever get to see their transcripts, and rarely do I ask them for follow-up interviews – hence no opportunity for second thoughts of the sort I'm having. Still, as I said, it *is* my book.

Fortunately, Elisabeth had the good sense and skill to pursue her own lines of inquiry, but she also did pose my pre-scripted questions, an act of kindness on her part. To the question about seeing things from the margins, I reply, "When I was growing up, it was with the assumption that I'd be of the elite that defined reality for others. When I dislocated myself from that, one of the costs was losing the comfortable assumptions that went with it. I think of it in a way as being inside or outside a castle. Inside, it may be dark and stifling, you have to dress right and say the right things, but at least you know your way around, you can function automatically. Whereas outside, where things are much less clearly defined, you're more exposed to all the elements of the earth. You have to be better able to improvise. That's the trade-off, security for freedom. Out here on the margins, if you've chosen to be here – so many people in the world don't have any choice – your energy can go into noticing how things work, who holds power, how people think, what they fear. You can certainly see the impacts more clearly than when you're inside the castle. That can be turned into a gift, where voices speaking from the margins can say things that might not otherwise be said."

Elisabeth says, "If you're a bird that sits on the tower, you can observe it all, you can fly off, sometimes you can be even fed by them." The journalist in her doesn't miss the irony. We share a laugh.

But now I wonder about this castle analogy of mine. Unlike the vast majority of my fellow earthlings, I live in a country where it's still possible to live well-insulated from harm, I have a mortgage-free home, a decent well, enough to eat, an abundant garden, woods to walk through and cut firewood from, a talented, loving partner, occasional income, national health care, even a car. Isn't it rather self-right-eous to portray myself as being 'outside the castle'? On the other hand, given global climate collapse and deepening drought, how long will our well last? Given our ages, how long can we continue to cut and haul firewood? How occasional will the income get? When and how much will we have to pay for privatized health care? How long will the car last? What will be left of the Canada Pension once the free-market vultures have had their fill of it?

Following on the inside/outside theme, Elisabeth asks, "How do you experience the outsider/insider role in doing interviews?" In oral history jargon, an "insider" interviewer shares fundamental group connections with the interviewee, and is thus, at least in theory, more likely to be trusted, and to elicit greater candour in the interview. For Elisabeth, an Austrian Gentile whose first formal oral history task was to conduct interviews with Jewish Holocaust survivors, the question is close to her heart.

I reply, "In my work in radio and film, generally I was an outsider. For example in talking with a union organizer in Mozambique, or a peace worker in Guatemala, or a traditional healer in Fiji, usually by phone – there I'm a big outsider. In those conversations, I would look for common ground. If I was to be a conduit, which is how I saw my role, I felt I needed to comprehend something fundamental about what the person was saying, so I could transmit it properly. That's part of the listening. Even as an outsider, there are moments when you can identify with someone because you recognize links to your own experience, or at least through imagination. At the same time, you have to be respectful enough not to pretend that you have an inside track on somebody else's experience. It's a balancing act."

A slight pause, then I say, "Uh, what was your question?" It's a hazard of the trade. In the thickets of a response, the original question can easily go missing. When I'm the interviewer, now and then even *I* can forget where we started. This implies a lapse in attention, a cardinal sin for any interviewer. But Elisabeth hasn't slipped. "About being an insider or outsider in interviews," she prompts.

Nudged back on track, I continue, "In the books where I wrote about gay and lesbian experience, there was a lot more common ground for me, especially in dealing with other gay men, and to some extent with lesbians – that was like visiting another province, but in the same country. When I dealt for the first time with transgender people, that enlarged the frame for me a lot. But still it's the same method. If I wonder about something – why someone would undergo highly invasive and still somewhat experimental surgery in order to get a penis, for example – I ask. That's my way of learning how the world works. It also reminds me that the ways people can be silenced can be much broader and subtler than someone holding a gun to your head."

Elisabeth pursues the insider/outsider question. "How do you think it influences the way an interviewee will respond to you?" I reply, "I suppose it could be said that you're always an outsider in a way. Even when I interviewed my own mother, I was an outsider, because you're not that person, you live outside their experience, even if you know something about it. Then it becomes a question of degrees of outsiderness, all the way from me interviewing Fijian traditional healers to my own mother."

Elisabeth questions, "Doesn't it also happen, for example with your mother, that you don't touch certain topics, whereas when you interview someone as a friendly stranger from far away, people may tell you things they might not to someone who's more familiar?" Probably, she's right, I say. "There can be safety in distance – as in the classic situation of strangers on a train, they tell each other all their secrets, on the assumption that they'll never meet again."

In our face-to-face encounter in New York, she asks how intrusive I'm prepared to be as an interviewer. "The clue seems to be in how well you pay attention," I say. "If you're being invasive, they may not say, 'It's none of your business' – many people aren't confident enough to do that. So you have to watch carefully to see if they're evading something, and if so, how far can you pursue that, is there a way to come at it from another direction? This is not an attempt to deceive, but to make it easier for them. If the same thing happens again, then maybe it's reasonable to ask, 'Would you rather not talk about this?' If they say, 'Yes, I would rather not,' then sometimes I will ask, 'Can you tell me why you'd rather not?' Sometimes that does it, it removes the obstacle, and out it comes." Elisabeth smiles and nods. "You, too?" I ask. "Oh yes," she replies.

She pursues the matter of intrusiveness – not surprising, given that much of her interview work has focused on people who've survived deeply traumatic events. "How far can you go in asking questions, when there might be a risk of retraumatizing someone?" Having had no training in trauma work, I know I'm out of my depth here but attempt a response from my own observations. "When I encounter people who've had bitter, difficult, or frightening experiences, intuitively I try to feel my way as to how much I have the right to probe. Given that we have made a tacit contract, and this is an opportunity for them to tell their story, how much right do I have – or obligation – to try to explore that story as fully as possible? Sometimes it does unnerve me how candid people will be with a complete stranger who lands in their life for two or three hours, then disappears. That's the strangers-on-the-train thing. Especially when you're not showing people their transcripts, you need to have pretty good built-in filters yourself."

Then Elisabeth asks another of my pre-scripted questions: "How does oral history serve as an antidote to despair?"

Some context: If I look only at the version of the world that comes down at us through the wires from Media Central, all I see is disaster, cruelty, hypocrisy, and terminal ignorance – the most fertile grounds for despair, in me and in other passionate, engaged people that I know. In my own experience, I equate despair closely with feeling helpless. In the absence of action, information becomes sediment, a dense, dark, overwhelming shroud.

"I think the authorities understand very well how to make us feel helpless," I reply. "When I saw *Triumph of the Will* [Leni Riefenstahl's 1934 filmic hymn to Nazi power], it was my impression that it sets out to convey an almost cosmic power, like the weather or God, that people would feel it's impossible to resist. Authorities do this all the time with their pomp, glitter, their 'Shock and Awe.' They project themselves into figures much larger than they really are, to make us feel, what can we do but support them or shut up? So I'm always looking for signs of the capacity, in myself and in others, to see through the lies, to think, act, resist tyranny, to find our own ways of acting rationally and compassionately. In people I've encountered for this book, I find confirmation of that. For me, that's very comforting, to find people acting compassionately and with reason – some of them under very difficult, even dangerous conditions – in what I would regard as a good human way to be in the world."

This line of thought leads to another question I've asked Elisabeth to pursue: Am I a parasite? She asks it with evident discomfort. I can't imagine her asking anything so rude, not of her own accord. In fact, it's the wrong question, a neurotic detour. I should have followed a line of inquiry I pursued with other people in this book: Is anything really accomplished by this work?

"It's so easy to live in illusion," I reply. "One of the illusions I worry about is the assumption that this work does have some effect, in 'giving voice' to people. But does it really? And then what? Do their voices just get ignored by the thugs who run this world, as mine does? Is all of this just self-serving talk, a make-work project for me? I don't know how to tell. How do you measure these things?"

Elisabeth retorts, "Does it need to be measured?"

I come back: "It's just that I'm so aware of politicians who say, 'I'm doing this for your own good,' which is something I heard all the time as a child. I was punished for my own good, they said, it would make me a better person, but nearly always the things I was punished for were authentic aspects of who I was. So here is a perfect self-serving illusion for the person with power. I struggle with that in own desire to feel I'm having some impact."

Elisabeth looks at me for a moment, then says, "There are several ways I see a person can have impact. You seem to be one of those I cherish the most, not a flashy superficial impact that maybe touches thousands, or millions, for fifteen seconds, or hours, or even weeks, but you have a transformative, silent impact on individuals that therefore goes far deeper, far longer."

I think to myself that this is an extraordinarily generous thing to say. Elisabeth is a generous person. Have I set her up? On the other hand, I trust her. It's a quandary. "I'd like to believe that, but I don't have any clear sense of it from within," I say. "That's what comes of being so at odds with the surrounding culture, which honours flash, celebrity, and quick satisfactions. When you set yourself at odds with that, there's very little way to affirm what it is you're doing, and it's hard to discern any gains from it. The kind of impact you're describing is so subtle, it's so hard to detect."

"But that's only because it's an immaterial, spiritual, personal impact you have," says Elisabeth. "It's not to be measured in numbers, you can't measure it like stocks going up and down on Wall Street, nor would you want to."

We continue in this vein for a while, Elisabeth arguing that the value of art can't be measured in concrete terms, and neither can human relations, I pursuing my own search for clarity on an impossible question. But then we're running out of time.

Now the tables have been turned, and we've interviewed each other. To wrap things up, Elisabeth asks, "Does the experience of being interviewed change the way we might do interviews? What do you think?"

I come at it indirectly, via a recurring theme: "My training as a child led me to always assess what I needed to do or say in order to be loved – or not to get into trouble, which I thought was the same thing. This became an automatic process with me, where everything I said was pre-thought, packaged to be acceptable to the adult, the authority figure. Given that experience, I'm inclined to think that for some people, especially ones who aren't used to expressing themselves, there may be a desire to read what the interviewer wants to hear. They will listen very carefully to your questions – 'Ah, so she wants to hear about my suffering, or how courageous I was, or she does *not* want to hear that I was *not* courageous.' That makes it quite crucial to be as un-leading as possible in the questions. When I'm interviewing people on projects in some way connected to my social/political interests, I have an agenda. Sometimes I will hear things in the interviews that support my agenda, sometimes not. The challenge for me is to avoid steering people toward sounding more like I think they should. Surely the whole point of it is, if a person hasn't had a voice, the voice that eventually comes out shouldn't be the voice *I* want to hear, it should be their own true voice, however that may sound."

I pause. Lost again. "What was your question?"

CHAPTER 13

A Really Tender One-Night Stand

There was a crippled paperboy, and he was gay. Some thugs decided to rob him one night and they took him out behind an alley and started beating up on him. This was right down where the Castle used to be. We saw this happening, got these two thugs, and beat the shit out of them. Meantime, somebody had phoned the police. They showed up and said "Oh, you're doing a pretty good job," turned their backs for a while, and said, "Go to it." They knew this paperboy was gay, and it was a gay crowd that was beating up on these thugs. The police were fair.

❁ N.S., born 1926, interviewed by Robert Rothon and Myron Plett for the *Tides of Men* project

ROBERT
AND MYRON   Returning to Montreal one summer from the cottage, the Rothon family stopped at a restaurant in the Laurentian mountains north of the city. Young Robert took an immediate shine to the waiter, and followed him on his rounds. The waiter told the boy this was his last day on the job; tomorrow he would

go back to school. Robert asked his father, "Can we bring him home?" "Why?" asked the father, a little surprised. "Because he's pretty!" said Robert. The memory is still clear with him, and by way of corroboration, he mentions that his sister also remembers the incident. Robert was four years old.

Robert suggested that we meet in the bar at the Hotel Vancouver, a convenient rendezvous for him and Myron Plett, coming from work. The hotel is an imposing baronial castle from the heyday of the transcontinental railroads. A man in a suit plays unobtrusive ballads on the piano nearby. We are all shocked to discover that a pint of beer costs $8.

Robert describes his coming out as "really breezy." Montreal was no paradise, he says, "but at least you didn't get that kind of vicious homophobia in political and cultural circles that's still fairly typical in some parts of the West. So really I never had much of a problem with being gay, no emotion-laden journey. That tended to skew my relationship to queer political movements – I don't respect them that much, though in some way I do understand them. As a Québecois, I'm familiar with the victimization discourse. It was drilled into me through childhood. But at some point you have to ask, does this really help me become who I wish to be, and to make my way in the world?"

For Myron Plett, coming out was far from breezy. He grew up in rural Manitoba in a family of conservative Mennonites. "The words 'gay' or 'homosexual' were never breathed aloud," he says. "By the time I could name these feelings, I was already seventeen or eighteen, and all I could say was they were horribly wrong. As many do when they're denying their feelings, I went to seminary and entered the ministry. By the end of the year, the anguish had reached the point where either I had to explore a new avenue or kill myself."

The new avenue he chose was Vancouver. Still in the ministry, Myron happened to meet a woman who, though also conservative, told him that the feelings he had didn't make him an evil person – it was only a sin if he acted on them. "Realizing then that I needed something more instinctive to go on than my inherited beliefs, I left the ministry in 1991, stopped going to church, and started to figure out who I am. It took me several years after that to accept myself as a gay man."

In 1994, during heated public debate over including homosexuals in proposed federal legislation on hate crimes, Alberta Member of Parliament Myron Thompson told a large meeting, "I do not hate homosexuals; I hate homosexuality." The controversial MP represented the riding of Wild Rose for the Reform Party, aka Canadian Alliance Party, recently merged into the new Conservative Party of Canada. Other Reform/Alliance MPs had made public statements along the same lines. One said that if he allowed a homosexual to work in his store, it would only be in the back, to avoid contact with customers.

Myron Thompson's "I hate homosexuality" comment attracted national attention, both for and against. Robert happened to hear it on TV. "Generally I wash my hands of bigots," he says. "But in this case I was really shocked that he could talk like that about people like me, people I know – we're perfectly nice people! I thought surely if these Reform bigots knew more about the history of gay people in Canada, it would be less easy for them to make such vile, annoying, and stupid comments, or at least to get away with making them, not to be called on them."

Myron happened to be working at a record shop that Robert frequented. "I knew of him as the only good writer at the time with the old *Angles* [a Vancouver gay newspaper, now defunct]," says Robert. "Otherwise it was drowning in gender-politic-speak, written by political wannabes. Myron could write, and he did good interviews."

"I had only recently come out of closet," says Myron, "and there was very little for me to refer to in the way of local lore or experience that I could relate to. Any stories I found were from the U.S. – 'over there,' a different place with a different culture and values. I wanted a map I could identify with. I concluded that if I couldn't find it, I would just have to write it."

One day at the record store, Robert raised the idea: Why didn't they do a history of gay men and lesbians in Canada? "Coming from Quebec, where history is such a big thing – though often it's manipulated for political purposes – I could see the need to develop our own history. I think it's folly to keep referring to the American experience as universal. Stonewall, for example, was an American phenomenon, not Canadian." The 1969 riots of queer street folk at the Stonewall Bar in New York are commonly identified as the spark that launched the contemporary gay liberation movement in North America. "As long as we keep using the U.S. experience as a universal template, we won't be able to read our own political and cultural landscape accurately."

But why pursue history at all, I asked Robert. What does it mean to him? "I find it utterly fascinating," he replies. "My interest in it started at my mother's knee – my favourite way of spending time with her was to ask her to tell family stories. I come from a large French-Canadian family, so she had a lot of stories, and she would tell them over and over. I never got tired of it. The result is that now I'm the archivist of our immediate family."

When he settled in Vancouver, Robert got a job at Radio Canada, the francophone side of the Canadian Broadcasting Corporation. "In five years as a researcher there, I did literally thousands of interviews with people, as backgrounders for on-air stories and interviews. So when I was spurred to action by Mr Thompson's intemperate comments, what did I know how to do? Research, interviews."

But still, why does history really matter? "Mammals die, we're a finite species," he replies. "To understand why things got to be how they are in the present, we need to know what went on before us. We can't aim for fairness and justice unless we have points of historical reference to help us understand what justice is, what is fair and what is not. That's one reason land claims are so hard in British Columbia – people don't understand the history of the First Nations and the European settlers. The Alliance Party says there should be no special treatment for First Nations. Instead they invite them to take part in our wonderful free market culture. But when some First Nations tried to do that in the nineteenth century, the Europeans wouldn't let them. They were barred from economic activities. Once you know that, it becomes harder to make such ignorant statements."

Myron was hooked. "I'd been quite dissatisfied with my work for *Angles*. I found them so obsessed with being oppressed, they're weren't really saying or doing anything new. When Robert started talking about doing the history project, it struck me as an opportunity for different voices to be heard, and a way to give others access to all kinds of information that I never had. Robert and I often discuss what seems a doomed-to-fail effort to portray the gay community as a single unified group – it's anything but, our interviews prove that – and to argue that we're constantly in peril for our lives, which is an exaggeration that doesn't wash. I propose that if the so-called leaders of the gay community changed their tune to talking about how progress for us, like relationship recognition, will result in benefits for the entire society and economy, you'd soon see a turn-around. That's one reason I did this project, to say, 'Here are the contributions of gay men in British Columbia to the fabric of Canadian culture. How can you say we should be working at the back of the store?'"

In the winter of 1995 the two applied to the Canada Council's Explorations section, a program that supported innovative projects. By this point they had narrowed their focus from queer folk across Canada to gay men in British Columbia, a much more manageable scale. "We proposed to interview a whole bunch of people," said Robert. "Originally we approached *Xtra West* [a Vancouver gay paper, new at the time], and asked if they would publish the interviews. The editor said no, he didn't think their readership would be interested. That was our first rejection – if we couldn't find a publisher, how could we do a book? Then Myron said, 'Why not use the Internet?' I said, 'What's that?' I didn't even have a computer!"

Myron adds, "The record shop had installed a computer section, so I could go on the Internet and learn my way around. I was pretty confident it would be the next big thing – this was before it turned into a shopping centre. I saw it as a good way to keep our delivery costs down, and to put the interviews into public hands, in an anonymous fashion, so people wouldn't have to go to a library and ask for the book. To our delight, the Canada Council said yes, they gave us

$15,000. They particularly liked the Internet idea. They said no one had used it this way before, to deliver serious Canadian content."

GLENN

Across the Atlantic, Dr Glenn Smith has been gathering stories of homosexuals who endured aver-
sion therapy in Britain from the 1950s to the present. When I heard of his work, I was immediately intrigued.

In 1968, while millions of people around the world were on the streets demanding peace and justice, I signed up to be tortured by a psychiatrist. Terrified that I might be homosexual, I submitted to a new regime called "aversion therapy." It didn't take – such tinkerings hardly ever do – and a few years later I came out.

Glenn Smith didn't go through aversion therapy, nor is he gay. He arrived by quite another route at his current job. In 1995 an adviser suggested that for his Masters thesis in human geography he write a critical autobiography of his own experience. At age ten, Glenn's kidneys had started to fail, and by seventeen he was on weekly dialysis. Two years later his illness went into remission, and eventually he was strong enough to continue his education, specializing in human geography, the study of how people interact with their environments. In his thesis, "Let My Silence Be Loud," he explored how growing up with a chronic illness had shaped his sense of self, as well as his relationships with other people and the spaces he inhabited. The perspective is social rather than medical; according to the social model, people are disabled less by the impairment itself than by obstacles and limitations in their environments. "This wasn't just an oral history on my own life," he says. "I tried to relate my own experience to a wider political perspective, especially in terms of masculinity and sexuality."

I ask him to be more specific about obstacles and limitations. "A lot of it is related to how people treat you," he says. "For example, in school or in hospital, you find yourself feeling trapped by people's assumption of how you should and should not behave, and how you should be treated as a boy growing up with an illness. People will throw heroic stereotypes at you – 'Look at this person with MS [multiple sclerosis] who manages to play soccer,' and such. If you don't live up to that, it's hard not to feel that you're lacking. It was only through reading a lot of material on disability that I could see my own experience in a larger context – it wasn't just me, I was doing my best. Suddenly you're aware of this other way of looking at all these assumptions of what's expected of you, or not, if you're ill."

One day at college he parked his car in a space marked with a wheelchair symbol. The security guard told him he couldn't park there. "I was on peritoneal dialysis at the time," says Glenn, "which meant I had to carry several bags of fluid to change during the day. They asked if I could walk. I told them yes, I could, but I can't carry these bags twelve minutes up the road. That kind of thing didn't fit into any of their accepted definitions of disability. I explained it to them, I showed them the bags, and finally, reluctantly, they let me park there. It can get tiring when you have to explain and argue like that." This is the stuff of human geography.

The way he relates to "normality" strikes a clear chord with someone raised in a world that dictates the only way to be normal is to be heterosexual. In his Ph.D. thesis, "No-Man's-Land," he writes: "I was often caught in a double bind. Because of my chronic illness I could not achieve the 'normality' that I was supposed to be able to. . . . On the one hand I had to accept my fate with good grace, stoicism, strength and individual morality, whilst at the same time behave and find my place as a 'normal' child. This had the effect of having to deny my own reality in order to appear 'normal.' This non-existent identity or, no-man's-land across which I had to negotiate my life, soon became difficult. I would often avoid places because of the difficulties and the energy involved in having to fulfil 'normal' expectations. Eventually the overwhelming pressures on my thoughts and feelings became instrumental in governing my use of places." It sounds familiar.

For his dissertation Glenn broadened the frame to compare the life stories of seven men who have a variety of conventionally defined disabilities and chronic illnesses. He concluded that it wasn't so much the lack of mobility that blocked people as the weight of expectations, their own and others. "One guy I interviewed had muscular dystrophy. He had picked up on all these expectations of him as a male – you pick up this stuff as a child, it's in the atmosphere. His father was very into being an individual man, pulling your own weight, earning a living and so on, he was very strong on that. As a lad, the son had worked Saturday mornings on a market stall, he did what was expected of him. But then he got muscular dystrophy, and slowly he went in the opposite direction from what was expected of him. Also, in his local area in the 1980s – Thatcher was around then – it was very conservative, a real go-getting area where people aspired to success and a wealthy lifestyle. Combined with the atmosphere at home, and at his school, which reflected the prevailing values of the local area, the whole atmosphere was about competition, and all of this was at odds with who this man was. As you can imagine, this tension became quite overwhelming for him."

Glenn interviewed Ahmed, a young man of a Bangladeshi family:

I was unconscious for two weeks and then I started to regain my consciousness. I looked at myself and I was a matchstick. I was like, all my eyes, everything, my legs you could see the bones. I had long hair at the time and all of it was falling off. I just felt so down. I thought, I've got to get out of this hospital. I'm going to die here of boredom and sadness, because the ward was a cancer ward. I was the only thalassaemia [an inherited anaemia, sometimes fatal; in Ahmed's case treatment had rendered it chronic]. Everyone was cancer people. When you see them people you feel even more down, because they're going through those stages: the sadness and pain they're going through, it's like everyone's sort of half dead, and that puts you down. . . . Times I was crying out and the staff said, 'You should be quiet because there is a lot of people down through them sad times. You should be quiet.' A person died on that ward after five days, and that got me scared too. I was in so much pain. I was screaming and they were saying 'Shh,

shh, stay calm, this is a ward, yer know!' But, I said, 'Look, how many hours do you have to wait for a paracetamol?'

Why did Glenn choose to build his dissertation from life stories? "For the same reason I did the critical autobiography on myself," he says. "When you read sociology, generally you get small vignettes, a few quotes. You don't really get a sense of development, the accumulation of small details that make a difference. With a life story, you can explore those in more depth. It's also important from the geography perspective. *Where* something happened – in a cancer ward at the hospital – is often crucial to shaping *how* it happened. With a life story you can also explore things better at the political level, why people think, feel and act the way they do. Without the full context, you can be a bit lost."

Doctorate in hand, Glenn went looking for a job, preferably one where he could continue to work with life stories. He heard that a researcher was needed for a new project in the Department of Psychiatry at the Royal Free Hospital Medical School in London. A three-year study on the history of aversion therapy in Britain, it was developed by Michael King, the head of psychiatry at the Royal Free Hospital, Annie Bartlett, who specializes in psychiatry and social anthropology, and sociologist/social historian/gay activist Jeffrey Weeks.

Funded by the Wellcome Trust, which supports projects on the history of medicine, the study would document the experience of aversion therapy patients and therapists from the 1950s to the present, especially the mid to late 1960s, when it was still illegal to be gay in Britain and behavioural therapy was in vogue. Says Glenn, "It moves from using estrogen in the '50s, then apomorphine, a drug that makes people feel nauseous, to mainly electric shock in the '60s. Then it gets a bit more mixed up with hypnotherapy and psychoanalysis, and tails off when the law changed, and identity politics and the rising social movement discredited that kind of thing. But even now – one man I interviewed still wanted to be changed, and he was frustrated that nobody was offering treatment anymore. The psychotherapists all say you have to accept yourself as you are, so he felt he was getting a raw deal."

As well as former patients, Glenn also interviewed therapists who administered the treatments, mostly electric shock. I want to know why the project initiators had felt it necessary to interview people who, from my own experience, I would regard as perpetrators, even torturers. "We wanted to learn why they did it," Glenn replies. "What were their motives, who were they, what were they feeling when they did it? Were they the bogeyman they're often painted? What was going on at the time that influenced them? All this is part of the history."

To find the therapists, he searched literature and professional networks, eventually finding about thirty willing to be interviewed. Not surprisingly, finding former patients was more challenging. "After doing my Ph.D., I was aware of the need to get a variety of people from different walks of life. I started with the gay groups, especially the older gay networks. There was a parallel project on gay sexuality going on in my department, where they had interviewed about two thousand people, so I asked them to let me know if any of them had had aversion therapy. Also, since I wanted to reach out as widely as possible, I used the general media. I wrote to every BBC radio station, about a hundred of them, including Scotland and Northern Ireland, and some of them let me talk on air about the project. I even did BBC breakfast TV! Media reads media, so *Time Out London* saw my article in *Nursing Times* – looking for people who'd been nurses to interview – and they did an article. Also newspapers like the *Glasgow Herald* and the *Manchester Evening News*. I quite enjoyed it, marketing the project, trying to make something thirty years gone sound relevant and interesting in the present time. Mostly I sold it as 'What happened to these people since, how did it affect them?'" Nearly all the people who contacted Glenn were men, which fairly represents the population most subject to aversion therapy.

A PRIVILEGED ARENA

When I was twenty, I fell very in love. I was still in the army and he worked on the coast boats and we had a hard time getting the same days off together. Anyway, I got out of the army and we moved in together. We made a nice

home and lived quite comfortably together. We were confident
that we were masculine enough, man enough, that there would
be no problems. But we had twin beds. We sort of made a joke
about it afterwards.

There was a time when I wouldn't even shake hands with a
person in public, and if there was a third person, no matter how
much I felt for somebody, I couldn't kiss them in front of anybody.
All of those things were hidden things we didn't do in public. Even
laughing and crying and joking. That's why I have a reputation of
being stone faced.

✺ Terry Wallace, born 1931, interviewed for *Tides of Men*

In Vancouver, Robert and Myron sought their first contacts at Prime
Timers, an organization of older gay men. When they interviewed
people, they asked them for leads to others. "We found that people had
very well established social networks," says Myron. "I think people's
connections tend to be more fluid now, more tenuous perhaps, but
with older men, even if they hadn't actually talked for years, they
would still say, 'Oh, I'll give him a call, it'll be all right, we've known
each other for decades.'"

A key early recruit was Terry Wallace, former manager of the Castle
Pub and a founding member of the Vancouver Gay and Lesbian Business
Association. "Terry was a real gold mine," says Robert. "He's a walking
history book. On the other hand he tends to keep pretty much to
himself. He's not the type you'd expect would tell his story easily to
strangers. We were lucky."

Myron adds, "In fact he was remarkably frank. He spoke of some
very tough things he had to deal with – the invisibility, the self-
loathing, the class divide between the average blue-collar gay man and
the richer contingent. It was an excellent way for us to get started.
Then in our later interviews we were able to ask better questions and
follow up themes that he raised."

Robert and Myron conducted interviews together at first, then
when they became overwhelmed with the volume, separately. They

started in the major centres, Vancouver and Victoria, then reached out to the interior of British Columbia, in a three-week trip to fourteen small communities. Outside the city, they counted on local gay and lesbian associations to provide leads. "In Vancouver, the structures that used to keep gay men and lesbians viable as a community are now falling by the wayside," Robert says. "Here we have the weight of numbers, we're outgrowing the community associations. Delaney's coffeehouse on Davie is a much more important rallying point for gay men in Vancouver now than the Gay and Lesbian Centre. But outside the metropolitan region, in Argenta, in Vernon, in the Okanagan and the Kootenays, community groups are still very important to people."

How did they select people to interview? "We didn't," says Robert. "Basically we said we'd talk to anyone who wanted to talk to us. That's how we got such a wide variety of interviews. After Terry Wallace and a couple of others, we were concerned that we might not get any more older people. We thought they might be too nervous, not comfortable to be in the limelight. But that wasn't the case at all. We got an abundance of interviews with people in their forties, fifties, and up, including a couple of octogenarians."

Did anyone turn them down? "In about seventy-five interviews I can only think of a handful where the subject was so antagonistic or guarded, they challenged our right to ask them questions," Robert says. Myron adds, "One young fellow said he didn't know why we were asking him all these questions, he didn't know what to say. It's too bad, he had an interesting life."

Robert continues, "There is one gap – we couldn't get any rich people to talk to us. The rich old queens said, 'Forget it, nothing doing.' Our theory is that at a certain point you stop being gay, you're just rich."

Myron: "One person said, 'It's far easier being rich than gay."
Robert: "So inadvertently our project is pretty much blue collar to middle class. Since there hasn't been much working class history done in this country, that gets us two under-valued groups!"

As it happens with a "finite species," as Robert puts it, they lost people along the way. "We made contact with a very nice First Nations man in Vernon," says Robert, "but before we could get back to him, he died. AIDS has created a huge hole in the demographic of some groups. Virtually a whole generation of First Nations men have disappeared. We were able to interview some younger ones, but when we asked if they could refer us to older men, they said, 'No, they're all dead.' We realized that doing this work was a bit of a race against time. That's why we went after the older men first."

I was keen to know how their experience of doing interviews with queerfolk compared with my own. Did they prepare? "Some of the interviews probably could have used some prior research," says Robert, "but then, we only had $15,000 to spend. Also I've found that the problem with prepping for an interview is that sometimes you end up directing it in ways that limit what you get. I had just spent five years doing interviews for the CBC, and I knew that if you ask the right questions, and you know how to listen, you'll probably elicit the information. Of course when you read the transcripts, you think sometimes you didn't pick up on cues at all, what an idiot! But generally you hit more than you miss. After the initial interviews, we would both pick up on things. For example, someone mentioned that they used to know a bunch of old queens, 'like Messy Mae.' By then we could say, 'Someone else talked about Messy Mae. Do you mind telling us more?' With oral history you can get this huge canvas, but you have to be able to appreciate every tiny brushstroke. It's in the details that you get the big picture."

Myron has to leave, he's due to play piano for a choir rehearsal. Robert and I continue to chat. On their road trip through the interior, he tells me, he and Myron did four to six interviews a day, each of them lasting at least ninety minutes and some as long as four to six hours. "You get punch-drunk after a while," says Robert, "and now and then you lose focus." I know the feeling.

How did they build trust with people they'd never met before? "We went into interviews with a basic kind of respect," says Robert. "We assumed that people were smart, and they had thought about their lives. So we'd asked them to speculate and come up with theories as to why things may have gone the way they did. 'You're in the lime-light,' we'd say, 'make good use of it.' An interview is a privileged arena, a special relationship. It's like a really tender one-night stand. We found that it could be quite cathartic, especially for gay men who had never talked much about their lives. Sometimes at the end of it people would tell us they never realized before what an interesting life they'd had. Some of them cried."

INSIDER/ OUTSIDER

I ask similar questions of Glenn Smith – for example, how did he prepare for interviews? "At first I'd make a list of the subjects I wanted to cover," he replies. "With the patients it was childhood, family, growing up, experience of sexuality, how they ended up having aversion therapy, what was it like, how long did it last, and so on. But the more interviews you do, eventually the list is in your head, at which point you get more relaxed and confident, you can focus better on what the person is saying. I would usually say something like, 'If you could start off from the earliest time you can remember in terms of your sexuality. . . .' People would start from their childhood, go into the future, maybe back again – but it never worried me, because by then I had in my head what I wanted to ask."

With the therapists, the starting point was their careers. "But there again, I'd have particular things to go after. What made them get into psychology, their thoughts about the treatments, what their families thought – if they talked to them about it, how did it affect their career, what do they think about it now, that sort of thing. I was interested in their emotions, their feelings, but often that was hard to tease out – as professionals they tended to speak with a sort of professional gloss. Sometimes I got a sense of the person behind the gloss – what did they really feel about homosexuality? Some danced around that kind of question, but some were more open."

An issue often raised in oral history circles is proximity of relationship between interviewer and interviewee. Is the interviewer an insider, by familial, social or cultural proximity, or an outsider to the interviewee's experience? It can be crucial in determining the quality of the encounter. In Glenn's case, I wonder how gay people react to being questioned by a heterosexual, clearly an outsider, particularly when the focus of the interview is an assault on the person's sexuality.

Glenn replies, "I was a little surprised that no one asked about my sexuality before the interviews, and only a few asked at the end. And when I told them I wasn't gay, no one said 'You shouldn't be doing this project.' The fact that no one asked me about it up front makes me think that if the interviewer had been gay, they might not have got any more out of the situation than I did. If they had asked at the beginning, I would have wondered if they were packaging things differently – 'Can I trust this guy?' To some extent I could draw on the experience of prejudice in my own life. You don't always need to have exactly the same experience to empathize with somebody."

In the academic realm where Glenn works, the insider/outsider question is taken quite seriously. "When I did my Ph.D.," he says, "identity politics was quite big, and my having a long-term illness was supposed to give me an inside angle. Of course it gave me some starting points, but when I was actually interviewing people, I found there wasn't much more connection than for anyone on the street. I've come to think it's probably good that people engage in research regardless of whether they're able-bodied, heterosexual, et cetera, as long as they're approaching it from the right perspective, with respect and from a wide angle."

With the therapists, he made a point of coming out as heterosexual. "I didn't want them to feel threatened, in case they got defensive and closed up. In fact some of them did worry there might be a political agenda behind the project and that what they said might be distorted. When I applied for the job, I said that my being heterosexual might actually be an advantage, at least in interviewing the therapists, because I'd be perceived as more neutral – my younger brother is gay, so I'm not really *that* neutral – but I could interview therapists without them feeling pushed into a corner." I can see his point. When I demanded an interview with my former torturer, the conversation did not go well.

I want to know how the therapists justified what they had done. "Many of them were junior at the time," says Glenn. "For some it was their first placement. They were given this task to do, and they didn't feel they were in any position to say no. They were scared of losing their jobs." Just following orders, I comment. "It was more than that," he replies. "You can't take this out of its historical context. It was a time of immense sexual naïveté, for both patients and therapists, and for many therapists at the time, the theories seemed to make sense."

Did any of them have doubts? "Some of them did feel uneasy, because it felt like a form of punishment, and that didn't seem what they had been trained to do. One guy I talked to, his social mix included gay men and women, and he couldn't relate what was going on in the hospital with what he knew of the gay world outside."

Some of the former patients that Glenn interviewed were forced into aversion therapy by the courts. With homosexuality still a crime in Britain, they were given the choice: prison or aversion therapy. The rest, who went into it voluntarily – people like me – did so in the repressive climate of the time. Many had never spoken of their ordeal to anyone before Glenn. "Some still felt a kind of stigma. A few of the older ones talked about how these strong emotions – shame, fear – hadn't gone away, they'd stayed with them all these years. For some it wasn't only the treatment, but other things going on in their lives at the same time, things they heard, the prejudice. All of it was over-whelming, and it left a deep sense of stigma, which to some degree had shaped the rest of their lives. Some people said that even among their gay friends now, they still feel uncomfortable. Their self-esteem isn't as strong as others they know who are gay. It's not exactly flashbacks they experience, a fear that they're going to be arrested or something like that. It's really more about how the experience knocked their iden-tify askew."

In my experience, when people who've been silenced for a long time are finally heard, the release can be intensely emotional. Like me,

Glenn isn't trained as a counsellor. How did he deal with that? "It did make me feel a bit uncomfortable sometimes," he replies. "There were quite a few sad stories, and sometimes people would cry. Apart from saying sympathetic things, I was never quite sure what to do. I wasn't going to give them a hug – that would break all kinds of professional rules. It reminded me in a way of own experience when I was in hospital and quite upset but the doctors and nurses had this professional boundary. I can see why it's there, but sometimes it can make you seem a bit inhuman. Now I'm on the other side, I'm supposed to be the professional. I suppose the thing I focused on in listening to what they said was to realize how many people who go through traumatic experiences actually come through it, and learn something from it. Often it's not all doom and gloom. In fact it can be quite inspiring. I suspect that may be the whole process of the human story, right there."

When people agreed to give interviews for the project, they were asked to sign consent forms agreeing to the use of short quotes, anonymously, in professional journals. As interviews came in, the project directors realized that the material was rich enough to warrant a book. Glenn contacted people again, for permission to use more substantial excerpts from their stories. He would send them an edited version of the transcript for approval, and ask if they felt anything was missing, or saw anything that might compromise their anonymity.

"I have to say, it's been a bit of a torturous process," he says. "A few people wanted to rewrite their whole interview! One man was quite upset when he read the transcript. He said it took him back to how he felt when we did the interview, which was over a year ago, but now he feels he's a changed person and he wouldn't say what he said then. 'But that's the point of oral history,' I replied. 'What you've recorded is a moment in time and yes, people do move on.' Our compromise was to insert some of the changes he wanted into the edited version of the original, and send it back again. But it does raise a few issues in getting the book done – where do you draw the line? You could keep on sending transcripts back and forth forever. And where do you draw the line in changing what people said? In talking about his boss, one therapist used words like 'God' and 'bloody,' as in 'that bloody guy,' but when I got the transcript back, he'd deleted them. He said he'd spoken about it to his family, and they said he doesn't normally talk like that. When I rang him up, I said, 'It gives a sense of your voice, your passion, and if we're talking about anonymity, wouldn't it be better to leave them in, because if you don't normally talk like that, people won't recognize you!' I got round it that way."

An obstacle he encountered among the therapists was their own fear. "Some of them were afraid to say what they really wanted to say about other therapists," says Glenn. "In the '50s and '60s this was a small world. There weren't many doing this kind of therapy, and most of the people I interviewed knew each other. The two leading people at the time didn't want to be interviewed, but most of the others talked about these two in rather derogatory terms. When I sent the transcripts back, some of them changed things because they said they were afraid of being sued – these people are still alive, though nearly all of them have retired. If I can't tell the full story because of people's legal fears, it means we may actually end up distorting the history. It's an issue in oral history that I haven't seen addressed much. Of course lots of stuff gets omitted in oral history, but here you're actually *changing* history. I find that a bit sad and troubling. The best I can do, I think, is make note of it in the introduction, as a methodological issue that warrants attention."

THE RHYTHM OF THE INTERVIEW

My brother was the first person I came out to, largely by propositioning him. Which did not sit too well with him. And that gives you some idea of my frustration that I would do that. I was eighteen or nineteen and he was about twenty-four, twenty-five. He found this psychologist and the guy was a hell of a lot crazier than I was – at least that's what I thought. He talked about himself for the first couple of sessions. He never asked me a question. But finally he encouraged me to talk about myself and he gave me sodium pentathlon, which does encourage you to talk about yourself without too many inhibitions. He made me cry as I recall. And that was the first time that anyone had been able to do that for quite a while. It was like a dam bursting. It was all coming out finally, I was able to actually talk to somebody about what was troubling me so much. In the end he was very supportive of me and I was grateful to him.

❁ Doug Ross, born 1926, interview
for the *Tides of Men* project

In their written agreement with men they interviewed, Robert and Myron specified that they would transcribe the interview, do an initial rough edit – some of the transcripts ran over a hundred pages – and then the interviewees would see the results. Nothing would appear anywhere, including the website, without their permission. If Robert or Myron wanted to use the material in any other form, they would have to seek further permission. Given the transience of life, this contract led to an ethical dilemma.

"One of our best contacts, Douglas Ross of Prime Timers, passed away recently," says Robert. "He was a really nice man. We sent him the transcript, then we spoke to him on the phone, and he said 'Yes, it's a good interview.' But before he could look at it for any changes, he died. Here's the ethical dilemma: Can I use his verbal approval, or do I have to go to his estate for written approval? We discussed it with other people who knew him quite well, and the consensus is, 'Go ahead, you have his okay.' So that's what we've done. But I do dread the thought of someone else dying who still hasn't checked their transcript, and then, God forbid, an unsympathetic estate. We'll just have to decide as we go what is the ethical approach in each case. Some of the interviews are quite frank, and we don't want to cause unnecessary pain to anyone."

In the beginning they did the transcripts themselves. "Myron is a wizard typist," says Robert, "but when you're nine-to-fivers, and in my case you type with two fingers, it could take forever. So we got some additional funding from the province that allowed us to look for people that specialize in this. We started with a legal secretary, but she was so thorough one transcript ended up costing us $500. After that we found a company that charges $250 for each ninety-minute cassette. They're used to dealing with the confidentiality factor. Our original agreement said that nobody would look at the interview till the narrator had seen it, so we had to go back and ask people if it would be okay for a third party to do the transcriptions. These things are important. It maintains trust, which is important if we want people to refer us to others for interviews. Also, I like the idea of being an honourable person."

How did they edit transcripts down to manageable size? "My journalistic training was useful there," says Robert. "Few people are born storytellers, most of us wander all over the place. So the goal was to edit in such a way that the person's real story could come out. If a transcript ran fifty pages, the final edit would usually run about a third of that. Our technique is to follow the rhythm of the interview, as long as it makes sense. When explanatory material is too long for an interesting read, we may simply do it for them with a piece of connecting text. It's an interventionist approach – with long narratives, you have to be firm to help readers get through the story. Occasionally I've even rewritten a long monologue, trying to adopt the person's voice. Then I'll give it back to them and ask, 'Do you think this is you, can you pick out what isn't?' Not a single person has said they didn't recognize their own voice, and most of them seem happier with the result. It's easy to be appalled by the way you sound on paper – what if you had a bad day and didn't verbalize well, especially with a stranger? We want this to be a good experience for people, from start to finish."

Robert takes ultimate comfort from the fact that the edited version which goes out into the world is not the only source. "I know the original audiotapes still exist, and so do the raw transcripts. They will always be there."

As it is for all community-based projects, funding is a challenge for Tides of Men. Aside from the two grants they got, Robert and Myron have subsidized it with their own passion and their own labour. Along the way, Robert acquired new Internet skills; he now manages a website devoted to the oral history of francophones in British Columbia, inspired, he says, by Tides of Men. But it's becoming harder all the time to get funding from government, he says. "There are really no programs aimed toward gays and lesbians in Canada, which is a real shame. Like any other minority, we've done much for Canada, and we have much to offer, but we don't get recognized by the multicultural model, for example, so we don't have access to funding the way some other groups do."

Even where government funding is available, most of it requires matching funds from other sources. "We've done lots of soliciting, but funding is very hard to find for a project like this," Myron says. "It's bad timing – when we would go to a corporation, they'd say they had just given to an AIDS conference. AIDS has taken up a lot of funding, which in other communities might have gone to community and cultural development. Aside from that, a lot of companies think the gay community is simply too insignificant to bother with."

Robert adds, "Sadly, it's also difficult to raise funds in our own community. The problem is that large amounts of money seem to be held by a few individuals, and they happen to be the same ones who wouldn't be interviewed! They don't give much to gay causes. Their first loyalties are to mainstream institutions, including the big mainstream charities."

Myron concludes, "So the lion's share of the matching had to come from what we put into the project ourselves."

The results of their work can be seen at the Tides of Men website, at http://www.tidesofmen.org. The opening page describes it: "Tides of Men is an online oral history of gay men in British Columbia, from the years preceding the second world war to the present. Seventy-five men from fourteen communities were interviewed, the majority between 1995 and 1996. Their stories will eventually find their way online before the end of the project, currently slated for 2005."

Glenn is hoping to complete his aversion therapy book by mid 2004. I ask him what kind of readers he wants to reach. "We're aiming it to have an academic feel," he says, "you know, footnotes and all that. But at the same time we don't want to lose the people who contributed to it. It's important that they be able to read it as well. The way I look at it, the stories are really interesting in themselves, so we're not going to analyze them; we'll only introduce them and then let people speak for themselves. I hope it will speak to different audiences: people who've undergone these therapies, people who are interested in gay history, academics, psychologists who may be unaware of the biases that have gone on in their own discipline. Also people who are interested in how science is shaped by the context of the time."

The last of these has been fundamental to the project, funded as it is by a foundation interested in the history of medicine. "These treatments could only have happened in a particular context," says Glenn. "Homosexuality was illegal. The media talked about it in a rather sensational way. Really, there was a sense of moral panic. Also, psychology was trying to compete with psychiatry, and aversion therapy was seen as one way to do that. Science is never neutral. It's always influenced by the laws and politics of the time – for example, who's funding what. They were eventually hoping to market aversion therapy on a wider scale, to deal with smoking and other behavioural 'problems' – some people actually saw a potential for making money off it. It's not much different from what's going on now, who funds what research, for what reasons, what gets left out, and what kinds of ideas get ignored."

Glenn came to my attention originally with a message he posted to the U.S. oral history list-serve. He questioned, in a mild English way, the volume of oral history being done on the September 11th attacks: Might it be a little excessive? Later I ask him to expand on this theme.

"I just wonder sometimes about collecting so many stories, and what do we do with it all?" he says. "I don't have an answer to that, but I do wonder sometimes what we're recording all this *for*. It's a bit like home video – people record miles of it, but then what? At oral history conferences I've been to in San Francisco and Florida, I get the impression that in America, they're recording a huge volume of oral history. It seems to be based on the idea that individual identity is the thing that really matters, which can be quite a conservative way of looking at life, not looking at the wider picture. With that highly individualistic approach, you tend to lose any sense of context or politics. That makes me a little uneasy. Can we become saturated with so many stories that people just switch off? And how does that help take us into the future? Do we risk becoming defined by the stories we tell of our lives? Can they become such a fixed part of our identity that we can't move forward? I do wonder if we shouldn't be exploring this connection a little more."

On the other hand, Glenn isn't done yet with oral history himself. "My original reason for using my own life story in the thesis was to have a voice, to say something I couldn't find said anywhere else, and to do it in a way that couldn't be done in a short paragraph. It needed the context, the whole life, to explain why and how I ended up feeling a particular way. I still see oral history as a good way to bring out the small details of daily life that can be extremely meaningful in how that life is lived. I also think it provides outlets for voices that might otherwise be written out of history, so that lots of people can have access to these voices, and hear what they have to say."

The last time I spoke to him, he had just landed a grant from the British Economic and Social Research Council, to do a project on naturists. For a moment I thought of birdwatchers, but in Britain naturists are nudists. "Not much work has been done on the subject," he says. "I've been a naturist for quite a while. There's been a lot of pressure here to change the sexual offences act in ways that could seriously limit a person's freedom to be naked, even in their own back garden. Partly it's in response to the current climate of fear around sexuality in Britain, which has a lot to do with pedophilia and people being fearful of anything that's not absolutely clear in terms of boundaries. I'm interested in using oral history, life stories, to explore the rather uneasy relationship between naturism and sexuality. My own experience is that there is an inherent sexuality and sensuality to it, as there is to many things in everyday life, but some people shy away from that completely. Even the word 'naturism' is a way of sanitizing it, it's much less sexually evocative than 'nudism.' So I plan to interview thirty to forty people of different ages and genders, to explore how and why people got into naturism, how they deal with sexuality in a naturist environment, and some of the more contentious issues around that."

A CUT DIAMOND

I think it's relevant for me to tell you that from quite an early age, maybe my late thirties or early forties, I've always used hustlers. And continue to. Their lives interested me and again it was the total contrast of their lives with mine that partially turned me on. This certainly produced a variety of reactions in my friends. "I would never do that." "I would never pay." To me it's a business transaction. I've been very fortunate; on those rare occasions where I sensed that things weren't quite right, I have broken it off and perhaps paid a portion of what we had agreed upon. No police harassment, and I've taken some chances, God knows. And I continue to do so and will.

❀ Doug Ross, 1995, interview for *Tides of Men*

I ask Robert what he had learned in putting together Tides of Men. "I went into it thinking I knew a lot about gay men, but I have to say, I've come out of it quite surprised, and immeasurably enriched," he replies. "That's what I like about oral history – unlike the conventional way of writing history, what you get with oral history is the amazing richness and variety of human experience. We'd have people talk about the same event, but they'd give incredibly different accounts of it. It's like a cut diamond, with every facet quite different."

What surprised him? "Some opinions I had were confirmed, but others I was forced to rethink or completely discard. For example, before the passage of Bill C150 [1968/69 federal legislation legalizing certain same-sex acts in Canada], I just assumed that life must have been horrible, one dark morass of oppression. But for many people, that simply wasn't the case. Illegal, yes, and people did go to jail. It was certainly no laughing matter. But despite all that, many of our older interviewees said it was more fun to be gay in those days, when you had a kind of secret society. Some of them also said that gay bashing didn't really exist until the bill was passed – suddenly we went from being individual perverts and particularly flamboyant men to a whole group of people, a much bigger target. One man told us that he was a real queen until 1969; then he started trying to act as straight as he could. People seem to be more tolerant of individuals than communities, and the power dynamics toward groups can be much more vicious, no holds barred. You see that in race relations, in linguistic groups, and you see it between heteros and homos."

Robert was also impressed by the human capacity for creative adaptation. "People were incredibly inventive in the compromises and solutions they came up with to survive on a day-to-day basis. They didn't have any sources, the books and such that we have now. They were like whittlers, whittling away on a piece of wood, and suddenly you have a sculpture, the arrangement by which you survive and deal with the universe. People lived much racier lives, in their behaviours and emotional arrangements, than I would ever have thought. Some were healthy, some unhealthy, some were so strange and wrong-headed I couldn't believe they were still alive! But regardless of how their choices strike me, I also really admire that people came up with them entirely on their own – the fertile human imagination!"

Early in the project, Robert ran up against one of his own prejudices. "I steered clear of talking to the politicos, the activists, basically because I think they're a pain in the ass. I think of them as social misfits. When you're a normal, well-balanced person, you can adapt to any situation. Even if the broader culture hates you, you can still find ways to get from it what you need. Misfits can't do that. They don't have the flexibility to adapt, so they do all can to change the hostile environment. That's my take on how gay liberation started."

Eventually Myron persuaded Robert that their project would have an odd gap if they excluded people who'd been involved in the Gay Alliance Toward Equality (GATE), founded in the early '70s, and the

Association for Sexual Knowledge (ASK), founded in the '60s. Myron also argued if it weren't for the misfits, we would all be culturally dead. "Okay," says Robert, "I realized maybe I should try to stop being a whiny, hate-politics kind of guy. The people who started ASK and GATE, the pioneers of gay liberation, were actually wonderful eccentrics. They could so easily have said, 'It doesn't matter, it has nothing to do with me, homophobia is their problem, not mine.' Instead, they had to change the world, though they might die in the attempt. The things they accomplished were wonderful acts of heroism. Normal people don't do these things. They don't have to. Really, we owe everything to the social misfits!"

At this point in our conversation I comment that, given my own role in 1970s and early '80s gay liberation, his category of "social misfit" would have to include me. We laugh. In a brief exchange of emails after my visit to Vancouver, Robert writes: "I thought you were very patient in the latter half of the interview when I got to babble about evil political activists – somewhat to my retrospective embarrassment I might add."

It's what I do in interviews: I listen, and hardly ever do I argue. But then too, once I filter out the rather sour judgment from his assessment of gay liberation, I think he's not too far off being right.

Now that he and Myron have become not only salvagers of gay history but part of it themselves with Tides of Men, I wonder how Robert measures the value of their work for the future.

"One should never forget one's history," he says. He doesn't wag a finger, but I can hear it in his voice. "Living in the present is one thing, but it should never be an excuse for wilful ignorance of our own history. As a francophone, it seems to me that English Canadians are particularly prone to historical amnesia, which is rather dangerous given where we live. As a gay man, I think it's particularly important to document our history – if we don't, soon enough it could be too late. We're told that Canada has become one of the most liberal places in the world on gay and lesbian issues. We may be gaining rights through the courts, but those gains need to be consolidated, which means we have to win the general public. I find the Alliance Party [ex-Reform Party, now part of the Conservative Party of Canada] quite frightening. They're foot soldiers for the American Christian right. I'm not looking forward to the day when they form the government of Canada. If we can believe the polls, they're clearly out of step with the majority of Canadians on gay issues, but that won't stop them from trying to legislate the things they believe in. I think that makes Tides of Men and other such projects very important now, for example in gaining access to provincial school curricula, to ensure that content like Tides of Men becomes available to everyone. I believe we have a small window of time to do these things, and I believe it's getting smaller each year."

I was living in Kitsilano and I got to know about five people. What I'd call close friends. Half the time they'd end up at my place, especially on a Sunday when everything else was closed. We'd have lunch, play games. I called it my own little gang. I was living in a rooming house at that time. If one of those friends decided to stay with me overnight, and then later on in the evening somebody else came over and realized I was in bed with somebody else, they'd sleep on the front porch on a wicker chesterfield that my landlady had on the front porch. I've woken up in the morning and found somebody lying there waiting for me. . . .

There was a couple that lived on the edge of Capilano Canyon. Right on the edge. . . . The parties were gorgeous. Never any trouble, other than stepping off the edge! A well-known character living near the canyon used to have live entertainers and movie stars the likes of Mitzi Gaynor at his parties. The sound would carry down the canyon, and the people at the other end would phone the police to complain. The police would send a car up and not hear another word from it. Send a second car to find the first one, and here's the cops enjoying the party!

– N.S., born 1926, interviewed for Tides of Men

CHAPTER 14

KEEP ASKING QUESTIONS!

In early summer of 1994, Dan Kerr was exploring his new neighbourhood, the East Village of New York City. A police car pulled up, and the officer went into an apartment building across the street. Dan stopped to watch.

A few days before, he had been to an emergency meeting at La Plaza Cultural, an abandoned lot that neighbourhood squatters were converting into a park. Newly elected mayor Rudolph Guiliani had given the New York Police Department carte blanche to harass and arrest low-income New Yorkers, including squatters and street people. Three had been beaten up recently by police, and strategies were needed to fight the escalating assaults. One man suggested storming the nearest police station.

"That was my first action in New York," says Dan. "I was kind of nervous. We went marching down the street, people kicking over garbage cans and making a ruckus. At the police station people tried to get inside, and the police were freaking out – they're not used to people trying to get *into* the police station!" He laughs, telling it. "They tried to shut the doors, then people started climbing in the windows. Then we all went back to La Plaza Cultural, we made a campfire, and people told stories – a kind of oral history of struggle in the Lower East Side."

Dan threw out a proposal: Why not develop a strategy of mutual aid? There were precedents, good models – the Wobblies, cop watches in other cities, the Mothers of the Disappeared in Argentina. Why not take an oath that if anyone was attacked by the police, others would go to their aid? "My impulse was simple: to build community by making a commitment to work together," says Dan. "They were interested, but a little uneasy. These aren't the kind of people who easily take oaths!" His proposal would soon be tested.

When the police officer emerged from the building, he was dragging a young man. Three people Dan recognized from La Plaza ran up the street, shouting, 'Why are you arresting Kenny?' "In typical New York fashion," says Dan, "the policeman said, 'None of your fucking business.' 'It is too our business,' they said, 'and we're not going until you tell us why you're arresting him.' A couple of them got underneath the police car, and grabbed hold. The policeman really freaked, he didn't know what to do. I went over, and he said, 'Tell them get the fuck out of there. This guy broke his partner's arm in a fight. It's domestic violence.' The people under the car said, 'If that's true, we'll get up.' So the policeman told me to go verify it with the guy's partner, who was now at this other police car. Of course she didn't know who I was, so she wouldn't talk to me.

"I came back and said if he let one of the other people talk to her, I was sure they could resolve it. Instead he called in about ten more cops, and they started to beat the crap out of these three people. I said to them, 'Why are you doing this? You could have resolved this whole thing in a non-violent manner.' One guy who was getting beaten up kept yelling, 'We will fight, we will win or we will die!' And this other woman who was getting beaten up kept yelling, 'Keep asking questions! Keep asking questions!' The police threw me into a paddy wagon, along with this other guy who hadn't said or done a thing. All through it, this woman kept yelling, 'Keep asking questions!'"

It's what Dan Kerr does. From the time he grew up in suburban Cleveland, he has been asking questions. On trips downtown with his parents, they'd drive from their own tidy streets, past the mansions on Fairmont Boulevard, then through streets of boarded-up, burned-out buildings, prostitutes on the prowl. Why were these neighbourhoods so different from his own? People around him said they believed in integration, but in his high school, though half the students were African-American, only one in twenty ever got into the "gifted and talented" program. Why?

He went looking for answers in history. For his major at Carleton College in Northfield, Minnesota, Dan studied the revolutions of 1848, Russian history, the civil rights movement, African-American history. But the professor who challenged him to ask the most searching questions taught philosophy. "With Maria Lougones, along with the traditional classics we read radical feminist philosophy, anarchist philosophy, Karl Marx," he says. "We'd actually sit and debate these ideas. For her, teaching wasn't a detached intellectual exercise. She wanted us to engage with the ideas in a personal way and figure out where we stood on them. In our final exam, the whole class had to present an argument as a group, each person adding a piece to it, and all of us would get the same grade. This was her way of getting us to work together collectively instead of constantly competing." Dan credits Maria Lougones with sparking his interest in academia.

In the wider world he was also encountering more questions. He joined the Committee for Responsible Investment, pressuring the college to pull its investments out of South Africa, still ruled by the apartheid regime. "I was surprised to learn how resistant the college administration and trustees were to divesting," he says. "And then after a series of date rapes on campus, their response was entirely geared to protecting their own liability, not at all to dealing with the pain that people were going through. These things got me asking more questions. They were my first formal training in politics and organizing."

To satisfy his curiosity about the Middle East – his father was born in Beirut – Dan decided to study for a term at the American University in Cairo. Three days after he arrived, Iraq invaded Kuwait. During the massive U.S. buildup to the Gulf War, he travelled through Jordan. "People I talked to in Amman had family and friends in Iraq. There was a lot of fear – would Israel be drawn in, would the war spread, would nuclear weapons be used? I got a real sense that people didn't know if they'd survive." He returned to Cairo via the West Bank, a month after Israeli soldiers killed twenty-three Palestinians at the Al-Aqsa Mosque in Bethlehem. "There was still blood on the mosque. I got a gut-wrenching sense of what these issues really mean to people's lives."

When the U.S. and its allies started bombing Baghdad early in 1991, Dan felt isolated and helpless. In Cairo he had been studying the history of poor people's movements in various countries, including his own. "I decided that what I wanted to do with my life was to help change the way society is structured in the United States, not just at the foreign policy level but very basically, from the ground up." Since there was little of use that he could do in Egypt, he went home.

"That was a formative moment for me," he says, "to come home with this very visceral sense of the impact that war has on people, and then to find this totally detached attitude in the United States, with people waving the flag, yellow ribbons all over, and when the war ended, people jumping up and down like we'd just won the Super Bowl! That was very disturbing for me, the intellectual detachment on campus, where people could talk about these things but obviously had no intention of doing anything about them."

A month after he returned to college in Minnesota, the notorious police beating of Rodney King provoked riots that left fifty-four people dead in south-central Los Angeles. Dan joined a small group of students grappling with the question of how college policies might relate to what happened in L.A. "Tuition was up and financial aid down, which cuts out low-income students," he says. "The material in the classroom was totally irrelevant to most communities, and there were no support networks for students of colour, so of course the drop-out rate was quite high among African-Americans and Latinos. We made a list of demands to change these things. After a few big rallies on campus, we went on strike, and then we invaded the administration building."

Soon after Dan graduated in spring 1992, he took to the streets. He had heard that in Minneapolis, homeless people were taking over abandoned buildings. "Around that time the Housing Now movement was very active across the county. It culminated in a big march on Washington, but that seemed so ineffectual to me. People would go down there, all these pop singers would get up and say they wanted to fight homelessness, then everyone felt good, they went home, and nothing changed. I really like the old Wobblies' saying, 'Direct action gets the goods,' so I was intrigued that these young street kids were quietly moving into buildings, not making a fuss about it, and creating their own kind of community."

He moved to Minneapolis, where he helped set up the Emma Goldman community centre. "Mostly it was people my age who considered themselves intellectuals, and then the street punks, who called themselves 'crusty youth.' I tended to side with them, so I ended up dying my hair five colours, in a kind of mohawk, wearing crazy outfits around town, and losing my job in a silk-screen factory as a result." He laughs. "Because I couldn't pay my rent, I lost my house and ended up living under a bridge – not entirely feeling like one of the street people, but certainly quite intrigued with what they were doing." From kids on the move by freight train, he heard that in New York City not only were people taking over buildings, they were doing it openly and fighting to stay put. By August 1993 he was in New York.

NEW YORK, NEW YORK

On his first trip to New York, Dan hung out in Tompkins Square Park in the East Village, living first in a college friend's room, then in a decaying bandshell in East River Park. He hoped to get involved in the squatter movement but instead ended up spending most of his time with young heroin addicts. "That turned out to be quite useful for me later on, getting comfortable hanging out with people on the street. You know," he says, "the people I found most open were the heroin addicts. There was an aspect of gentleness about them, not at all like people into cocaine. Sometimes I'd help them inject the needles into their arms. But they all warned me, 'Don't ever try it, you'll like it too much – at first.'"

With no home, no squatter contacts, and winter closing in, Dan returned to Cleveland. He kept to himself, wrote a series of zines, and applied to universities to do a graduate program in history. Accepted at Case Western in Cleveland, he got permission to defer his entrance. "I wanted to get out of Cleveland, but I didn't want to burn my bridges here. My plan was to go back to New York in the spring, but if it didn't work out – if I ended up with drug addicts again – I could still go back to school!" He laughs. Dan's laugh is full out, from the belly. Usually it's provoked by his own quirks.

Second time around, he got quickly and deeply involved in the East Village squatter movement, at first sharing a squat on 13th Street and helping out at a free kitchen run by his host. "Unfortunately he started to drink excessively, and eventually it became unbearable," says Dan. "He got abusive, people wouldn't come to the kitchen any-more, and I started moving into this other abandoned building that several of us opened up on East 3rd Street. The kitchen fell apart, and basically he drank himself to death, which was really sad, because when he wasn't drunk he had great sense of humour, and he was highly talented. He'd go down the manholes and surreptitiously hook up squats to the electric network. But finally the whole shit of every-day life just wore him down."

When a drug deal went sour between two members, the 3rd Street squat also began to disintegrate. "Even so, I did like that people were into trying to figure out how to deal with our own problems," he says, "not always in the best way, but amongst ourselves. A couple of years ago near here [Cleveland], a guy died in his apartment from a heroin overdose, and for ten days no one knew. In the squatters' movement, no one would ever have been left alone that long. We were always in each other's business, not always for the best, but I think overall for the better."

The 3rd Street squat had a huge iron grate that barred entry by the front door. Weary of clambering in through the back, one night Dan and about a dozen others tried to remove it. Police arrived and arrested them for trespassing, possession of burglary tools and several other charges. While they were in jail, the building was boarded up, front and back, unassailable.

In Dan's next home, a big squat that housed close to a hundred people, chaos reigned among the residents – street punks, hippies, undocumented workers from Latin American, and people with mental illnesses and on a variety of drugs, who had settled into conflicting cliques. Just before Dan moved in, a woman pulled a gun and threatened to shoot a neighbour during a meeting. Shortly after he moved in, a gang of residents forcibly evicted the same neighbour. With amused understatement, Dan says, "There was a serious issue of morale going on."

Along with Dan and Ayr – a friend whom Dan describes as "a wonderful person, very generous, and very politically astute" – a few people in the building formed a coalition and called a meeting to develop some rules for the squat. "For example, we wanted a rule saying that evictions could only be decided in community meetings, and if anyone tried to force other people out, that in itself could be grounds for eviction. There was lot of debate on whether there should be evictions at all in a squat, but at least people came together to start talking about these issues. At first it was mostly 'I can't stand so and so,' but then gradually people got into the issues – how to deal with the big leak in the roof, water pouring down the stairwell, no electricity on the fifth floor, drains not hooked up and so forth. We managed to get work crews together, fixed all kinds of things, created a community space on the main floor with a stage, and people started painting murals in the common spaces. It was an amazing transformation, from this bleak, dark, dusty atmosphere with animal poop all over the place to a setting where everyone was fixing up both their own and the shared spaces. In the end, this building had one of most politically active groups of all the squats in the lower East Side."

This, I'm learning, is a recurring theme with Dan Kerr: If we organize and work together, we can fix anything.

Along the way, one afternoon when they had nothing else to do, he and others seized a branch of the world's largest bank. During the

mid '90s peso collapse in Mexico, an internal report at the Chase Manhattan Bank advised that if the Mexican government wanted a loan
guarantee for U.S.$40 billion, it would have to demonstrate its control
of the national economy, and to do that it would have to "eliminate"
the Zapatista rebels in the southern state of Chiapas. "Some of us saw
ourselves as part of an international movement connected to the Zapatistas," says Dan. "We felt we should be doing in New York as the
Zapatistas were doing in Mexico: creating opportunities for people to
take back the commons for the people." After an encounter with the
NYPD ended in a rare, sudden withdrawal by the police, the squatters
found themselves with a lot of adrenalin and no opposition. "To the
Chase!" someone shouted. For a few giddy minutes they occupied a
busy downtown bank in one of the world's major financial centres,
then sensibly melted into the large crowd that had gathered outside,
just before a dozen police cars screamed onto the scene.

In the meantime, the Guiliani regime was escalating its eviction
campaign, and the squatters' movement its resistance. In May 1995,
squatters learned that the city intended to evict five well-established
squats on 13th Street that night. Close to a thousand people gathered
at the buildings and set up barricades. The city sent in riot police –
Dan estimates over one thousand of them – in full military gear, along
with a tank, three helicopters, and snipers on top of nearby buildings.
Lawyers friendly to the squatters told them that if they could hold off
the police until the courts opened in the morning, they would get an
injunction to block the evictions. Through the long night, it was a
standoff, with local media broadcasting live from the barricades.

"So 9 A.M. rolls around, and people were saying, 'Hey, we won!' So
we found ourselves, about fifty people left on the barricades, but still
on the other side, a thousand police – oh no!" Dan laughs. Eventually
the remaining defenders were arrested and carted away to prison.
"They did take the buildings, but it cost them an enormous amount of
money, which was part of our object. If we couldn't actually save the
buildings, at least we could make it as politically and financially costly
as possible, to protect other buildings. We had the impression that a

fair number of people were receptive to what we were trying to do – the mayor's approval rating dropped significantly during the evictions." A few weeks later, squatters re-entered the buildings, and fought another running battle with the police.

In a 5th Street squat where Dan lived for a while, he happened to be working in the ground-floor bookstore when city workers arrived to evict the residents. "I said to these guys, 'Didn't you read the papers? You can't evict people without a tank and at least a thousand police!' You could tell they didn't want to get involved, these were people on minimum wage, welfare-to-work people. They said it's what they'd been told to do. They said, 'Do you have any dogs here?' Some squatters are obsessed with big dogs, and this building happened to have one of biggest Rottweilers I had ever seen, so I mentioned that. The city workers said, 'Oh no, it's against union policy to go in there.' They called their supervisor, who called their supervisor, who called *their* supervisor – finally somebody said, 'Forget it, we're not going to evict.' But it was a brief victory. Eventually that building burned down – arson being the most effective way for speculators to get at these buildings."

When the city moved to clear peddlers off the street, the people at La Plaza Cultural let them move in. "Then the neighbours started getting *really* upset," says Dan. "Already they wanted to convert our park into a green thumb park – there are a lot of nice ones, community gardens, but most of them close at night, and they have very strict rules. Ours was a different idea, a free space where people could actually live. Now the neighbours on the block were threatening to evict this park. So I started going to block association meetings and suggesting that it might be better if they got more involved in the park, if they got to know people, so we could talk about the issues. But they didn't seem to have any interest in dealing with the thing reasonably. At one block meeting, one guy said he'd stab me if I went in. Then they called the police, who dragged me away, even though *I* was the one who'd been threatened!"

With four arrests and now a threat on his life, it was time for a change. Dan believed no less in revolution, but he now understood that to create a system where all people were treated fairly would require an enormous, fundamental transformation in social and political thought. "It was clear to me that if this kind of social change was to take place, people would need to work wherever they are – not just in the exciting metropolis but in towns like Cleveland, everywhere. Also, those questions I had growing up in Cleveland were still in my mind, not answered." Not long after he left New York, the city evicted his last squat and made deals with other squats to become legal. In Dan's eyes, the movement had peaked.

He signed up to begin his Ph.D. work at Case Western Reserve University in Cleveland. "Going back to school, with a grant and a stipend for teaching, would provide me with the sense of structure, the stability I needed to explore those questions." From Maria Lougones he had learned it was possible to do engaged work in an academic setting, and from his own reading on popular education, he had learned that formal research methods could play a useful role in social change. He would start work on the Ph.D. in the autumn of 1996.

But first he wanted to reacquaint himself with Cleveland. Late in 1995 he rented a two-bedroom flat on the South Side. To the west it faces the vast gloomy hulk of an abandoned steel mill, and to the south, vacant lots and a neighbour's chicken coops. I spent a couple of days with him in November 2003. He's tall and angular, with a gentle handshake and what sounds to my Canadian ear like a midwestern twang. The flat is small, brightly painted, and crammed with books, papers, video cassettes and CDs, the roots and products of Dan's work. On a wall in his tiny office is a 2003 award from the Cleveland branch of Jobs with Justice, "for rank and file activism." Vibrant paintings on the wall are by Tatiana, his wife, away studying that week in New York. Wobbly the cat comes and goes at will, a free spirit. He was born, Dan tells me, in an East Village squat.

A sharp wind off Lake Erie threatens rain. Driving from the bus station, we pass monuments to urban renewal – the stadium, the State University Convocation Center, the theatre district, office towers, a luxury hotel – all built on land that used to be a neighbourhood, low-income and predominately African-American. On a street of tastefully renovated houses we pause at the Jay Hotel, Cleveland's last SRO – single room occupancy, affordable accommodation. After a long fight to keep it open, the householders prevailed at City Hall, so gentrification can now proceed. A roughly hand-lettered sign is stuck to the door with duct tape: "Congratulations Ohio city neighbours you won we're closed but in your victory against us you've managed to put too many people homeless and 12 more people out of work as if there isn't enough people out of work. We hope everyone sleeps well. PS God is watching you."

First question for Dan on his return to Cleveland: Six years after the massive Housing Now protests in Washington, both the number and desperation of homeless people in Cleveland had continued to rise – why? More important, what was to be done?

PUBLIC SQUARE

In January 1996, Food Not Bombs began serving Sunday suppers at Public Square, a monumental civic space in the city centre. Food Not Bombs is a loose network of urban activist groups that resist federal and state policy on two fronts – the insanity of military production, and the resulting impoverishment of people. "Right after I got back here I was bit of a hermit," says Dan, "but when my friend Ayr came to stay for a month, he pushed me to get this thing started, going over to the West Side Market and asking people for food. He knew how to do that kind of thing from running a free kitchen. And there's an obsessive aspect in me, so once the thing was going, I kept it working."

Winter is a grimly fearful time for people on the street. The Sunday meals were timed to fit the winter circuits of homeless people seeking shelter and warmth. "They can sit in the public library, as long as they don't fall asleep," says Dan. "But the library closes at five on Sunday, so everyone tries to sneak into Tower City [an office and shopping complex] until the shelters open for the night. And some people refuse to go to the shelters at all – they have tents tucked away in the nooks and crannies of the city. I see it as a kind of resistance to the institutions of homelessness."

Along with Dan, fifteen to twenty volunteers would collect, cook, and serve food in Public Square on Sundays at 4 P.M. to anywhere from fifty to one hundred people. Most of the volunteers were high school and college students. "The younger folks tended to hang out with each other pretty much, but I was more interested in developing relationships with the people who showed up, and finding out from them what was going on in the city," says Dan. "I would just sit down and eat with people, and after a while conversation would develop. Usually it started with something like, 'How come there isn't any meat? What are you, hippies?' It was those growing connections that motivated me to keep coming, week after week. Eventually most of the others dropped out – chopping and cooking vegetables, bringing the food down to the Square every week, that's a lot of work." By the time Dan met Tatiana, some days the two of them were the only volunteers.

As the conversations evolved, it occurred to Dan that he should record them. He started with a $30 microcassette recorder. But in transcribing the tapes, he began to feel uneasy. "People's life stories can be pretty overwhelming. They were telling me all kinds of things, some of them so personal it seemed like they should be confidential – 'I'll tell you this but you can't tell anyone else.' That kind of intimacy started to frighten me a little. I'm not equipped to be a therapist, and also I didn't want the conversations to be that private, to end with me. It occurred to me that people should really be talking to each other. But this raised a problem – either it's very expensive or very time-consuming to make transcripts, and anyway, who wants to wade through a big pile of text?"

This dilemma prompted two shifts in the project, one in technology, the other in the kinds of questions he asked. Taking advantage of electrical outlets that allowed church groups to proselytize in Public Square, Dan brought a camera and monitor from the university and started recording the interviews on videotape. Each Sunday he would show the interviews he'd taped the previous week. "This gave people a sense that they weren't just speaking to me but to each other – and to anyone else who might see it. Eventually they were requesting replays of particular interviews, and they wanted me to show the tapes in other places, such as the shelters."

A deeper shift occurred in the way that Dan approached interviews. "Gradually I went from seeing them as personal life narratives to conversations about how people placed their own lives in the overall historical picture – in other words, how have we got to where we are? I wanted to know and I wanted other people to know how each person's experience connects to the others'. When I started to steer the interviews in that direction, people got less intensely personal. They started to relate their own experience to a larger political analysis. For instance, if I asked how a neighbourhood had changed over time, that would draw out their interpretations of local history, which inevitably includes their own experience within it. I'm sure there are ways that exploring personal issues can be transformative too, but this is the kind of oral history I'm interested in now – transformational, at a collective level."

> It takes the efforts, man, of all of us homeless people to get together and try and come up with solutions. But they don't want to hear our ideas. We go on homeless marches. We go on homeless outings. And we tell them what's the problem. We know what the problem is. But they don't want to listen to us. You know why? Because there's big dollars involved now.
>
> ❁ John Appling, interview, September 1999

Visiting Dan's street-based world, it's easy to forget that he's also working towards his Ph.D. at Case Western. I ask him how he integrates the academy and the street.

His dissertation title, "Open Penitentiaries: The Rise of the Institution of Homelessness in Cleveland, Ohio," captures both the content and his engaged approach to research. "It's not as directly connected to my work with homeless people and day labourers as I'd like," he says. "I do quote material from the oral histories, and they definitely provide the thematic backbone, but they aren't the central focus of it. That's one of the limitations of academic work – when I was doing my Masters, people made it clear to me that if you're going to market yourself as a historian, you need to have this very traditional research aspect to your work. So I did a lot of hard-core archival research that starts in the 1870s and runs through to the present. The oral histories only deal with the most recent piece of this. But part of it is my own desire for the grand narrative. Maybe that goes back to those questions when I was growing up – what happened earlier that led to this? I wanted to examine what happened before the oral histories began, in some way to validate what they said, through these earlier sources. I feel I've succeeded in that. What homeless people say is going on, and why, certainly makes a lot more sense than anything we hear from the so-called experts."

In the archives Dan found ample evidence to confirm the suspicions of homeless people that, as John Appling put it, "big dollars were involved." Says Dan, "The documents make quite clear how certain areas are allowed to deteriorate, and therefore these areas become abandoned. Then they're turned over to private developers who make a fortune off so-called urban renewal. My archival research has helped me understand that this pattern didn't start in the '60s, it was already well underway in the '30s – really, it's just capitalism at work. But still, the interviews with homeless people remain the most damning material. They really put the finger right on it."

Dan also concluded that his dissertation would not be the only product of his work in Cleveland, and perhaps not even the most important aspect. "There are already quite enough books in libraries with all kinds of great ideas that are totally collecting dust, and my guess is if I get my dissertation published, eventually it will become another one of those."

As he continued to accumulate interviews, and people kept urging him to spread the word more widely, he turned to radio. It was far less costly than TV and more accessible. He knew that a fair number of people living in shelters, under bridges, and on the streets carry portable radios; via radio, their voices could also reach households and cars throughout the city and suburbs. In the summer of 2000, he launched a weekly one-hour radio show, broadcast live Tuesday mornings on WRUW, the radio station at Case Western.

> I've seen people die out there on the street, they die on the church steps, and people will come by, they'll look at you, but they don't stop, they don't care if you're dead or alive. Everybody keeps walking past, walking past, going about their business. They have no time to say, 'Are you okay, do you need something to eat?' Finally some homeless person like me comes along and finds out you're dead. Don't you think people could stop?
>
> ❖ Robert Jackson, radio interview, November 27, 2001

Dan questions Robert Jackson about his involvement in the Poor People's March on Columbus, the capitol of Ohio, after deep cuts to welfare put many more lives at risk.

ROBERT: Forty-seven of us walked from Cleveland to Columbus.

DAN: That's a long way. How long did it take you?

ROBERT: Six days. We walked in rain and snow, but we made it. Then Voinovich [Ohio governor at the time, now a U.S. senator] wouldn't see us. We got a lot of flack up there, people said if you can walk you can work. But we made the national news.

DAN: And what came of that?

ROBERT: They promised us work on the Gateway Stadium [under construction at the time in Cleveland]. But when we went there, they escorted us out.

DAN: I heard there was some –

ROBERT: Yeah, they escorted us out at gunpoint. They forgot their promise, they got amnesia. Everybody wants to improve their situation, and you keep hoping, but it's all empty dreams.

"The primary goal in all those interviews at Public Square, and the radio show, was to let people hear each other and develop their voices," Dan says. Some of the interviews had unexpected impacts. Just before Christmas in 1999, a regular at the Sunday meals, Jason Maiden, told Dan in a video interview that homeless people were being arrested. It had been going on for a couple of days. "No one else seemed to know this was happening," says Dan. "Because of the terrible conditions at the shelters – it was even worse then than it is now – people had started sleeping out to avoid having to go into the shelters. But now the mayor [Mike White at the time] was trying to force everybody back into the shelters by arresting them if they were found outside." Dan wrote a leaflet reporting that 3,500 to 5,000 people were living on the streets in Cleveland, and more than a quarter of them were children under eighteen. He also mentions that the projected cost for the new football stadium in Cleveland was likely to exceed $400 million.

> The police come down and tell us we cannot lay on the sidewalks, period. . . . Now they want to come around the holiday season and get homeless people off the streets – to show things off for the people from the suburbs. That's all they want to do is see things pleasant. They don't want to see us lying on a bench, try-ing to get money. I think it is uncalled for. Now we must find places where they can't see us.
>
> ❀ Jason Maiden, interview, November 28, 1999

Dan says, "We found that to avoid arrest, people were leaving the steam grates and moving into secretive places where they risked freez-ing to death. This was a very dangerous public policy." He called a reporter he knew at *The Plain Dealer*, a Cleveland daily newspaper, which resulted in a story on the arrests. "We also discussed it with our group on Public Square: what should we do about this? Since they were arresting people so Christmas shoppers wouldn't be disturbed by their presence, we decided to set up a tent city on Public Square. That was our first organized act of civil disobedience. The night before Christmas Eve, we set up a big tent, we brought blankets, food, a kerosene heater, and we put up some banners. We were there for about nine hours, then the police shut it down." Eventually, activists won a court ruling that police could no longer arrest homeless people for sleeping on the street.

One Sunday afternoon in 1998 at Public Square, Dan interviewed Ralph William Pack, who calls himself "the barstool philosopher." Dan guesses his age as late sixties, early seventies.

RALPH: In a city where nobody will speak to you on the street, these communal meals are the only place where people can get together to network and exchange tips about things, like where you can get the best food. This is one of the great services, a lot more than just food.

DAN: All right. Do you want to maybe tell me what you think might be some of the causes of the present situation people find themselves in?

RALPH: In a so-called economic boom [before the dot.com bubble burst], too many Americans are doing well. During the Depression, so many were suffering, they all collaborated and helped each other out. When the majority think the stock market is going out of sight, they think they're going to be part of it, and they forget those who haven't quite got on the bandwagon. Besides, they've torn down nearly all the low-cost housing in the city – they tore them down for the various stadiums. Now instead of $3 a night hotels, we have $300 a night hotels, for people from New York, Toronto, and L.A. that have a thousand bucks to spend in a weekend. The majority of poor people have simply been priced out of the housing market. Jesse Jackson said it, "After the civil rights movement we now have the right to enter any hotel, but we don't have the money to."

DAN: How about the criminalization of the homeless, what do you make of that?

RALPH: It's criminalization of the poor. Today there's only one crime in America – that's being poor. Police stop everybody, clearing the streets. Something I really resent, these guys from the suburbs who come in, cruise around the poorer neighbourhoods, and automatically assume that every woman they see on the street is a prostitute. That's demeaning, a criminalization of people because of their economic status.

Through the 1980s and '90s in North America, an already tenuous social safety net was shredded by governments in Canada, and much more aggressively in the United States. By 1995, U.S. social expenditures represented just 17 per cent of the gross national product, a little more than half the average level of ten comparable Western nations. In 1998, already the thirteen thousand richest families had as much income as the twenty million poorest households. Then came the Bush regime's worldwide "war on terrorism," enormous tax cuts for corporations and the wealthy, and now a new space race, all financed primarily by the deepening misery of low and no income Americans. In 2002 another 1.7 million slipped below the poverty line, bringing the total to 34.6 million – one in eight Americans. Over 13 million of them are children. The United States now has the worst child poverty rate and the worst life expectancy of all the world's industrialized countries.

At the same time, while violent-crime rates have consistently fallen in the U.S., the Justice Department reported in 2003 that more than 5.6 million Americans – one of every thirty-seven adults – were imprisoned, the highest per capita incarceration rate in the world. Though African-Americans account for only 12 per cent of the U.S. population, they constitute 44 per cent of all prisoners in the United States; an African-American male has a one in three chance of going to prison during his lifetime. For a Hispanic male, it's one in six; for a white male, one in seventeen. Since 1980, incarceration rates for women have increased at nearly double the rate for men, almost entirely due to increasingly punitive drug policies. Nearly one in three women in prison is serving a sentence for drug-related crimes.

The barstool philosopher's analysis clearly supports Dan Kerr's contention: "What homeless people say is going on, and why, certainly makes a lot more sense than anything we hear from the so-called experts." The next step was to act on this belief. "At this point," says

Dan, "it seemed important to bring all these ideas I'd been hearing into some kind of group setting where people could develop their own themes and issues. This meant I had to negotiate with the directors of drop-in centres and mail sites, the kind of institutional involvement that I'd intentionally avoided. Until now, it was just myself with home-less people in public settings."

At about the same time, Dan spoke on the Cleveland Homeless Oral History Project at a conference in Istanbul, Turkey. "There was this woman on the panel who did oral history in prisons," he says. "She talked about how she had to negotiate everything with the guards. I thought, Well, if she can do that, surely I can at least figure out a way to do this thing, for example, to find a space that's accessible to home-less people, near to where they already are, as opposed to a room at the university where no one can get to."

After getting permission to use a room at Bishop Cosgrove, a drop-in centre and emergency shelter in downtown Cleveland, he put up flyers at other drop-in centres and mail sites and announced during meals at community centres that a series of workshops would be held. About a dozen people showed up for the weekly sessions through the winter and spring of 1999–2000. With Dan facilitating, they watched video interviews, listened to radio programs, brainstormed on the problems that homeless people faced, and finally wrestled these into six major themes: public policies that destroyed working class neigh-bourhoods, the replacement of SRO hotels by downtown "revitaliza-tion" projects, gutting of the welfare system, criminalization of the poor, the inhumane shelter system, and the rise of for-profit tempo-rary day-labour agencies.

THE LABOUR GUY

They decided to tackle the last of these first.
Through hundreds of interviews, Dan had been
surprised to discover that a high proportion of people living in the shelters work at paying jobs, whenever and wherever they can find

them. Corporate "rationalization" in the '80s and attacks on the welfare system in the '90s had combined to generate a large pool of available workers with no access to permanent jobs, and thus no choice but to do "mind-numbing, back-breaking, sometimes dangerous work for poverty wages and no benefits or health care," as an article in *The Plain Dealer* put it. They work in factories making car parts and toys, they clean hotels, restaurants, and office buildings, and they help bury the dead. After the temporary agencies take their cut of one-third to one-half of the worker's wages, few can survive on what's left.

In another series of workshops at the men's shelter, 2100 Lakeside, about twenty people decided to form the Low Wage Workers Union, later renamed the Day Labourers' Organizing Committee (DLOC). "Everyone there was a day labourer except me," says Dan, "and this one other guy that I'd interviewed, an eighty-year-old radical labour organizer from the 1930s. We talked about everything – the name of the organization, how to address the issues, and what our strategies should be. For me these second workshops were the turning point from the popular education approach, where people come together to figure out their issues, to an activist approach, where you actually build an organization to address these issues."

To spread the word, the DLOC published a pamphlet outlining the problems that day labourers face, and the goals of the committee. "We can effectively cut out the labor predators," it said. "We believe we can develop a co-operatively run labor agency that pays workers a full living wage, including benefits." Over the next several months, the committee created a questionnaire, and day labourers set out to interview other day labourers on wages, hours, safety concerns, harassment, and discrimination. They got petitions going to stop the temporary agencies from recruiting in the shelters. Then they put together a report and went to City Hall.

"That was an amazing process," says Dan. "A couple of city councillors agreed to hold a hearing on day labour. We asked who would be interested in testifying. Everyone knew there would be risks involved, but eighteen people volunteered. Then we had workshops to decide what issues they thought should be brought forward to council, and how. People divided up the twenty-three grievances we'd listed on the blackboard – it was like the collective final exam I had at college, with each person providing a piece from their own experience. The group decided they would push for two policy solutions: a community hiring hall and fairness legislation. In the actual hearings, all I said was, 'Listen to them.' Eighteen day labourers got up and spoke. They were very articulate on the issues. It was spectacular and gut-wrenching."

The risks were real. Some of the people who spoke at the hearing got blacklisted by the temporary agencies, which meant no jobs. "A few were upset, but I don't think anyone blamed the DLOC," Dan says. "I think the ethical key is to be completely forthright with people and not push anyone into a position that will put them at risk, especially if they're unaware of it. But in the end they have to make the decision."

Plans for a community hiring hall moved ahead. A local union agreed to help the blacklisted people find cleaning jobs at Cleveland hotels with union contracts. "The DLOC," says Dan, "was on a big high."

Then two planes slammed into the World Trade Center in New York. Air travellers panicked, and hotels across the country virtually closed down. Within a few months the hiring hall plans bogged down in a tangle of bureaucratic wrangling over partnerships and funding, as well as internal questions about how jobs would be found and who would get them. People became frustrated and discouraged; a string of personal crises also got in the way.

The DLOC decided to switch its energies to its second priority, the day labour fairness law. "That was an important transition," says Dan. "There's massive unemployment out there, and it's risky to be seen as a source of jobs. It's really not a good position for an organizer to be in who's trying to interest people in the issues: what if someone does get a job, will they be satisfied and lose interest in the bigger issue? Or if they don't get a job, will they be upset and lose interest anyway? I've never been in a position to dole out any jobs, but the perception is certainly there that I can."

In the short time I was in Cleveland, Dan got several calls from job-seekers. When we sat in on the fried chicken lunch at the West Side Catholic Center, a man looked at him, looked again, then said, "You're the labour guy, right?"

"Well, kind of, " Dan replied.

"What's happening with that?" the man asked. "You got any jobs?"

"Not really," said Dan. "But we're hoping that Local 10 can maybe get some contingent jobs in the parks next summer. They say there could be as many as five hundred." The man nodded and resumed his lunch. Dan pulled out a leaflet. "Maybe you'd be interested in this petition for a day labour fairness law?"

Based on similar legislation in Atlanta and Chicago, the Cleveland Day Labor Fairness Law would provide for the municipal licensing of all day-labour agencies, and the establishment of minimum operating standards, to ensure that day labourers were compensated fairly and treated with respect and without discrimination. Operators of any agency that violated the ordinance would face fines and be subject to having their licence revoked. By January 2003, over fifteen hundred individuals and organizations had endorsed the proposal, including most of Cleveland's city councillors. In March a councillor agreed to introduce the legislation, but failed to follow through. The petition drive continues. It now includes the signature of the man who asked Dan for a job in the West Side Catholic Center.

In the meantime Dan hasn't given up on the community hiring hall. "It's struggling right now, and it may not come to fruition. But if we can get it set up somehow, it could be a tremendous resource, not only for the obvious practical reason – to provide a viable alternative to the for-profit agencies – but also from a popular education point of view, it could open up all kinds of other alternative grass-roots economic development strategies."

I tagged along with Dan to a meeting at the United Labor Agency, a small non-profit inner-city agency set up by three unions. It provided the funding to hire a development director and to launch a twelve-week hiring hall pilot project involving twenty-five day labourers. The test run had just concluded, and this meeting was to plan an all-day evaluation session the following weekend with people who'd taken part. Several logistical questions came up: How could people be contacted who have no home and no phone? They could be reached via their voice mailboxes, provided by the North East Ohio Homeless Coalition. How would people get to the evaluation session? The United Labor Agency would provide bus passes. How many people would come, how much food was needed?

Over the twelve weeks the pilot project ran, it had become clear that for a hiring hall to survive, more jobs would have to be found. All the hirings in the test run were obtained through union shops, mostly hotels, where the union had been able to negotiate a clause in their contract specifying the community hiring hall as first source for temporary workers. People at the meeting agreed that most employers who wanted a reliable source of labour at minimum cost would tend to see a community hiring hall as more of a threat than an asset. How could this obstacle be addressed?

Dan argued, "The best source for direction on that question is the day labourers themselves. They're in the best position to evaluate what worked and what didn't." Others looked doubtful: If the day labourers were asked to identify problems, wouldn't it just turn into a griping session? Eventually it was settled. The evaluation question would be: What needs to be done to make a future hiring hall work most effectively?

In an academic paper that Dan wrote on the Cleveland Homeless Oral History Project, he refers to the importance of "shared authority" in doing such work. Rather than the classic roles of active researcher and passive subject, shared authority implies a relationship of equals. Though I agree with the theory, I do wonder how it can work in practice. After all, it was Dan who asked the questions, who kept all the tapes and CDs, and who would write the dissertation. "There's no easy answer to that," he admits. "Even on the radio show, I went through the radio training program, I determined who came on, I had the car that got them to the studio. But even then, in the actual interview process, there was shared authority in how the interviews were structured. They are the experts, not me. What I'm providing is the outlet, so they can be heard. In the workshops, it's true that I'm the one who can book the room, the one who has resources to print flyers and so on, but my goal has always been to create situations where people could come up with their own conclusions. At certain moments, I have to admit, I did seize the reins – 'Okay, we've got this idea.' I'd put it on paper, then I'd try to get things moving. In retrospect, I think I might do things a little slower. But there's a big Catch-22 here: if you do things too slowly, people lose patience and get frustrated, and if you do things too fast, they can become overly dependent on you to get things done!"

He also argued in his paper that for the homeless people's movement to survive, they would have to lead it themselves. But again I wonder, given the overwhelming challenges of day-to-day survival that homeless people face, is it fair or realistic to expect them to lead their own movement? Is it possible? Dan nods. "I think it is. What it needs is a supportive atmosphere, but that can be cultivated, which is partly what this whole process has been about."

Two years ago homeless people launched a petition drive, collecting massive numbers of signatures to kick out the Salvation Army, which runs the shelter. Dan played no role at all in organizing the campaign. "There was this prison mentality at the shelter. People were getting beaten up the security guards," he says. "So the Salvation Army got called down to city council. They were actually threatening to strip the contract from them. I was at that meeting. All I said was that in all other neighbourhoods they have block club associations to decide issues that matter to them, but in the shelter they're not supposed to meet or decide anything. It's actively discouraged; any control taken from the Salvation Army is fought tooth and nail. Well, after all this, they ended up firing the director of the shelter. The building and the conditions are much the same, but the attitude has changed. The new director has done some interesting things, like now they have a room where people can have meetings, which are encouraged but not led by the staff. They've divided the shelter into something like affinity groups who live together – the work group, the addictions group, the group that doesn't want anybody to bother them, and so forth. In this way people can support one another better. And it's entirely the actions by homeless people that led to these changes."

Two weeks before my visit, homeless people organized a march from the shelter to City Hall. "With so many people homeless now, the shelter is way overcrowded," Dan says. "This protest was organized entirely by homeless people themselves. I had no role in it at all. The new shelter director calls them 'the DLOC people.' It's only DLOC in the most grass-roots sense – we didn't have a meeting and decide, 'Let's have a march.' They just went ahead and did it. They chanted something like, 'Get us a place to stay, or we'll sleep at City Hall!' And they had their own spokespeople designated to talk with the press. I didn't say a word. That was very empowering for me to see."

Dan expects to complete his dissertation over the next few months. He'll move to New York, where Tatiana is studying. He's already started to apply for teaching jobs around the country. Where does he see oral history fitting into his future? "I think it will matter more and more in my work as a historian. I'll continue to use archival research for context and background, but what really fascinates me is the oral history part. Once I get a tenure track job and I can do whatever the hell I want" – he roars with laughter – "I'll continue to do interviews with people, particularly ones who are in some kind of crisis situation. It could be homeless people, it could be undocumented workers – it will depend on the issues I find in whatever community I'm in. But wherever I am, the most important thing for me, like that woman in New York said, is to keep asking questions."

I've told Dan that before I return home to Canada, I'd like to meet some of the people he works with. We miss Ralph William Pack at lunch but run into Tony Hall and his wife, Jay, first at lunch in the Westside Catholic Center, then again at the library. The Westside Center was built by the church, Dan tells me, as penance for destroying the neighbourhood when they expanded St Ignatius, an imposing private

Catholic school across the street. The lunchroom is packed – much more crowded than it was a few years ago, Tony says. The food is served up by smiling volunteers: fried chicken, white bread, macaroni salad, beets, and two brightly coloured cookies.

Jay doesn't say much, but Tony keeps up a running commentary, a stream of consciousness, through the meal. He mentions that in 1992 he started the *Cleveland Grapevine*, a newspaper by and for homeless people. "That was my creation," he says. "It was valuable in the beginning. It helped to keep people informed, but then it was taken over by the [North East Ohio Homeless] Coalition."

"You can get your breakfast at St Augustine's, your lunch here, and your dinner someplace else, but what I really want is to eat in my own home. Why can't I do that?

"They say people are homeless because of drug abuse. So how come rich people hooked on cocaine aren't homeless?

"In this country, convicted felons aren't eligible for any jobs or programs. That's all part of the criminalization of African-Americans."

Tony's nephew, an American soldier, is in Iraq. "He's at risk of being killed over there. Instead of all this war, why isn't the government addressing the needs of the people here at home? This country, it's a cyclone going the wrong way."

That evening Dan takes me along for his regular office hours, 7 to 8 P.M. Wednesdays in the DLOC office, upstairs from the Catholic Worker storefront. A sudden storm has blown in off Lake Erie, with flashes of lightning and lashing rain. He doesn't expect anyone to show up, but just in case. . . . People wait outside, crowding as close to the door as they can. The drop-in will open in another ten minutes. For homeless people, this is a regular stop on the circuit.

The office is basic, two small rooms with a table, a desk, and a couple of chairs. Someone broke into it recently, took the computer hard drive and the printer. No one shows up while we're here.

Downstairs, the drop-in is now open. Bright-eyed young people offer sandwiches, soup, coffee, and pastries. In one corner, a battered-looking man huddles in a chair, asleep. In another corner a woman sits by herself, laughing quietly now and then. Next to me on a sofa, two men strike up a lively conversation about Bush and bin-Laden. "Bin-Laden is an Indian," says one.

"What do you mean?" the other asks.

"He's an Indian, I swear to God. That's why he hates white people – three hundred years ago they stole his country."

Dan circulates with the Day Labor Fairness Law petition on a clipboard, asking people if they'd like to sign it. Some do. The man beside me says he can't. "Okay, but can I ask why?" Dan asks.

"I just can't," says the man. "It's confidential."

"Okay," says Dan, and he moves on. Eventually he settles at a table with another man and two women. One of the women talks to Dan for a while, then leaves. I join them. The other woman is a volunteer. Her cheerfulness strikes me as a little forced. We play Hearts, a card game three of us know and the other man says he can learn. He laughs a lot. He's a little drunk. Dan tells me later that he's a skilled welder who used to work in the Cleveland shipyards. About thirty years ago he was convicted of a minor felony. Since the yards closed – the jobs have gone to Asia – he's found very little work. Under the new Homeland Security regime, police checks are routine, and now he's rejected for most jobs, even the low paying ones. "He has two daughters," says Dan. "They're teenagers, and they want things, but he can't buy them. So he drinks."

Now and then, as we play, Dan asks him a question. Nothing too personal, "I was just wondering. . . ." It's what he does.

CHAPTER 15

A MAP OF THE HOLY LAND

On the time-smoothed slopes of Mount Carmel, Efrat Ben-Zeev used to lead groups of Israeli children along the winding paths of antiquity. She pointed out age-old springs, mysterious caves, small, tough oaks and terebinthes, almond trees and prickly pear cactuses gone wild, figs, grapes, carobs, and pomegranates. "Just down there on the coast is Caeserea," she told her young listeners – Caeserea, capital of the Roman province of Palestine, its aqueducts, theatres, temples, and fortifications beautifully preserved. Then she led them through one of the early Zionist settlements, now more than a century old. "This," she told them, "is where our national enterprise began."

Adult Israelis are required to serve two years in the military; like most women, Efrat was assigned to a non-combat post, in her case as a guide with the Society for the Protection of Nature. She conveyed to wide-eyed tourists the natural, historical, and biblical features of the Mount Carmel ridge, much of it now protected as a Gan Leumi, a national garden. Along the way she mentioned Abraham, King David, Jesus, the Crusades, the occupations – Turkish, then British, and finally, modern Israel. This was the official version, just as she had learned it. But roaming the ancient landscape, she began to notice other signs in it, signs that got no mention in her practised patter. She looked closer, and began to ask questions.

"It's astonishing what you can overlook, and for how long," she says. "Israel is a historically saturated place. The remains of former landscapes are everywhere. In school I learned a lot about the ancient – King David, the Temple, the Crusaders – and a lot about the modern – the Holocaust, the founding of Israel, making the desert bloom, the wars. But in between, nothing. Look, the mountains are terraced, and the terraces are handmade. It's obvious that someone was there before the Zionists. Everywhere you can find the ruins of houses, you can make out where cemeteries were, water mills, mosques, whole villages. I even lived for a while in a house that had been part of an Arab village, and we collected fruit from trees that were planted by Arab farmers. But I had no mind to pay attention to the fact that those trees were planted by real people who had lived there until quite recently. The only map I had ever known for this place was the Zionist map."

I met Efrat Ben-Zeev in June 2001 at Columbia University's Summer Oral History Institute in New York. Her work as an anthropologist relies heavily on oral testimony. She had come to the institute, like the rest of us, to compare notes on the whys and hows of doing this work. I was drawn immediately to her intelligence, humour, and the bright intensity of her engagement with her surroundings. She was also the first Israeli I had met.

From childhood I had absorbed the same images of her country that Efrat used to offer the tourists. Mine were derived from church, school, and the media: the Promised Land, the Holy Land, the Holocaust, the Exodus (Paul Newman and the other beautiful, tanned freedom fighters), the Six Days War – brave little Israel, surrounded by Arab hordes bent on driving the Jews into the sea.

In my *Bible Reader's Encyclopedia*, a Sunday-school prize from 1956, black and white photos depict key Bible sites: Nazareth, Bethlehem, the River Jordan, the Sea of Galilee. The people inhabiting those stony places are clothed as they might have been twenty centuries ago, barefoot, unsmiling, most of them bent under heavy bundles or water jars on backs and heads. To the eyes of a Canadian child they look timeless, or fixed in time, unevolved, quite unlike the vibrant images of modern Israelis, the people who made the desert bloom. I had no name for those timeless people in the photographs, not until the 1960s when some of them hijacked airplanes. Even then, all I learned was that they called themselves Palestinians, and where I lived, they were called terrorists.

In New York, Efrat and I went for long walks through warm evenings, shared dishes at Thai restaurants, and talked with the easy intimacy of strangers far from home – she from Jerusalem, I from rural Ontario – about our work, our backgrounds, our given and chosen families, our sexualities, hope, and fears. I read her doctoral thesis, she read one of my books. By habit we asked each other many questions.

For this book, we recorded two long interviews about Efrat's work, one in a park by the East River, another overlooking the Hudson. We explored the new map of Israel that has gradually revealed itself to her in the ruins, military archives, and stories she gathers from the lost tribes of Palestine.

NARRATIVES
OF EXILE

Born in Israel in 1964, Efrat travelled with her parents in the mid-1970s to Australia, India, Nepal, Thailand, Hong Kong, and the Philippines. "I found it quite fascinating to encounter these rich cultures that I knew nothing about, and people who lived so differently from us." The experience gave face and body to her childhood fascination with maps, for the stories they tell, and – as she would discover – the stories they conceal.

For her Masters thesis in anthropology, she assembled an oral history of Abu Ghosh, a Palestinian village that still exists on the road from Tel-Aviv to Jerusalem. There for the first time she heard Palestinians tell their own story, in their own words. Later she worked at a facility under transformation into a museum of co-existence, and met more Palestinians.

In 1995 she began research for her doctoral thesis; eventually, after two years at Oxford University in England, and shortly after the second Intifada erupted, she published the finished work: "Narratives of Exile – Palestinian Refugee Reflections on Three Villages, Tirat Haifa, 'Ein Hawd and Ijzim." All three villages were occupied by Jewish forces in July 1948 and destroyed soon after. As an academic study the thesis explores a complex mesh of displacement, exile, and memory; at a deeper level it challenges some of the most cherished founding myths of Efrat's own people.

While Jewish Israelis celebrate 1948 as the year of liberation from their long exodus, Palestinians mourn the year as *al-Nakba*, the Catastrophe. According to the United Nations Relief and Works Agency, some 800,000 Palestinians were forced to flee from farms, towns, and villages into Jordan, Lebanon, Syria, Egypt, Iraq, and other more distant places. Nearly all of them left with virtually nothing, believing that they would soon return. The 1967 war triggered another massive wave of uprooting and dispersal. The UNRWA reports that the current Palestinian Diaspora numbers over four million refugees.

For those who live in the West Bank and Gaza Strip, things have gone from bad to worse. In September 2003, Amnesty International reported that "Closures, blockades, checkpoints, roadblocks, curfews and other restrictions have had a disastrous impact on the lives of Palestinians in these Occupied Territories, and have crippled the Palestinian economy. Some 60 percent of Palestinians in the West Bank and Gaza Strip live below the poverty line of $2 per day and unemployment is close to 50 percent."

Under the circumstances, I ask Efrat, how did she manage to find Palestinians willing to be questioned by an Israeli? She says she started with friends of friends, then knocked on doors in a Haifa refugee quarter, asking in her halting Arabic, "Who here comes from Ijzim?"

"Sometimes I would have to go back two or three times before people trusted me enough to talk. Sometimes I would phone to say I was coming, but when I got there nobody was home, or they wouldn't open the door. Some of them would joke with me, they would ask, 'Do you work for the Mossad [Israeli secret police]?' One man told me that when I first came to his village, he was sure I worked for the police because I had a white car with two aerials on it. It's funny, because it's so hot here that half the cars in Israel are white! But then it's hardly surprising that they would be suspicious. There is always the secret police, Israeli, Jordanian, whatever. You never know who might be an informer."

Efrat conducts some of her interviews in English, usually with younger people, but most are in Arabic. "I'm aware that my lack of facility in Arabic has been a defect in my work. I could ask how many goats a person had, but could not engage in a proper discussion of anything more complicated, such as identity. But it was either do it this way or not do it at all."

To compensate, she pays close attention to what she calls "the external dimensions" of the conversation. "I make notes about how the room looks, how the person looks, how they relate to other family members, and other things going on around the interview. I make additional notes when I return from the interview and have time to reflect on what happened – why someone from the Islamic movement agreed to talk to me, for example, and what use he might make of our contact, that kind of thing. I also note some of my own emotional responses to situations, although I'm not yet skilled enough in doing this."

When she and her husband returned from England, Efrat proposed that they rent a house in an Arab neighbourhood. There could be no better way to learn the language; each time she goes to Jordan to do interviews, she notices how rapidly her Arabic improves. Out of the question, her husband said: What would happen when he came home in uniform from his turns of duty with the army reserves? Efrat continues to take classes in Arabic at a small bilingual school in Jerusalem. "To speak Arabic well is quite challenging," she says. "Usually Israelis who are really good at it have worked either in the army or intelligence. At least mine is learned at the school!"

As people came to trust her a little more, they would refer her to relatives in the West Bank and Jordan. Usually she went to meet people in their homes, some of them in refugee camps. She described a camp in Irbid, a city in the north of Jordan. "Before 1948 it was hardly a village, but then suddenly came this huge wave of refugees. At first they had only tents, then little huts. Now the houses are made of cement, but the poverty there is very apparent and quite deep. Even after half a century everything still looks makeshift. The roads are narrow, sewage runs into the streets, the houses are so small. It's very crowded there. In one house I sat with maybe twenty people in the same room, mothers, babies, neighbours – everybody came to watch."

Venturing as a woman into a culture where women and men lead quite separate lives has pros and cons. In one way it has made Efrat's work a little easier. In one of her interviews she asked a man named Munir if it mattered whether she was a man or a woman. "No," he replied. "Well, perhaps. With a woman it is nicer. A man can be dangerous."

"Threatening?"

"Threatening, yes. You are not a direct threat but an indirect one. You are thought of as being 60 per cent of a man. Because a man is 99 per cent from the secret police, a woman 70 per cent. Whoever walks into this village and speaks to someone, people will say, 'Someone from the secret police came to see him.' 'But they are not,' the man will say, 'they are writing a book.' 'Yes, all right, I know, but they are from the secret police.'"

In the introduction to her thesis, Efrat acknowledges the respect she developed for Munir. "In spite of fits of skepticism and ongoing cynicism," she writes, "he relentlessly acts on behalf of others, relinquishing personal comfort for altruistic aims." Munir lives in the "unrecognized" village of 'Ein Hawd. Its survival is a testament to endurance. A few kilometres from the site of the original village, the new 'Ein Hawd was built without approval from the authorities. Though technically its inhabitants are citizens of Israel, for years their village has had no electricity, phone, roads, water, or sewage system.

Munir is a pseudonym, as are nearly all the names used in "Narratives of Exile." Efrat never pushed people to use their own names, and many didn't. Though she always stressed that she wasn't a journalist, enough of her narrators had learned from prior experience to fear their stories would appear the next day in an Israeli newspaper, with unpredictable but usually negative consequences.

Palestinians – both men and women – have often asked her, "Why is a woman like you out on her own doing this work, instead of being at home with her husband and children?" On the other hand, her apparent independence leads some men to sit with her and talk as they would with a man. Other men won't talk to her unless a second woman is present. The company present determines the topics of conversation. With older men Efrat can explore "male" topics like history and politics, and with older women, family stories, folklore, food, the practicalities of day-to-day survival. With younger people, the separation is less defined.

I return to my original question: Why would any Palestinian trust an Israeli stranger with their story? A similar question comes up in my own work, though I live in a much less dangerous place. The bus drops me off in a small town, I share a meal with a vulnerable person I've never met before, we record a conversation about intimate aspects of life – childhood wounds, isolation, loneliness, fear, sexuality – then I get back on the bus and likely we'll never meet again. But I have the tape, and I will write a book. With stakes so much higher in Israel/Palestine, why would any Palestinian trust Efrat?

"I often wonder myself," she says. "I was surprised by the distinction that Palestinians were able to make, even the most simple poor people did it – to them I represented Israel in some way, but somehow they were able to deal with me also as a singular person. Some of them said to me, 'I can still hate the Jews but I shouldn't make you into a representative of your people.' Often in interviews people would say, 'You Jews did such and such, we had a lovely life until you came and took it away from us.' On the other hand, people were incredibly kind to me. I haven't been able to decipher exactly why. Partly I think it has to do with Arab hospitality."

The distinction between representative and singular person can reach bizarre extremes. In September 2001, a year into the current Intifada, Efrat was doing research on Sarafand, another village obliterated by the Israeli army in 1948. Its ruins are tended by the Islamic movement. The man in charge of the Islamic holy places at Sarafand had agreed to an interview, their second meeting. "He was very nice to me, and very open," she says. "Then he started to say the most fanatic things – that the Jews have deserted the way of Moses, and therefore they are not entitled to be the people of God any more. One day there will be a war in Palestine, he said, the Moslems will extinguish the Jews and they will build a Moslem state in the place of the Jewish state. All of this came out in a very quiet and friendly manner, as if somehow he couldn't imagine how any of it could cause any harm to the person sitting in front of him."

Given this deep gulf, I wonder even more, why would any Palestinian consent to talk with her? I watch her thinking. On the darkening East River a tugboat rumbles by. "I think first of all that people are people," she says. "If we can overcome our animosity and fear, and it's clear that someone is ready to listen, most of us like to talk, to convey our side of things. Beyond that, some Palestinians tell me they hope my project may improve the chances of making even some small change. They've been silenced for so long, in so many ways. And despite everything, I think that a lot of Palestinians still believe in non-violent, political methods of changing things. Perhaps they think I have more power than I actually do, but at least they know I have the potential to reach a wider public – especially an Israeli public – than they can. Some people actively encourage me to do more than I do – people such as you!"

Since shortly after we met, and especially after reading her thesis, I've been nagging Efrat: These are such powerful stories, they need to be heard beyond the confines of the university. Why don't you make them available to a wider public? How will Israelis ever discover those other maps unless people like you provide them?

At the oral history institute in New York, we grapple with the responsibility we bear towards our interviewees or narrators, without whom – no oral history. "Of course I feel responsible," says Efrat. "I barge into people's lives, some of them I see only once, and I ask them very personal questions about the most difficult time of their lives. Usually I come out of interviews quite moved, and sometimes almost shattered by what I've heard. I've grown to like many of the people I've interviewed, and to appreciate their way of life – I keep wondering how they manage to remain humane under these terrible conditions. Yes, I feel responsible. But I don't know how to translate that – what is it that I should do?" Her frustration is palpable.

I start again: "These are such powerful stories. . . ." Eventually I'm embarrassed by my own nagging, especially from the comfy cushion of a rural Canadian. "I'm sorry," I say, "I feel like your mother."

Efrat smiles. "My mother would never push me as you do."

MACRO/MICRO

Another magnet for me with Efrat is her passion for exploring how "ordinary" people read their world, in the shadow of the grand official narrative handed down by the authorities. In fact she didn't set out to oppose the two versions – which she called macro and micro – but to investigate how they might compare. She also reminds me that there are actually two official versions, the Israeli and the Palestinian. The Palestinian official version tends to be as selective and packaged as the Israeli, relying as it does on the views of leaders, prominent men, parties, and social institutions – "the grand politics," as she puts it. In both official versions, the experience of common people, especially villagers, tends to go missing.

To see how personal memories of *al-Nakba*, the Catastrophe, compare with official Israeli accounts of the 1948 triumph, Efrat negotiated permission to view relevant documents in the archives of the Israel Defense Forces. By law all such documents were sealed for fifty years, but in preparation for the fiftieth anniversary of the founding of the state, historians prevailed on the government to declassify some materials earlier. Still, access remains daunting. Efrat approached the archives as a university researcher and listed her requests: documents pertaining to the war of 1948, with specific reference to campaigns in and around the villages of Tirat Haifa, 'Ein Hawd, and Ijzim. Then she waited four months while an archivist selected the relevant files, a fairly quick process, and the censor screened them, a very slow process.

When her documents were ready – close to five hundred of them – she found that some she'd requested were missing entirely, replaced by a cryptic form, and others had sections, sentences, or words cut out by the censor. "It's not hard to guess from the context that it's mainly the names of informers, or actions such as the expulsion of civilians that the archive still wants to conceal."

The documents included battle accounts, intelligence reports, interrogations of prisoners, and reports from Arabs who provided information to the Jewish forces. "The censor did a lousy job on some of those," says Efrat. "Some of the names are still there, which is very irresponsible. A lot of collaborators were paid off with permission to stay in Israel, and their children are still there. Even now this information could be dangerous or at least very uncomfortable for them."

Many academics, particularly historians, tend to regard oral testimony as unreliable. Efrat was surprised to find how closely the accounts of villagers, their micro versions, converged with the military records, which also represent micro versions from the other side – they begin as detailed account of life "on the ground," then they are selected to form the macro version, the grand narrative. "When it comes to war or other traumatic experiences, it seems that things imprint more strongly on our memories," she says. "War, the loss of one's home, one's land: what could be more traumatic than that? Also there's a lot of research to suggest that autobiographical memory – memories of your own life – is the most reliable kind, and apparently people remember best from their youth and early twenties. People that I interview can remember incredibly small details from 1948: the names of Israeli prisoners caught in the fighting, what was growing in the field where they were caught."

Where micro and macro diverge, radically, is in interpretation. "On the macro level, Zionist rhetoric always claims that the Arabs were so weak, so scared, when we approached, they fled, and that was that," Efrat says. "But when you look at the actual records – and here the army documents agree completely with the oral testimonies – in some places there were battles, villages were bombed heavily, then finally the villagers fled. That's quite a different story from the official rhetoric."

In a nation that regards itself as being under constant threat of annihilation, to question the official rhetoric strikes me as an intensely political act. "Anthropology for me *is* a political act," she replies, "in that it teaches you that people differ and you should be humble enough to respect those differences. At the same time, I also know that there's a delicate borderline between speaking about my research and making political statements."

How does she know where that borderline is? "Intuitively I know. One has to balance very gently between description and interpretation – both that of the researcher and that of the researched. Because my material is so inherently political, I try to be more descriptive than interpretative in my work, more grounded in facts, things that I can see and hear. But at the same time I hope to lead readers toward grasping reality in a certain way. This is in contrast to someone who spells out the conclusions clearly. Such boldness is bound to be more controversial, I think."

How can she grasp reality herself when she's dependent on quite varied, even contradictory memories and interpretations of fact? "If you take fifteen different interpretations, and you look at them closely enough, you will often find recurring patterns," she replies. "Even though I said that the conclusions of my research on the Mount Carmel villages were only relevant to those particular villages, I have discovered since that similar patterns hold true for many Palestinians. For example, tensions between the first and second generations are very consistent, with the younger people accusing their elders of having left their land without putting up a fight, then not being rebellious enough after the expulsion. Once I'm aware of patterns like this, I try to check them in my further encounters with Palestinians, to see if they reverberate."

In conversation, I've noticed that Efrat often follows a statement with a qualifier: "And yet. . . . although. . . ." Then she'll introduce a new, sometimes conflicting idea on the subject, a gentle reminder that there are no easy answers. "I would say that my anthropology is relativistic," she says. "How you stand in relation to someone or something determines your perspective. I am not looking for objective truths or wide generalizations from the outside but trying to see things as people see them from within. Later I may try to see them from a greater distance and try to draw some conclusions from that, but the first part of the game is to immerse yourself as well as you can in the ways that people live their lives."

MEMORY

Since she completed her thesis, Efrat has deepened her exploration of the role that memory plays in the Palestinian struggle to maintain a sense of land and nation, when both are out of reach. A favourite act of commemoration is to visit the site of the former village, even though most of these were wiped off the map long ago. When Efrat has gone along on these visits – pilgrimages, really – people tell her "So-and-so's house was here, the men would meet over there, here I saw a snake, I was only five at the time. . . ." "They re-imagine the place. It's a way of preserving memory, by rooting it in places and things, in their bodies," she says.

"This is not about nostalgia, at least not in the western sense, which seems to mean wrapping some former era in a vague, golden haze. This kind of remembrance is much more complex, more balanced. When people spoke to me about a particular spring, not only would they tell me how sweet the water was, and how they used to walk there and pick mushrooms, but parallel to that they would also say things like, 'Shit, I was only six years old and I had to carry water on a donkey, in pots made of clay that would hit the trees and break, but I couldn't say anything because then people would consider me not a man.'

The Islamic movement has become the leading force in the return to villages and maintaining what remains of them – a few graves, the skeleton of a mosque. "By roaming the village and uncovering its pre-1948 remains, Palestinians make themselves present again within what has seemingly become an entirely Israeli landscape," Efrat says.

In Sarafand, on a low hill by the coast, a small mosque somehow remained standing, but needed repairs. People began to work on it. "One night somebody came with a D10," says Efrat. "These are huge tractors that the Zionists love, you can pull whole mountains down with them. They pulled down the mosque. Probably it was somebody semi-official from the nearby Jewish settlement. But then the people who care for the mosque decided to rebuild it. When they couldn't get permission to rebuild with stone, they put up a tent on top of the foundation, they brought chairs, carpets, and for over a year now they've had a guard there day and night. Many of the people that go there are in their seventies or even older, but they bring their children and their grandchildren. A lot of youngsters are joining the Islamic movement – they may not be particularly religious, but in their eyes at least it's trying to do something."

Not everyone wants to go back. Fatmeh was born in 1928 in the original 'Ein Hawd and gave birth there to her first child, a daughter, during the 1948 war. When the Jews conquered her village, people fled into dense forest on the Carmel slopes. There Fatmeh's daughter died. Fatmeh has lived the rest of her life in a refugee camp on the West Bank. She has since had an opportunity to visit the site of her village, but chose not to go. She would probably die of a heart attack if she saw what the Israelis had done to 'Ein Hawd, she told Efrat.

When commemoration is effectively blocked at the state level, it still finds expression in the community or the private realm: "Every home, shop and café becomes a museum." A witness told Efrat that in the refugee camp at Irbid, two glass containers stood on a shelf in a fruit juice shop. The shop-owner explained: One jar contained a handful of earth that he had scooped up on a visit to his former village, at-Tireh, and the other held the sole of a shoe with which he trod on the ground of at-Tireh.

In a paper titled "The Politics of Taste and Smell: Palestinian Rites of Return," Efrat studies food as an especially pungent vehicle for preserving memory. Here she pays close attention to what she calls "the external dimensions" of her interactions with Palestinians.

'Abd al-Malek and Ramziyyeh, a couple originally from the village of 'Ein Hawd, now live in an Arab village in the Galilee. At their front door is a small patch of dry land that 'Abd al-Malek has turned into a garden. Efrat describes a meal that Ramziyyeh prepared. "The main dish was *kufta*, and with it we ate fresh thyme salad made from a bush that 'Abd al-Malek had transplanted from the mountains into his garden. Ramziyyeh also served a mallow salad, made from leaves she had collected in the wild. The lemons came from a tree that grew behind their house. In the refrigerator 'Abd al-Malek kept a liquid brewed from water and *za'ator farisi*, another plant from the mountains that they would drink if they had a cold or were feeling sick – it's known to contain an antibiotic component. All of these foods help bring the past to life."

Qasem lives near the Haifa beach, a few kilometres from his original home, at-Tireh, where he was born in 1931. He visits the ruins regularly and tends to his father's grave as well as he can, in a cemetery that's gradually disappearing under a Jewish settlement. One visit left a particularly vivid imprint on him. Every autumn he and his children would go to pick olives from a few trees his grandfather had planted near the entrance to al-Tireh. "Olives are the Palestinians' most treasured fruit," Efrat writes. "They're grown throughout Palestine, from the mountainous area of the Upper Galilee to the southern Hebron Mountains. The harvesting of olives in autumn, after the first rain, is a family occasion with countrywide traditions – everyone helps, including children and the elderly. People sing while they work, and shared meals are served at the olive grove. Especially since 1948, the olive is probably the closest thing to a national symbol that the Palestinians have."

On the visit he remembers so well, says Qasem, "An Iraqi man, a Jew, saw my children picking olives and thought that the children were alone. He didn't see that I was on the tree. He passed by with his car and then he made a reverse and came back. I came down and he said to me: 'Oh, it's you.' I said: 'Yes, it's me.' 'Are you the owner here that you come every year and pick olives?' I said: 'These are my father's olives. My grandfather planted them and we pick them every year.' He said: 'No, they used to be yours. They aren't any more.' I said to him: 'You came from Baghdad yesterday and now you think it is yours. My grandfather planted these trees, and yet you say they aren't mine. I will come every year to pick the olives, and you can do as you please.'

Says Efrat, Qasem's clear memory of this small act of resistance is all the more striking since it happened more than thirty years ago, and at a time when Arabs in Israel were under direct military control and very tight surveillance.

INTIFADA

When the oral history institute ended in New York, Efrat and I went our separate ways, she to Jerusalem, I to rural Ontario. We continued to talk by email, partly for the sake of this book, but more, apparently, because it fed some need in each of us. Unlike the brisk efficiency of most email exchange, our correspondence has the reflective quality of old-fashioned letters. "Your letters move me deeply," I write in one message. "Your letters open my heart," she writes in another.

As the Intifada deepens (the Arabic word *intifada* translates loosely as "breaking away from something that binds") and Israeli state repression escalates, Efrat's life and work blur in ways she doesn't like but can't help. Early one morning – usually the only time of day when she's free to write – she says that she will only have a minute because the helicopters circling overhead will soon wake the children.

She writes about a colleague at Hebrew University whose kids decided at the last minute they'd rather eat lunch at a falafel place in town than at the university cafeteria. At precisely the moment when they would have been eating their lunch, a bomb exploded in the cafeteria, killing seven people and injuring dozens more.

In return, I write to Efrat about my work, and life in rural Canada – planting garlic, cutting firewood in the forest, the golden radiance of sun through autumn leaves. Then I apologize for being so trite by comparison with her chaotic reality. She writes back that I have no reason to apologize. "It brings me much joy to know that people somewhere live a proper life, especially when it is my friends." We write back and forth about despair and hope, the repetitiveness of history, the numbing power of religion, the ease with which apparently sane people can be induced to vote for psychopaths.

After reading my third book, *Eating Fire: Family Life, on the Queer Side*, she writes: "It opened a whole new world to me, a world that has been and still is very foreign. I must confess I find it very intriguing and almost exotic. I now find myself looking at people on the street and wondering about their sexuality. And on this frank note – my curiosity for Palestinians is probably also motivated by this attempt to understand something that, at least from the outside, seems very different."

This is how Efrat sees the world, I think, as she did the rough signs of Arab civilization on Mount Carmel: first curiosity, then looking closer, then drawing parallels and investigating patterns. "When I mention that I'm reading about alternative families, people get curious but when I say it is about homos and lesbians the curiosity transforms into something else. Through these reactions I can learn something of the experiences of hostility you and your interviewees describe. These negative reactions to homosexuality, reactions signaling 'I don't want to know anything about it,' are common among my Palestinian friends, perhaps because they have not internalized political correctness."

In February 2002 Efrat reported her first encounter with the Israeli police. They had piled up a wall of mud and stone across the only road into Issawiyyeh, an Arab village near the university. As these blockades do throughout the West Bank, it functioned as a prison. When a group of Israeli-Jewish and Arab activists set out to dismantle the roadblock, a friend persuaded Efrat to go along. "I don't usually get involved this way," she says, "but this village is just two hundred meters beyond the valley near my home, I can see it from my balcony."

The police called in reinforcements and charged the crowd. "No one really hit me badly, but I did fall to the ground and then got pulled up violently by a policeman who wanted me to move away," Efrat says. "They hate it when you are on the ground, especially when there are photographers present. As soon as the policeman let go of me, this woman took me to the side. She was younger than me, probably a student, and Palestinian. It seemed that she's been through these things before. And it reminds me that the dividing line is not the national one. But still, the more I touch on the real things that are going on here, the more I lose hope. Even the violence and hatred that I felt within myself towards the policeman who was holding me now worries me."

In April, after bombing and shelling Bethlehem, which is Palestinian territory, Israeli tanks invaded it. Fifteen Palestinians died during the incursion, and 198 Palestinians sought refuge in the Church of the Nativity, reputed to be built on the birthplace of Jesus. Contradicting Israeli authorities, the Vatican announced that those Palestinians inside the church were non-combatants seeking sanctuary, and that the forty-five priests and nuns who had remained in the church were not hostages but were hoping that their voluntary presence would prevent a full-scale Israeli assault. A month later the siege ended, but the city remained under tight blockade by the army.

In August a group of Israelis and Palestinians prepared to enter Bethlehem for a joint rally. By now Efrat had become involved. Formed in autumn 2000, the group calls itself Ta'ayush, from the Arabic for "life in common" – "a grassroots movement of Arabs and Jews working to break down the walls of racism and segregation by constructing a true Arab-Jewish partnership. . . . through concrete, daily actions of solidarity to end the Israeli occupation of the Palestinian territories and to achieve full civil equality for all Israeli citizens."

The group decided that instead of entering Bethlehem secretly, partly because it could endanger their Palestinian counterparts but mainly to make a point of transparency, they would simply walk past the army roadblock. It is generally assumed that Israeli Jews have freedom of movement. "The army knew in advance that we were coming, and they put up a new roadblock very close to Jerusalem," says Efrat. "They brought horses and a special car with a water cannon to disperse us. We clashed with them a little, trying to push the soldiers and policemen, and some of us were hurt. Then we gave up and had a rally at the roadblock, while our Palestinian partners had a rally near the Church of the Nativity. We spoke to each other by phone. Altogether we felt it was a failure, but the consolation was that it got a lot of media coverage, much of it portraying us favorably."

In her emails, Efrat often expresses frustration with the Israeli media, which consistently upholds the official version, and helps keep the public ignorant. Journalists only tend to be interested in Ta'ayush activities when there's a good chance of violent confrontation, she says. In contrast to the August rally, hardly any media showed up at the much larger October 2002 protest in Abu Dis, organized by Ta'ayush and other peace groups. The notorious new "separation wall" cuts through this Arab neighbourhood in East Jerusalem, isolating sixty thousand Palestinians, most of them with Israel residency papers, from their work, relatives, hospitals, pharmacies, schools, and holy places in Jerusalem.

Efrat reports, "Because we knew the army would try to block us, we had the buses let us off on outskirts of the neighbourhood, and walked fast so they couldn't stop us with the usual roadblocks. As we walked, people from the neighbourhood started to join us, and by the time we reached the wall we were about seven or eight hundred. Then the army decided to crack down on us. Some said a few Palestinians threw stones at them, but I didn't see that. Suddenly the army started shooting tear gas at us and charged the crowd. We dispersed into the side streets. The protest reassembled, and concluded without any further confrontations. I was very sorry that nobody from the media bothered to come."

I ask if she feels anything was gained at Abu Dis. "The Palestinians loved it," she replies. "They said, 'Can't you come back every week?' It shows them they aren't completely alone, and at least some Israelis realize how badly the system treats them. Something very important happened to all of us together there. I felt a sense of solidarity that I have never felt anywhere else."

In addition to organizing rallies and protests on many fronts, Ta'ayush groups work with Palestinians to repair water lines destroyed by Israeli settlers and the military, harvest olives, build playgrounds, plant trees, and deliver emergency food by human convoy to villagers under blockade.

I ask Efrat how she would define the mission of Ta'ayush. "That is not very clear," she replies. "When people tried to write a constitution they couldn't agree and the whole thing nearly fell apart. So instead of people who agree on an ideology, what you have is people who share a need to *do* something, to be politically involved, to put a humane dimension into this terrible situation. The injustices brought about by the occupation are so many and so depressing, it's easy to feel completely overwhelmed. We want to put forth an alternative viewpoint, to demonstrate that Israelis and Palestinians can work together and can agree on many points. But mainly I'd say our mission is to act. If a curfew makes life impossible for people we should demonstrate against it, if a village has no water supply we should intervene, if Jewish settlers try to prevent villagers from harvesting their olives we should go there to help them."

Inevitably Efrat's work as an activist spills over into her home life. Occasionally Ta'ayush meetings will be held at her house, and since Palestinians aren't allowed to enter Israel, activities will often be planned by phone in the evening. "This means that when the children want me to be available, often I'm not," says Efrat. "When I travel with them I tell them, 'Look, there was a village here, this is the story of that village.' Sometimes they tell me, 'Mummy, stop lecturing, we don't want to know about that.' Still, now and then I tell them stories of what I've seen. One time Jamil asked us to come to his cousin's house in Bethlehem. The army had arrived in the night, they said they were looking for someone. They shot every window on the first floor, then they made everyone come outside and stand in the rain while they went in to search. I saw the house afterwards, it was a mess, all the cupboards spilled out, many things broken. Sometimes I tell the children stories like this, and they remember."

When other parents at her son's kindergarten decided to hire a security guard, to protect the children from terrorist attacks, Efrat refused to contribute. She argued that there were too many armed guards on the streets already, and they didn't seem to have much effect on suicide bombers. If people were a little more friendly to their Arab neighbours, she said, then those neighbours might be less inclined to support armed Palestinians. Reactions from the other parents were almost entirely negative. One woman snapped, "Oh, you pacifists!" Another warned that this conflict among the adults could threaten friendships among their children.

"I know this was not an idle threat," writes Efrat. "Because of my views and activities, there are parents who already won't invite Gidon to their homes or allow their children to come to ours. It's bad enough, the feeling of being despised by these parents myself, I could hardly sleep last night. What is my motivation, I ask myself, that I would risk my child's well being and happiness too? Maybe I am just enjoying being the lunatic, the outsider that is saying things that are completely meaningless to these people?"

I write back the same day. "First, you may be an outsider, but you are certainly not a lunatic. As I understand it, an important part of your work and your struggle is to help build an Israel, a world, in which your children can be safe, as much as that is possible anywhere. You can see from experience that a whole army of security guards can't make them safe, and it's hard to imagine how an intelligent person like you could now pretend that you don't see it – now that would be lunatic. I also think one of the most valuable gifts any adult can give a child is the example they set."

Efrat writes back a week later to say she has talked with the woman who issued the warning about relationships among the children. "I couldn't persuade her to share my worldview but it really didn't matter. We talked of other things and that dissolved the tension. It should've been done earlier. And I also decided to make an effort to contribute extra time and money to the kindergarten, to make a point that I'm not a free-rider, as they seem to think."

When there are silences from her, I worry, especially after reading of another Palestinian suicide bomb in Jerusalem, or that Israeli settlers have attacked Ta'ayush activists who went to help Palestinian farmers plow their land. I send a note: "Just to let you know I'm thinking of you. I recall you saying that you Ta'ayush people will place yourselves between Palestinians and the army because you believe the soldiers will think twice before shooting Jews. How complex and challenging, even dangerous, your life must be. And how much I respect the way you live it. My warmest wishes to you. Michael."

Efrat replies the same day. "If there is a God, then it is he who sent you to me. Whenever I want to disappear, whenever I think every little act is worthless, that this place will only become more fascist and dangerous, I receive these small notes from you and am comforted a little. Your friend, Efrat."

THE HOLY COWS
OF THE DAY

In June 2003 Efrat was invited to Ottawa for an international conference on Palestinian refugees, and after it ended she came by for a few days' visit with Brian and me, a few hours' drive from Ottawa. She brought photos I had asked her to take, allowing me glimpses of her world. Yoav and the three kids, at home. A neighbourhood grocery. One of her classes, mostly women. A Ta'ayush meeting, in a Palestinian living room. A valley near Bethlehem, olive groves below, terraced land above. A Palestinian village, under a hot sky more white than blue. A road, blockaded by the army. The view from her balcony – on the right, a rocky hill and the Hebrew University where she is an associate fellow at the Truman Institute, and on the left, the village of Issawiyyeh, site of her first action with Ta'ayush. On a map of Jerusalem she points, Here is my office, my house is here, Yoav's parents live here. . . .

We went walking in the woods and on stone beaches by Lake Ontario and picked strawberries at an organic farm. Efrat marvelled at the lush green forests and fields, and the exuberance of our garden, by then in full early summer glory. She questioned everything: "What kind of trees are these? How does this work? Who owns this land?"

On her last day in Prince Edward County, we sat in the generous shade of the elm by our garden, and recorded another interview. I asked Efrat to tell me about her work as a teacher and how it relates to her research. In 2003 she taught a new course, Identity, Myth and Collective Memory. "In the second term the students did a research project in which they were to study some form of commemoration – a museum, a monument, something like that. The students were so good and so serious that at the end of the year I suggested we make a trip to see one of their projects. The students organized everything. Two of them had interviewed some Yemenite Jews who used to live next to a kibbutz dominated by Ashkenazi Jews near the Sea of Galilee in the 1910s and '20s, until the Jewish settlements agency managed to kick out the Yemenites. We saw the museum that the kibbutz had established – of course in their account the Yemenites hardly existed – and places where the Yemenites used to live. It was a very good experience. With this group of students I felt I had actually had some impact on their worldview. They've become disenchanted to some degree with things that are supposed to enchant them, things like nationalism that they're supposed to accept without question."

As far as I can tell, learning to accept without question has become the primary goal of most contemporary education everywhere. In such a dark age, every door that Efrat opens for students is a huge gift. But I worry for her too, particularly in a place where people are being bullied into ever-narrowing polarities.

"Because of my subject, and the source for most of my examples, automatically it becomes more radical," she admits. "A lot of academics will tell you they're trying to get the students to think critically, but usually they're not touching the holy cows of the day."

When I nagged her in New York about making her work more widely available, she told me she didn't think she could face the criticism that would inevitably result from taking a more public role. Yet now she confronts not only the holy cows but armed soldiers and, at least as dangerous, Israeli settlers. "Facing soldiers or doing illegal things that are justified in my opinion is very easy for me. I admit that I am frightened at times, but then I say to myself, although I try not to be naïve, I enjoy life because I trust people. If I lose hope and confidence and trust, there is no more use for me in living."

Though she grows more confident, Efrat continues to avoid the spotlight. "I still don't see myself as an effective spokesperson," she says. "I don't think fast enough, so I know that I would lose in public debates. On the other hand, I've found that I can be effective in other ways, listening to what's going on, and responding to it as a mediator or organizer. The Palestinians are very isolated, they lack outside contacts and networks, and this stops them from getting what they need. In some ways we can connect them to Israeli society and the larger world."

We've covered a lot of ground, so I return to our original point of contact and the subject of this book, oral history. Efrat continues to believe it crucial to the way she reads the world. "It gives you access to dimensions of human experience that other methods do not. You can read a good book, you can learn from it and enjoy it, but that's a very different experience. The direct interaction between people is the most valuable kind we can have, and each one of these interactions is completely unique. It always amazes me."

Recently, she has begun to seek oral testimonies from Jewish soldiers who fought in the Palmach during the 1948 war. Formed in 1941, and partially trained by the British, the Palmach is described by the Jewish Virtual Library as "the elite striking force of the Haganah, the Jewish underground military organization. The Palmach launched pre-emptive strikes into Syrian and Lebanese territory, frequently sending members fluent in Arabic in Arab dress into Syria and Lebanon to sabotage and scout targets."

Efrat started this new project by interviewing her father, a Palmach veteran. "Over the years he has told me stories about the war," she says, "but now I can see that he is getting old, and I have never asked him about his experience in any systematic way. I do know that when he meets with fellow soldiers from his unit, they tell stories that differ from the official narrative. Maybe for them it's a way of coming to terms with what happened in the war. It is those other stories that I hope to hear."

Given what her father knows of Efrat's work, isn't he a little leery about how she – or the Palestinians – might use the material? "He didn't put any conditions on the interviews," she replies, "but I realize he's quite nervous about it. Under the current conditions, I think he wonders what use the Palestinians might make of what he says. So I said, 'Look, Dad, unlike any previous research you will be able to read my article before I give it to anyone else.' On the other hand, I didn't promise that I wouldn't publish it."

Still, under the circumstances, past and present, why would he co-operate with her at all? Efrat pauses, then chooses her words with particular care – this matter is very close to home. "Because they are intelligent people, my father and his unit, and they know that there are multiple histories. Because they believe in justice, and they know that injustice is being done. I want to believe that this is their motivation. For me the heart of the issue is that this bunch of people have a whole set of different stories to tell, all kinds of strange stories, about their fear – they were seventeen, eighteen years old, many of them – about the anarchy of war, about their astonishment when they discovered that people were actually dying in these battles."

A NEW POSITION

Two years ago in New York I asked Efrat what it was that drove her. She told me then, "This whole adventure is my attempt to understand the Palestinian perspective. A very nationalistic Palestinian friend always fights with me, she says I can never understand. She's right in a way – growing up where I did, I don't have any scars on my body. But I do think this is what should be done. Peace is not just about signing contracts between politicians in Oslo. Solving a problem requires putting yourself in a new position. That is what I try to do."

Again and again in our conversations, it strikes me that she's working in a very dangerous minefield, on the border of two clashing sets of national myths. "It's true," she says. "In fact the strongest motivation for my work is to dismantle this whole concept of the other, the enemy – myself as enemy to the Palestinians, and them to me. In general, to deal with myths you try to realize first that they are fiction, and that they have been constructed, so you try to deconstruct them. I think that when you work at the local level, close to people, you realize how different things look, and the myths no longer stand up."

She stops a moment, then continues. "My ambitions aren't high, I'm not aiming for a revolution. But look, I play basketball every Monday, mostly with girls who come from a right-wing religious background. I catch a ride with this one girl who believes the popular story that there were no Arabs in Israel until the Jews arrived, and then they all migrated here to work! I told her it's bullshit, we know that Arabs have a long history here. Four hundred villages were uprooted, thousands of people were pushed out by force. But this woman grew up with that other story, everyone around her confirmed it, so why would she think otherwise? This kind of ignorance has to be overcome. We need to reach out to good people in Israel, people who block themselves off from knowing what's really happening. Somehow we have to make them listen, and see for themselves."

History, it seems to me, can be used in many ways. It can obscure or clarify, paralyze or inspire. In Israel/Palestine, Efrat sees it primarily as a burden. "It makes it very hard for people to think in new ways, to be creative. The Palestinians, especially the older people, get stuck in the good old days, and also in this endless argument, who was here first. You can understand why people do it, but it never goes anywhere, and accomplishes nothing. My own people are overwhelmed by fear, this feeling that the world always has been and always will be anti-Semitic, and all the Arabs want to massacre us. When Israel sends F16s to bomb civilians, it's not because this fundamentalist guy went into the street to blow himself up because his life is impossible, it's because we've been persecuted for two thousand years, and Israelis can only see themselves as victims. We have to be reminded there are other victims too."

The question of who victimizes whom is spectacularly embodied in a colossal serpentine structure that advances day by day across the landscape. Eventually it's expected to stretch 650 kilometres and enclose the entire West Bank. Eight metres high and up to seventy metres wide in some sections, it will be equipped with underground sensors, armed patrols, aerial surveillance, trenches, and landmines. The Sharon government calls it a security fence, "a component of the Israeli government responsibility to protect its residents against a wave of terror originating in the West Bank."

Palestinians and some Israelis call it the "apartheid wall." They accuse Israel of devising a route that legitimizes illegal Jewish settlements and steals thousands of acres of productive Palestinian farmland. Already, critics say, the wall has imposed a new layer of suffering on the besieged Palestinians.

In the Israeli newspaper *Haaretz* on October 27, 2003, journalist Amira Hass writes: "Farmers cannot make their way to their land; hothouses and orchards have been destroyed; olives are left unpicked; teachers and students fail to get to school because the gate of the separation fence is not opened on time; feed for the livestock does not arrive consistently – and the animals are being sold or slaughtered, or left to die; water pipes for drinking or irrigation have been cut; siblings and parents are not permitted to visit; garbage trucks are unable to complete their routes; cesspits are not being drained on time. All of the above examples have been documented, with a hundred different variations, in all of these trapped communities." A recent World Bank report on early impacts of the wall confirms this view.

According to the Israeli peace group Gush Shalom, the wall is "a prison with no warden." The Sharon government's long-term goal, they say, is to leave "hundreds of thousands of Palestinian farmers with no means of sustaining their families, to the point that will force many of them to simply leave their homes, and try living elsewhere as refugees. This is quiet ethnic cleansing, the sort that cannot be photographed, but nevertheless as effective and devastating. In short, it is intended to be a death blow to any possibility of a viable Palestinian state."

In November 2003, Ta'ayush groups joined with Gush Shalom and other Israeli peace groups in yet another protest against the wall. According to polls, most Israelis support it. Despite occasional mild quibbles about its route, so does Israel's chief backer, the United States.

In one of her emails, Efrat wrote, "There is so little hope here, so much despair, not only from the fate of the conflict but also from what it has done to us and our morality."

She has told me she can't function without hope. I want to know, where does she find it? What sustains her? As usual, she's quiet before she speaks. "I'm not optimistic," she says. "I have few signs of hope. But I think I have two choices: Either I really try to shed my Israeli identity and come to Picton and have a nice rural house and teach at a small university, or I remain in Israel – in a way I think that's inescapable – and then I feel obliged to participate. The situation is so bad, and such bad things are coming out of humanity there, I do not want to be a passive person who only participates by passivity."

For over a year she has been working on a project to help a village south of Bethlehem deal with its water problems – old, inadequate pipes, dirty water. Ta'ayush, whose ranks include plumbers, agreed to finance and help install new pipes. At the last minute, their contact in the village said that if Israelis came there to work he couldn't guarantee their safety. Then two retired French hydraulic engineers arrived in Jerusalem; with a group called Hydroliques sans Frontières, they wanted to help Palestinians solve their water problems. Efrat took them to several villages. In one they stumbled onto an internal power struggle and in another a legal obstacle. "The original plan was to connect illegally to the main pipeline, which belongs to an Israeli company," says Efrat. "Then, as other villages have done, they would negotiate to pay for the water. But the French said 'What's all this ille-gal business, we want permits in place up front.' These are two elderly men, very dedicated, but they had no idea how complicated the occu-pation makes everything for the Palestinians."

Finally Hydroliques sans Frontières decided to take on a water project in Ma'asara, a village trapped between two expanding Israeli settlements that was plagued by repeated water shortages. In October 2003, Efrat reported: "The French have completed the water project in Ma'asara but are still in Israel/Palestine, seeking more projects. We are having a small solidarity day in the village on Friday. Meanwhile they are staying in my house." Of the work day in Ma'asara she wrote a few days later that, despite many difficulties, "People were happy to come to this remote village and be in touch. Such encounters between Israelis and West Bankers are almost non-existent nowadays."

Early one morning on her visit here, I watched Efrat walk to the edge of the woods. She stood for several minutes, scanning: a broad-reach-ing sugar maple, the dense wall of prickly ash, a remnant of cedar-rail fence, plump milkweed pods, the abundant life of a meadow left to its own devices. I imagined she was committing it to memory.

After returning from a hike one day in her own country, she wrote: "What I love most here is that there are human signs every-where – ancient human signs. Anat [an old friend from her guiding days] and I walked in the Judean hills today and found caves, including some Roman burial caves, dug into the hard rock. All over the barren rocks we found diggings – round ones like bowls and rectangular ones. We imagined how happy we would be if we could have one of the ancient people explain to us what these diggings are for. There are lovely handmade stone terraces on all the mountains, ancient paths, stone fences. But we also wondered why it is called the land of milk and honey; the summer here is very long and hot and growing things needs so much hard work – digging wells and cisterns, carrying water, building terraces. Still, maybe because we are surrounded by desert this part of the country seemed fertile to the ancient people. And in winter, when the rains come, it is a miracle how things sprout. I wish I could show you this place one day – it is astoundingly beautiful!"

On another hike Efrat and Anat discovered an old spring from which the villagers of at-Tireh used to draw water. Beside it stood a few aged fig trees, survivors from another time. To the knowing eye it was clear they had been planted well before 1948. But still they endure, still they bear fruit.

Canadian Oral History Association: Official
publication: *Oral History Forum d'histoire orale*.
http://oral-history.ncf.ca/

*Guide to Oral History Collections in Canada Guide/Guide des fonds d'histoire
orale au Canada*, compiled by Normand Fortier. Ottawa: Canadian Oral
History Association/Société canadienne d'histoire orale, 1993.

International Oral History Association. http://www.ioha.fgv.br/

National Oral History Association of New Zealand/Te Kete Körero-a-Waha o
Te Motu. http://www.oralhistory.org.nz/

Oral History Association of Australia. http://cwpp.slq.qld.gov.au/ohaa/

Oral History Association, U.S.A. http://omega.dickinson.edu/
organizations/oha/contact.html. Official publication: *Oral History
Review*. http://www.ucpress.edu/journals/ohr/

Oral History List-Serve. http://www.h-net.org/lists/subscribe.cgi?list=
H-OralHist

Oral History Productions, New York. http://oralhistory-productions.org/

Oral History Society, U.K. http://www.oralhistory.org.uk/. Journal: *Oral
History*. http://www.oralhistory.org.uk/#journal

September 11th 2001 Oral History Narrative and Memory Project,
Oral History Research Office, Columbia University, New York
http://www.columbia.edu/cu/lweb/indiv/oral/sept11.html

Ta'ayush, Arab-Jewish Partnership, Israel. http://www.taayush.org/

Testimonies of Pain and Courage, Project Counselling Service, Peru, and Inter
Pares, Ottawa, Canada. http://www.interpares.ca/en/photo_essay/2/
index.php

Tides of Men, online oral history of gay men in British Columbia.
http://www.tidesofmen.org

Workers Arts and Heritage Centre, Hamilton, Ontario.
http://www.web.net/~owahc/